Sun Over Ol' Starlin

Great Smoky Mountain Stories
and
Sun Over Ol' Starlin

by

W. CLARK MEDFORD

The Overmountain Press
JOHNSON CITY, TENNESSEE

Other books by W. Clark Medford

Biography of R. A. Sentelle, 1959

The Early History of Haywood County, 1961

Mountain People, Mountain Times, 1963

Land O' The Sky, 1965

ISBN 1-57072-159-9
Original Copyright © 1966 by W. Clark Medford
Reprinted 2000 by The Overmountain Press
All Rights Reserved
Printed in the United States of America

1 2 3 4 5 6 7 8 9 0

Preface

No wonder that the early settlers, on pushing westward and south-westward into this high Western N. C. Plateau mostly stayed — when they finally got here. Because they found protection behind these mountain walls; a haven from the scorch of sun and bitter cold; also from blizzard winds, raging floods and havoc of wind storms.

They also found here, generally, a rich soil, good 'woods and water' — and the good hunting ground which they were also looking for.

We are speaking particularly of the area including the counties of Buncombe, Haywood and Henderson (where the bulk of our population is found), as the area most unique in this respect. It has been said, that if the spiritual application of Psalm 121:1 was changed to a material one, the people of these three counties could well say: "I will lift up mine eyes unto the hills," from whence cometh our good tourist dollars. Also there are other counties here that benefit from the "good tourist dollars"; because Nature has so wonderfully bestowed her blessings in this respect on all Western North Carolina, more or less.

THE BALSAM RANGE

We take this range as an outstanding example — there are other mountain ranges adjacent to the Great Smokies which are perhaps of equal importance.

In general consideration and reference, the Balsam Range extends from Tri-Corner Knob in the Smokies to Tennessee Bald, a distance of forty five winding miles, and constituting as it does, a high mountain wall, dividing the Counties of Jackson and Swain from Haywood on the east. It thus affords with other mountains, two wonderful valley drainage systems, that of the Tuckaseigee River in Jackson and Swain Counties and the Pigeon River in Haywood.

Crossing the Balsam Range are two or three commercially important and historic road-gaps, Balsam and Soco, the latter having already been mentioned herein (See Story); then there is Black Camp Gap — not so important, but having an altitude of 4,522 feet.

Taking mountain peaks of the Balsam Range into consideration, we find the following, all over 6,000 feet: Tri-Corner Knob, 6,100 ft.; thence going south-eastward, Lufty Knob, 6,216 ft.; Balsam Corner, 6,002 ft.; Amos Plott Balsam, 6,292 ft.; Jones Knob, 6,245 ft.; Richland Balsam, 6,410 ft.; Rhinehart Knob, 6,100 ft.; Mt. Getty Browning, 6,110 ft.

This high, irregularly continuing mountain range, with other elevations under 6,000 feet, forms the west and south boundary "wall" of Haywood County.

Now, this mountain section (as all civilized sections of our country) has played an important and rather unique part in all phases of the growth and development of our great country — in its natural resources, climate and health, industry, agriculture, scenic attractions, history, social culture, etc.

Our History Began Late

The beginning of our history here in far Western North Carolina came late, compared with most other sections of our United States — east, north, south and west; since our settlements did not begin until around 1790. Therefore, our white civilization is only 175 years old. Also we had 100 years of almost total isolation: That was up until the coming of railroads and telegraph in the 1880's. By far our greatest development, progress and culture has been made since then — in the last 75 years, as you will understand.

However, our pioneer ancestry wrought well — even though the 100 years was a period of comparatively slow growth.

Now, with the above preface — concerning the location, geography, topography, together with a little early history of our country, we shall make only a brief introduction to the book.

INTRODUCTION

This is the fourth of our works, in regular book form, about this west-of-the-Ridge section of Western North Carolina — its history, people, customs and traditions, folklore, etc. But the greater part of this has been directly and especially about Haywood County and her people.

The first part of this book "GREAT SMOKY MOUNTAIN STORIES", is a continuation of historical stories of the type we ran in our 1965 volume, "LAND O' THE SKY."

Part two, "Sun Over 'Ol' Starlin", is our first venture into pure historical fiction — of any considerable length. This part has its own introduction.

In part three, "UNCLE ABE," is to be found a revised reproduction of quite a number of the articles by that name which has been running for thirty-two years in the WAYNESVILLE MOUNTAINEER off and on—just "for the fun of it."

W. Clark Medford

Waynesville, N. C., July 25, 1966.

CONTENTS

PART ONE

Miscellaneous Stories

PART TWO

Sun Over Ol' Starlin

PART THREE

Uncle Abe

ILLUSTRATIONS

Chapter I

Relations With The Cherokees In Colonial Times

THERE was a time when nearly all of this Southern Appalachian Country was dominated by the great. widely extended and powerful tribe of Cherokee Indians. That was in the Colonial years of the first three quarters of the 18th century. At the time of the ending of this period of Cherokee domination the white settlers had extended their settlements all around this Indian-held territory — in Virginia, the Carolinas, in present East Tennessee and in upper Georgia. White settlers had pushed close up — even to the foothills of these then British-owned colonies.

At the outskirts of the white settlements the colonists had erected enclosed forts, built of logs with outlook rifle stands, all enclosed by a strong wall with one gate entrance. The forts were kept supplied with food and other provisions and, of course, with ample supplies of guns and ammunition. The guards kept night watch and there being a change of guards at certain intervals. Also patrols were regularly made.

In case of an Indian uprising, warnings could be given to the white settlers nearby so that all necessary precautions for their safety may be taken. At Old Fort in McDowell County there was one, another was near Tryon, and perhaps about the same number of forts were in the other provinces, upper South Carolina and Georgia, and East Tennessee.

For there was fear in the land in those days—continuous, suspended, tragic fear! The men folks had to work, and also hunt to make the living; and yet they were afraid to leave their cabin homes and families. So, often they would take, not only their gun or guns, but also the family of women and children into the field with them. But if the women folks must be left alone, there was always a strong bar inside the door—and a rifle left for them to use if necessary.

Look what happened to Samuel Davidson on the upper Swannanoa, and to the Kirk family near the Indian town of Chilhowee, in Tennessee. Those were only two instances out of many such raids. Fear of the wild animals of the forests was as nothing compared to the fear of the Indians.

CHEROKEE TRIBE WAS LARGE AND STRONG

The Cherokee and some others of the aboriginal tribes grew to be strong here in the Appalachians. They built up a fairly lucrative trade with the white traders of the colonists, of which there were many; also British and French traders, adventurers and prospectors who made friends with the Indians. These traders would exchange articles

1

of clothing, trinkets, guns, powder and lead for the Indians' hides and furs, blankets and beads and sometimes roots and herbs.

Trails and Travel

The crude, winding and worn Indian trails extended throughout the domain of the Cherokee Nation. These were the much-travelled principal trails—like the long transmontane Appalachian, and other Indian trails mentioned in this book. There was the Indian Gap Trail (now New-found Gap), the Cataloochee, and the Overhill of the Upper Little Tennessee River Country, and the Soco ("So-cah") Gap trail. Also there were numerous cross and intersecting trails.

All this intricate system of Southern Appalachian Cherokee trails was well known and used at that time before the Revolutionary War —when the tribe dominated this region. It served them in warfare, in hunting and transportation and communication in general. Because these trails were strategically and advantageously laid out, affording as they did, view for outpost sentinels; also meeting, camping and watering places.

It is interesting to note that now—less than two hundred years later, and about one hundred thirty years after the Great Removal (of the Cherokees), a great, powerful, highly civilized and progressive mountain 'empire' is to be seen here—in the very midst of which is the Great Smoky Mountain National Park, leading any of the rest of our parks in number of visitors.

* * *

"Let us go over and possess the land." (This, our 'Caanan', has already been gratefully possessed!)

NOTE: As you will see from the following, the state of North Carolina stepped in when the National Government failed — and rewarded Chief Junaluska for his friendly services.

AN ACT IN FAVOR OF THE CHEROKEE CHIEF "JUNOLUSKEE" (sic)

Whereas the Cherokee Chief, Junoluskee, who distinguished himself in the service of the United States at the battle of "Horse-Shoe," as commander of a body of Cherokees, as well as on divers other occasions during the last war with Great Britain, has, since his removal West of the Mississippi, returned to this state, and expressed a wish to remain and become a citizen thereof;

Sec. 1. *Be it enacted by the General Assembly of the state of North Carolina, and it is hereby enacted by the authorizing of the same.* That the said Junoluskee be, and he is hereby declared a citizen of the state of North Carolina and entitled to all rights, privileges and immunities consequent thereon.

Sec. 2 *Be it further enacted* that the Secretary of State be, and he is hereby authorized and directed to convey unto the said Junoluskee, in fee simple, the tract of land in Cherokee County, in District No. 9, tract No. 19, containing three hundred and thirty seven acres; which

2

said land the said Junoluskee shall be empowered to hold and enjoy, without the power to sell or convey the same, except for the term of two years from time to time: *Provided, nevertheless* that he shall have full power to dispose of the same by devise only.

Sec. 3. *Be it further enacted,* that the Public Treasurer be directed to pay unto the said Junoluskee the sum of one hundred dollars, out of any monies in the treasury not otherwise appropriated.

Sec. 4. *Be it further enacted,* that this act shall be in force from and after its passage.

Ratified the 2nd day of January, 1847.
(Laws of the State of North Carolina Session 1846-47, p. 128);
Thomas J. Leman, Printed, Raleigh, N. C.

Chapter II

The Story of Abraham (or Abram) of Chilhowee

THIS old half-breed Cherokee warrior and his Mohawk slave wife lived in the aboriginal Indian village of Chilhowee in East Tennessee, adjoining Great Smoky Mt. National Park, which covers the upper section of Cade's Cove.

Old Abraham lived not far from the mouth of Abraham's Creek (named for him) in a large bottom. Here cultural remains of this ancient village may still be found, such as potsherds, stone chips and other objects.

Adjacent hereto are Abraham's Ridge, Abraham's Falls etc., all tending to show the deep and lasting imprint made by the remarkable life of this old warrior on the community in that day.

The identity of Abraham's white father is pretty well known. He was said to be Nathaniel Gist, who married Werteh, a sister of Chief Old Tassel.

Here the Wilburn paper (March 1940) notes: There were many English and Scotch traders, adventurers and explorers (in those Colonial days) who settled temporarily on the Little Tennessee River from about the year of 1700, and later. Some of these traders became actively associated in the Indians' affairs. And they often had great influence upon the chiefs and warriors by forming a rather intimate alliance with, say a sister or daughter of some chief or noted warrior. From such unions many outstanding mixed blood Cherokee families are to be noted. For instance: Ross, Rogers, Bushyhead and Gist, George Gist (Sequoya) being the son of Nathaniel Gist and Werteh, the daughter of Chief Old Tassel, who was massacred along with Abraham in 1788.

Abraham A Contemporary of Washington

The date of Abraham's birth is not known. However, it it believed from existing records, such as Old Abraham's letters to President Washington, etc., that he was born in the 1730's. This would make him a contemporary of Washington—actively so from about the time of the French and Indian wars on up to the time of Washington's presidency.

So, Old Abraham lived in the vicinity mentioned above from the 1730's (his near birth date) and on up until 1788. Sometime during the middle part of this period Henry Timberlake, a British Army officer, visited in the Chilhowee settlement and made records and maps of the village.

Old Abraham, A Loyal Ally

Now let's see what part this half-breed warrior, an ally of the American colonists, played in behalf of our cause.

4

He was first heard of as a soldier in the Colonial Army in the 1750's. By his own statement, Abraham was present on the Ohio frontier and in the final taking of Ft. Duquesne, then Ft. Pitt in 1758. This service lasted for at least one year. After this it is recorded that Abraham, with other Cherokee Chiefs and warriors left for Virginia in September 1758.

Next, we see him, with other Cherokee Chiefs, on the Watauga River at the treaty ground, March 1775, the occasion of the Henderson purchase of Kentucky. He was one of the chiefs who authorized the signing of the treaty for the entire Nation to the Henderson Company. Following this sale there was dissention in the Cherokee camp. Chief Dragging Canoe and other young warriors seceded from the nation, and taking their families, moved to the vicinity of Five Nations near Chattanooga. This dissention continued increasingly because the whites were already pressing the Cherokees by settling over treaty lines on Indian lands, so much that the dissatisfied Cherokees were fighting hard against this violation of treaty lines.

To make matters still worse, British Agents, at the outbreak of the Revolutionary War, incited the Indians to secretly make simultaneous attacks against the White frontiers in Western Virginia, East Tennessee and Western North Carolina, and also in upper Georgia and South Carolina. General Rutherford's expedition, Sevier's and Williamson's were hastily made (in September 1776) vs. the Cherokees.

In these expeditions, especially these made by Rutherford and Sevier, it seems, that the "scorched earth" policy was used.

Hostility had been stirred up to such a high heat amongst the Indians that even Old Abraham had been induced by the British to forsake his white allies and lead a raid against them. This was on July 20, 1776, about two months before the sending of the white armies mentioned above.

NANCY WARD COMES TO THE RESCUE

Abraham, with a party of some 40 warriors were assigned the duty of reducing the Watauga settlements. In spite of secrecy, Nancy Ward, a friendly Cherokee woman, had sent out warnings so that the Wataugans were partially prepared to defend themselves.

Abraham made his attack on the fort July 20, 1776, and continued it with little success for two weeks. In the confusion of the onset of this attack, in the early morning the gates were shut before some of the women engaged in milking the cows, could get inside the fort. Catherine Sherrill ran desperately to get in as the Indians approached and opened fire. She was gallantly assisted over the palisades by Col. John Sevier as officer in command at the fort.

(Four years later she became his second wife)

Several whites who ventured outside during the siege, in search of wood, were killed.

Young Jas. Moore was taken prisoner; also Mrs. Wm. Bean was captured and taken to the Indian camp and questioned as to strength, supplies, etc., of the fort, under threat of death. But later she was told

5

by Abraham that she would not be killed, but she would be required to teach the Cherokees to make butter and cheese.

Not long after this the siege was given up, and the two prisoners, Moore and Mrs. Bean, were taken as prisoners to the Cherokee settlements on the Little Tennessee River. Both were condemned to death by fire. Moore was taken to Tuskegee; Mrs. Bean was carried to Toque, about 5 miles up the river and tied to a stake at the top of a large mound. The fire had already been kindled when Nancy Ward, the Beloved Woman, came to her rescue. Mrs. Bean adopted into her (Nancy Ward's) family, where she taught Nancy and other Cherokee women how to make butter and cheese.

NOTES

As a result of the attacks upon the white colonists — Old Abraham's being only one of them, the expedition of Rutherford and others mentioned, was sent against the Cherokees.

The "sorched earth" policy was used, the result being that, so thoroughly were their towns and crops destroyed and the inhabitants scattered that the main body of the Cherokees sued for peace.

At this treaty of peace, which was held at the Island of Holston, near Kingsport, Tennessee, July 20, 1777, Old Abraham was there — and signed his name (by mark), as did also other Chiefs and leading warriors of the Cherokee Nation.

In May and June 1785 another treaty was signed at Dumpling Creek on the French Broad River, where the Chiefs and other leaders of the Nation met with John Sevier and other representatives of the State of Franklin. This treaty was not as effective as it might have been, since Franklin was a lost state. The treaty was soon followed (November 1785) by the Treaty of Hopewell. This was entered into by and between the United States Government and the Cherokees — when they became wards of the Federal Government. This was the first dealings the Cherokees had had with the (now new) United States Government. Many of the whites along the frontiers became alarmed, because it provided for their removal, and set the line far back from the areas they had considered their own by reason of settlement and claim.

Now, in the midst of these perilous times — 1782 to '85, Old Abraham (or Abram) and Old Tassel (veterans both), but still active, became to be recognized as the principal chiefs of the then peace-loving Cherokees.

OLD ABRAHAM APPEALS TO HIS "ELDER BROTHER"

It was also in these trying times that Abraham appealed to General Washington (now President), whom he called his Elder Brother. The letter was entitled: "Letter from Chief Abraham of Chilhowee to General Washingon, September 1787." It begins:

"My White Elder Brother: I look upon the Beloved men of Chota (Cherokee Capitol) to be my Elder Brothers as well as you.

6

This day we have heard the good talks, and smoked out of your pipe, and my young warriors were pleased from their hearts to hear such a good talk from you. And they will keep it in their hearts as long as they live. Our young warriors of all the Nation look upon Chota as their Beloved Town, where the fire of piece is always kept burning.

We will always keep the good talk, that our children may grow up in piece and live in piece. And the good talks that you sent us, that the path should not grow up in Thorns and Briars, and be kept clean by you (My Elder Brother) and your young warriors, and our young warriors will also assist to keep it clean on our End of the Path. We are all proud and happy in our minds Receiving such good talks.

Brother, I hope you will listen well to what I am going to say: When you were appressed by your enemies, the French and the Indians You sent in the war-hoop (Whoop) for me to assist which I did with my young warriors and helped subdue your enemies which you should not forget, that it was a long time ago. I hope you will send this letter to Congress. I make no doubt thare is some thare remembers this well, so if it is in power to help, not to put my talks aside. I am in hope you and Congress will hear this talk good. And you must remember that time we went hand in hand Against our Enemies Towards the Ohio and took Pitt. And I hope you havn't forget we were willing to help you in Distress. We hope to live in piece but thar's Other Nations of Indians at variance with you, but hope thro your wisdom to make piece with all nations (Indian Nations). Brother, I am in hopes you and Congress will Boath Heare this talk and not throw it aside that my young people may grow up in piece and increase.

This talk from Half-breed Abraham and the young warriors of the Cherokee Nation."

(Signed) Abraham of Chilhowah
8th of September 1787

DEATH OF ABRAHAM

The last episode in this story involves the massacre of Abraham, his Mohawk son, Chief Old Tassel, and peaceable, loving Cherokees of that day.

Here follows: In the Spring of 1788 the Cherokees came into what is now Blount County, Tennessee and murdered the family of John Kirk — Kirk was away from home when the massacre took place.

He returned in the night time, and on entering the cabin, stumbled over the bodies of his murdered family — wife and children.

Kirk gave the alarm, and John Sevier gathered a force at Craig's Station and marched into the Indian country; crossed at Citico, where his men killed 4 Indians. Then they went up to the river to the Chilhowee towns. They saw some Indians on the way and Colonel Hubbard killed one as he was running up into the mountains, Hubbard putting his horse into a full gallop.

As the troops were going up the Tennessee River, Corn (Old) Tassel, who was then King of the Cherokees in company with an Indian called Old Abram, crossed the river with a flag, bringing with him

7

some other Indians. Kirk's son, who had been absent with his father at the time of the murder of the rest of the family, was in the company— and burning with revenge on account of the murder of his mother, brothers and sisters. He sought an opportunity while Colonel Sevier was absent to slaughter all the Indians that came over, except the squaws, Abram's wife and daughter. Abram's son was in the company, a lad of 15 or 16 years. Kirk killed him with others. Abram's wife was not a Cherokee, but a Mohawk whom Abram had captured in some of the skirmishes between the tribes. She could speak fairly good English, and put forth loud and mournful lamentations for the death of her son. Abram's wife and daughter, were taken prisoners, together with another squaw and her child. They were found in the river concealed under the bank of the water, the squaw just holding her mouth and nose above the water, and keeping her child in the same position.

ANOTHER VERSION OF THIS RAID AND SLAUGHTER

In order to give some more details, not mentioned (by Brezeale) above, the following is taken from Ramsey's History of Tennessee.

On the next day they (the Kirk crowd) went up the Tennessee River to the towns on that river, killed several Indians, burned the towns and returned to the station. Tallassee on the upper part of the Tennessee was one of the towns burned. The Indians fled from their different towns into the mountains; but they were pursued by the troopers, and many were killed.

Abraham, a friendly Indian, with his son who lived on the north side of the Tennessee, had declared publicly that if the Indians went to war, he would remain at his own house and never quit it. When the troopers went to the south side, Hubbard sent for him and his son to come over. They came over to the troops accordingly. Hubbard then directed them to return, and bring with them The Tassel and another Indian that he might hold a talk with them; they also held up a flag inviting those Indians to come to them. The Indians did so and were put in a house. Sevier was absent for some time on business, and in the time of his absence those who were left behind permitted young Kirk, the son of whose family was killed, to go with a tomahawk into the house where the Indians were enclosed, Hubbard being with him. There Kirk struck his tomahawk into the head of one of the Indians nearest to him. The Indian fell dead at Kirk's feet. The other Indians, five or six in number, seeing this, immediately understood the fate intended for them. Each one cast his countenance to the ground; then one after the other received from Kirk, on the upper part of his head, the fatal stroke of the tomahawk, and fell, as the first one had done.

Chapter III

Mount Pisgah Overlooks A Fine Land of Promise
(Condensed from an article by H. C. Wilburn)

It is a fact worthy of note that such a prominent peak as Mount Pisgah has no known connection with Indian mythology or tradition relative to the origin and significance of its name.

This is especially true when it is recalled that Pilot Mountain, Tennessee Bald, Devil's Courthouse and other points in the Balsams only 10 or 12 miles distant from Pisgah, figuratively sizzle with Cherokee folk-tales and legends.

The French Broad and Pigeon valleys, over which Pisgah stands sentinel, had been well nigh deserted by the Indians before white settlers came into the area and began to mingle with them.

Most, if not all, who have commented about Pisgah and the source of its name agree that it came from the Bible. No one, however, has come up with a definite answer as to who, and just the time when the name and the mountain first got acquainted. Nor has research in this study brought to light any definite record that pinpoints the question.

A number of years ago, while "digging" into the details of General Rutherford's expedition against the Cherokee Indians in September, 1776, I was impressed with the idea that some member of that 2,400-man army, was impressed, and immediately pronounced the name, "Mount Pisgah!" This must have been as the intrepid, patriotic soldiers swung along the well beaten Indian trail (since known as the Rutherford Trace), as they began to mount the flat hills a few miles west of Asheville where there are a number of vantage points from which Pisgah sticks up on the sky-line "like a sore thumb".

The chaplain of Rutherford's army, and at the same time, Captain of one of its companies, was the Rev. James Hall, a young, vivacious, and patriotic Scotch-Irish Presbyterian minister. Hall had graduated from Princeton College (now University) two years before, and at that time was in charge of several churches in the upper Catawba and Yadkin area including the one on Fourth Creek, now Statesville, N. C. So trigger-keen was this preacher-captain-chaplain that, as the army advanced along the narrow trail, when a Negro slave ran out of a trader's cabin and started away, he immediately shot him down, thinking he was shooting an Indian. Preacher Hall must have been at the head of the moving army strung out along the trail for the reason that the Negro slave, in all probability, took fright and tried to get away on its first approach. This incident must have happened near the head of Scott's Creek in Jackson County, as the Indians at that time were ensconced, for the most part, behind the Great Balsam range.

It is also recorded that on Sunday, Sept. 15, while the army was encamped near the present day Franklin, Hall preached a sermon to the men, which Dr. F. A. Sondley says must have been the first sermon preached in the mountains of Western North Carolina. Trigger-sharp also was the mind and tongue of this well educated Scotch-Irish preacher. So, it seems likely that it might have been he who first caught sight of and named Mount Pisgah.

Dr. Sondley, in his "History of Asheville and Buncombe County", says: The name seems to have been given about 1776, but by whom is not known.

The latter statement coincides with my belief as to the time, and is not out of accord with the idea that Hall was the man.

In "Hunter's Sketches of Western North Carolina," quoting Ramsey on the Rutherford Expedition, it is recorded that "he (Rutherford) crossed the French Broad, passed up Hominy Creek, leaving Pisgah on the left".

This reference seems to indicate that the name, "Pisgah", was well established a good many years prior to 1800. Others in Rutherford's army were the first persons to take up lands in the present day counties of Buncombe, Haywood, Jackson and Swain.

The name, Pisgah occurs some eight or nine times in the Bible. The Hebrew meaning is "the hill". Its location is about eight miles east of the mouth of Jordan River. By reason of its situation and not its elevation (2,644 ft.), it has an extensive outlook or overlook, from which Moses viewed the Promised Land. Clingman's Dome may be viewed from the top of our Pisgah.

Pisgah of local fame also owes its prominence and popularity more to its situation than to superior elevation. Standing nearly two miles off the main divide between Pigeon valley to the west and French Broad to the east, it looks directly down South Hominy and East Fork of Pigeon; and toward the north, the main lower valley of the Pigeon and its tributaries, Fines Creek, Crabtree, and others.

It affords a telescopic picture of Asheville. Also this noble peak is high enough to look over the main divide and its neighboring highlands into Henderson County, and toward the east and south into the head streams of the French Broad as they finger out to the crest of the Blue Ridge. Toward the north and west Pisgah peeps over the lower sections of the Great Balsam range, and reveals a chopped-up picture of the Great Smokies from Clingman to Guyot.

Had Preacher Hall ascended the North Carolina Pisgah as did Moses of old the Bible Pisgah, he too might have "viewed a Promised Land," figuratively, "flowing with milk and honey," literally with activity and money, as well as other good things: Invaluable forests; fine farms; live stock on a thousand hills; industry, Champion Fibre, Enka, Ecusta, and many others already here, and more to come. Also Schools and colleges; religious culture, Blue Ridge, Ridgecrest, Montreat, Lake Junaluska, Kanuga, Bonclarken; a playground of America; and last but not least, a prolific reservoir of human resources that has helped to people many far places, and advance the American way on all its frontiers.

10

THE CATALOOCHEE ABORIGINAL TRAIL AND ITS USE
AND DEVELOPMENT BY WHITE PEOPLE

Roughly, this old trail skirts the Northeastern border of the Park for 2 miles or more; running from Cove Creek Gap, via the mouth of Little Cataloochee Creek, Scottish Mountain, Mt. Sterling Gap, post office, Davenport Gap. (NOTE: See "South End of Cataloochee Trail", following this)

From Davenport Gap Northwestward the primitive road thru that section which was abandoned some ten years ago for the present Highway, Tenn. 75, coincided closely with the location of the aboriginal trail. Some two miles Northwest from Davenport Gap, a branch leads Northeastward to the Big Pigeon River in the neighborhood of the present Hartford where there were Indian settlements. This paper deals mainly with the seven miles of the aboriginal trail that lies between Cove Creek Gap and Mt. Sterling Gap, for the reason that it is wholly within the Park.

HISTORY: The Cataloochee Trail seems to have been well known in early times, the first known reference in literature being that of John Strother at the time of his survey of the State Line in 1799. He described it, even at that early date as "The Cataloochee Turnpike".

Another well known reference is that found in the journal of Bishop Asbury. In November, 1810, he and a party traversed the Cataloochee Trail during his annual tour through the South. He recorded "At Cataloochee I walked over a log But oh the mountain height after height, and five miles over; After crossing other streams, and losing ourselves in the woods, we came in, about nine o'clock one night, to Vader Shook's (present Clyde, N. C.) What an awful day."

William Davenport, under the commissioners, Alexander Smith, Isaac Allen, and Simeon Perry, representing the State of Tennessee; and John Mebane, Montford Stokes and Robert Love from North Carolina, completed the State Line survey in 1821, beginning at "Cattalucha (Sic) track". This description by Davenport would seem to indicate a road of less importance than that described by John Strother twenty two years previously. However, by 1821 there must have been frequent travelers on this route. Numerous settlements had been made in the Cosby section of Tennessee and on Jonathan Creek in North Carolina. It is known that hunters and cattle rangers, if not indeed, permanent settlers, were already in Cataloochee, Big Creek and Tobes Creek by this time.

However, the Indians claimed these lands as their hunting ground until the Treaty of 1791 and the State of North Carolina protected them in their rights by legislation, both in 1778 and 1783.

These acts forbade hunting, ranging of cattle, and other forms of trespassing, as well as land entries on these lands that had been reserved for the Indians. But the fact that Bishop Asbury and his party, in 1810, chose this route in their passage from settlements in the Newport area to those in Haywood County, North Carolina seems to indicate that the Indian laws were disregarded.

11

LATER TIMES. No doubt some efforts had been put forth by the pioneer settlers, and by the land speculators who had long since purchased all the lands along this route, prior to the sitting of the North Carolina Legislature in 1846-47. It is well known that many had made permanent settlements in Cataloochee, Big Creek and Tobe's Creek; and that outsiders regularly frequented these areas for the purpose of hunting, and some had established extensive cattle ranging businesses.

The Legislature of North Carolina, in 1846-47, passed an act creating the "Jonathan Creek and Tennessee Mountain Turnpike Company," whose purpose it should be to construct a road from Waynesville, N. C. to the Tennessee State Line. Specifications were that the road should be not less than 12 feet wide, and not steeper than one foot vertical to 8 feet horizontal which would be a grade of 12%.

When the road should be completed according to specifications, the Company would have the right to erect toll gates and collect the following rates of toll; a 6-horse wagon, .75, 5-horse wagon, .62½, 4-horse wagon or coach, .50, 3-or 2 horse wagon or carriage, .25, 1-horse, cart or carriage .20, man or horse, .10 each; hogs and sheep, .01 each.

In 1851-52, the original act of 1846-47, was amended, providing that as soon as the "Catalucha Road" is completed 4 feet wide, the Company would have the right to collect the stipulated rates of toll, and that they should be permitted to use such sections of the old road as it found necessary or advisable.

Of Indian or White Origin?

Indians occupied areas along the route as proven by Indian sites along the way. The extremities of the trail were thickly populated by Indians necessitating a communicating passage way; also the fact that the first record of this trail (1799) before many whites were in the area, seems to indicate that it was a well marked route of travel. Tradition is 100% on designating this as an Indian trail.

NOTES

There's an old ford, just below where Highway, N. C. 284 crosses Cataloochee Creek. The United States Geological Survey, in 1930 constructed a weir gaging station here, the weir being just a few feet below the old passage way across the stream. I was at, or near this place where, November, 1810, Bishop Asbury crossed the creek on a log and exclaimed about the height of the Mountains and the longness of the way. The old Indian trail may have crossed a few hundred feet lower down, near the mouth of Little Cataloochee Creek.

Indian site on Palmer Creek (Old name, Indian Creek) of Cataloochee Creek. This site was known by the local people as "Indian Flats." This location is just above the late Turkey George Palmer's home, and at the mouth of pretty Hollow Creek. Mr. Palmer stated to me that when he and his father, sometime prior to 1875, first came upon this site with an idea of purchasing it, there was much evidence

12

of Indian activity. This evidence consisted of a small field that had been cleared, but at that time was growing in briars, brush and small trees. Also there had been an old "fireplace", stones and pottery pieces.

Part of the old trail, possibly the first "dug" road. The location is some 800 feet North of the mouth of Little Cataloochee Creek where the trail "topped out" in a gap in the ridge. From this point the trail followed the flat top of the ridge for some distance. Indentation in the surface here, is shown by a dead log lying across the trail.

A grave is in the gap where the trail "tops out" at a point, about 80 feet North of the mouth of Little Cataloochee Creek. This is said to be the grave of one, Williams, a traveler who sickened and died at the Kerr place sometime prior to the Confederate War. Graves of negro slaves belonging to O. A. Kerr, first settler at the Kerr place, are said to be located here also.

"Flint" "chips" were picked up beside a trail leading down Hogland Branch which trail branches off from the main trail at Hogland Gap. It is thought that the aboriginal trail leading into the middle and upper reaches of the Cataloochee basin followed down Hogland and Winding Stair branches. The spot where these "chips" were found is on a slightly elevated flat near a small stream and constituted, in all probability, a wayside camping place. The aboriginal traveler or hunter, no doubt, while resting, spent his time "chipping" flints to replenish his supply of weapons.

The Cataloochee Trail was mostly in Haywood County. It is usually spoken of as running from Cove Creek Gap to Cosby Creek in Tennessee. (H. C. Wilburn, "Cataloochee Trail").

But this trail really started about the old Davis place or Kimsey Howell place on the Cove Creek side above the old Jacob Owens Mill, which was the turning off trail leading into Cataloochee.

South End of Cataloochee Trail

The Cataloochee Trail was first an Indian and animal trail — mostly cattle, that were being driven thru to the good range there by citizens of Jonathan's Creek in the spring of the year. After being ranged until late in the fall, the cattle would be driven back for winter feeding.

"About two miles of the trail was along an old dug road, which was probably done by early pioneers to improve it for a cattle road". So says H. C. Wilburn in writing about this trail. This is true, it was mostly done by the Jonathans Creek herders, mentioned above, but the digging and improving of the trail was done after the real early (first of the century) days, along about the late 1820's.

The citizens of Jonathans Creek — Reuben Moody, Joshua Allison, Howells, Leatherwoods, Davidsons, Owens and others formed a little stock company. Then they blazed out, cut out and dug out wherever necessary to make easier and safer driving for their cattle, and also as a bridle path and for pack horses.

Allison was made keeper of the toll gate, which was erected across the trail at a closed in place, said to be near the Reeves place.

13

A small fee was here collected from all other travellers and herders, not belonging to the company.

At Cove Creek Gap a most wonderful view is afforded — of a big portion of the Great Smokies range, looking North and West.

From the time of the cattle road, some improvements were made, that is during the settling up of Cataloochee, it was made into a rough wagon road. Since then the major change was the widening and grading in places, then surfacing with gravel, making (now) a fairly good road for its limited travel.

In the old times before the coming of white settlers into this area, a well-beaten Indian trail passed through the Cataloochee and Big Creek valleys from Davenport in the Smokies via Mt. Sterling Post-office, Mt. Sterling Gap and connected with other trails in the Waynesville area.

The ranges visible from Cove Creek Gap are Noland Mountain, the Short Bunk, the Long Bunk, Cooks Knob, Rough Ridge, Indian Ridge; and against the skyline, Mt. Sterling, flanked on the right by Mt. Sterling proper, and on the left by Big Cataloochee Knob.

These place names are reminiscent of early settlement days and the hunting and cattle ranging activities of the Davidson family and others which began, possibly as early as the establishment of Haywood County in 1809.

In 1807 William Davidson conveyed a tract of 300 acres to William Mitchell Davidson on Jonathon's Creek. The description in the deed mentions the Indian Path and Indian fields.

From the mouth of Laurel Creek the trail followed up Stateline branch for some distance, then bore to the right to the top of a flat ridge, and passed through Davenport Gap into Tennessee.

But the ancient Cherokee passerby on the old trail were not content with a distant view of the Cataloochee area. They penetrated its wilds and roughs in quest of game and fish that have ever made the streams famous. Cultural material that has been picked up at a number of places along the streams is evidence of campsites and frequent occupancy. Scattering finds (arrowheads, etc.) along the ridge tops and in gaps mark this as a notable hunting ground long before the coming of the white man.

By the treaty of Holston in 1791 the Cherokee gave up title to all the land in Cataloochee and Big Creek. Five years later, in 1796, a state grant of 176,000 acres was made to one John Gray Blunt. This grant covered the area in question, and much more besides. About 96,000 acres of this grant is included in the bounds of the Great Smokies Park. Soon after it was issued individuals began to take up the choice lands, mainly along the streams, both in Cataloochee and Big Creek. The earliest settlers, probably in the order named, were: Davidson, Hannah, Palmer, Caldwell, Bennett, Woody, Sutton, Conrad, Messers, Hall, and some others.

At the time of the inclusion of this area in the park there were approximately 56 families living in Cataloochee, 25 in Big Creek, representing altogether a population of 390 persons. At the present time there are only three families in Cataloochee. In Big Creek, however, a

14

John Hannah House on Cataloochee

This house was built later than the others shown, because Cataloochee was settled later than most other sections of Haywood. However, it was standing and in good repair when the Great Smoky Mountain National Park lands were acquired in the 1930's.

number of families remain for the reason that all the lands in that area were not included in the park.

Editor's Note: The 176,000 acres mentioned above (granted to Blount) was the tract, parts of which Col. Robert Love acquired later. The tract even extended across the mountain into Jonathon's Creek and included the Purchase Mountain. But this land was not soon settled up along the creeks. Except for herders and hunters it lay idle for years, settlements having begun in the early 1830's.   W.C.M.

"The commonly accepted form of the place name 'Cataloochee' is the white man's pronunciation of the Cherokee word 'Ga-da-lu-sti.' James Mooney says that the word means 'standing up in a row'! It is my belief that the word is descriptive of the several ranges or ridges of mountains rising one behind and beyond the other in a row or series."

Chapter IV

Mills and Milling In Smoky Mountain Section

Note: We are indebted to Mr. H. C. Wilburn for these Articles on Milling.

From remotest time, and among all races of mankind, grain and the crushing of it for food to satisfy primeval needs, has played an important part in economic and social well-being. Indeed a study of the appliances from the crudest stone-age mortar and pestle to the machines of modern milling, runs parallel with the advancement of civilization. Such a study reveals a step-by-step advance, or evolution toward our modern machine age, and is not an uninteresting story. These "steps" may be represented by: (1) Stone, or wooden mortar and pestle: (2) quern: (3) pounding mill: (4) tub-mill: (5) over-shot, or other type of water power mill.

It seems quite remarkable, and of great interest that all of these "steps" should be found in use, or at least in existence in Great Smoky Mounains National Park at the time of the taking of lands for its making. To be sure, the stone mortar and pestle had been largely displaced by its wooden successor such as the one illustrated in the pen drawing by Douglas Grant, which drawing accompanies this account. The transition from the stone to the wooden type essentially marks the introduction of European cutting tools among the American Indians, although long before the use of such tools, the natives by means of fire and stone, or bone, scraping tools were able to manufacture good and useful wooden mortars and pestles for use in reducing corn, beans, nuts, and other food materials, to meal or flour which they used for bread, mush, or other prepared dishes.

Several different kinds of stone were used out of which they made mortars. Sometimes a water-worn boulder of suitable size and shape, with a depression also etched by water action, was used in its natural state, or possibly improved by deepening the hollow, or otherwise altering it to suit the wishes of the artisan. Most specimens however, were evidently quarried from sandstone, quartzite, soapstone, or other workable outcrops. A vast amount of labor, time and artistic skill was required to produce a well fashioned and decorated mortar. This is evident when it is recalled that only by a "chip-and-peck-and-grind" process with other stone tools, was the task accomplished. It has been said that the older men after they were unable to be active in warfare, or even in hunting, spent many of their declining years in making a single object, such as a fine mortar, or perhaps a gaming stone. This persistent effort was motivated by a wish to be of some service to family or tribe to the end, and to leave something behind

16

by which to be remembered after they had departed for the happy hunting ground.

Some years ago while I was exploring the country adjacent to the park for any object or evidence of historical or cultural remains, I visited, examined and photographed Judaculla Rock near the residence of the late Milas Parker on Caney Fork Creek in Jackson County, N. C. Mr. Parker told me about certain evidence of quarrying and shaping of the soapstone outcrops he had observed on the ridge 400 or 500 feet up the steep slope above Judaculla Rock. What I saw up there was both amazing and enlightening. The entire underlying rock seemed to be an impure or low grade soapstone or steatite formation, the same substance as the notable rock itself. Many jagged points or projections knee-high to shoulder-high stuck up out of the ground. The amazing thing was that several of the projecting masses had been "worked". Some of them showed signs of having been more or less smoothly cut off, and the pieces carried away. One in particular, that was photographed, and now recalled, had been carved into a nearly complete mortar. The tray, or depression had been dug out; the excess stone at the front had been chipped off, and back of the tray had been girdled, and nearly ready for removal. Why it was abandoned and left in that unfinished state is an unsolved riddle.

Some other pieces were observed that had been separated from the parent rock, but seemingly by mishap, had been spoiled and abandoned as worthless. Much fragments and chips littered the ground where work had been carried on. The surface of the rock that had been worked was not different in appearance, from the surface that had not been disturbed. That is to say, time and weathering had erased any evidence of recent activity. In all probability the "workings" may have been coeval with the carvings on Judaculla Rock.

A wooden mortar and pestle such as that illustrated in the picture, and still in common use among the Cherokees on the Reservation adjacent to the park, is not difficult to construct. Usually a hardwood block about three feet long is cut out of a log two feet in diameter, and set up on end. A fire is kept burning on it for several hours, the edges being banked with clay, until a cavity is burned out. This is then chiseled and scraped down to a funnel-shaped hole.

The pestle is of seasoned dogwood or hickory, about the size and shape of a wood-splitter's maul. The large, heavy end is for added weight and crushing power when "muscled" up and down by an operator. Such work is slow and laborious. The operator tires out by the time she had made enough meal for a day's supply.

THE QUERN

Since the quern is an ancient rotary-stone type of grinding device maybe it should be classed higher up in the scale of progress toward more modern efficiency; but as it was always hand-operated contrivance it should precede the pounding-mill, which was water-powered.

In an article that appeared in the old "Outing" magazine, January, 1920, Horace Kephart gives the following paragraph on the quern:

QUERN,—This is a picture of a quern in operation, from an illustration contained in an article by the late Horace Kephart, January, 1920. Mr. Kephart labels his illustration, "Kentucky Mountaineer Grinding with Quern", In refering to the Pounding Mill in this article Kephart mentions an article in the National Geographic Magazine of July, 1919.

"Another photograph in our series shows a Kentucky mountaineer grinding corn with a quern or hand-mill such as was used in ancient Britain. The nether stone is set in a hollow log similar to a bee-gum. The upper one has a hole through the center, where the grain is fed by hand, and is turned round and round by a driving-stick, the upper end of which is held in position by a right-angled arm". Douglas Grant's pen drawing that accompanies this account was copied, in part, from the picture in "Outing" magazine.

In addition to the quern in operation, as shown in the picture, there is also illustrated the grinding surface of a light stone as was used in a quern, and in a heavier form, was the prototype of those used in water powered mills. The pattern of the furrowing or grooves on its face is of such design as will gradually drive the grist from

18

the center toward the exit spout at the edge of the stone as it revolves.

It can not be said that querns were in actual use here in 1920, however, several of the old settlers were familiar with them, and had seen them in use in earlier times.

Mr. Wilburn says: While "exploring" in a very secluded, and almost inaccessible area, some six miles down the Tuckaseegee River from Bryson City, there I found a pair of very crude quern stones. It was well known in local tradition that a number of Cherokee Indian Families had "hid-out" in this area during the removal period in 1838 and following; and that they eked out a most perilous existence for several months in the period in which Tsali and others were being hunted by United States soldiers. Only one family lived in the area at that time. He had, a good many years previously, used the querns as cap-stones on high wooden pillows under his barn. I helped him prize up the barn and replace the querns with other stones.

As previously stated, these were of the crudest sort of querns. There was no sign of furrowing; the working faces were smooth and showed signs of abrasion by much use. They were about sixteen inches in diameter, three inches thick; roughly circular in shape, only the angular corners having been "pecked off" with a hammer, or most likely, with another stone.

Discussing the probable use of these stones with the owner, he thought that they were used only for crushing parched corn; and that the grinding was accomplished by lateral abrasing action rather than revolving the stones.

Querns are still extensively used by backward peoples in remote sections of Mexico, Central America, and no doubt, in sections of the East and in Asia.

Bible commentators believe that hand-mills, querns, were in use in Palestine prior to the time of Christ. Quite likely they were also being used by neighboring peoples. Matthew 24:41, says: "Two women shall be grinding at the mill; one shall be taken, the other left."

THE WONDERFUL OLD POUNDING-MILL

In an article in old "Outing" magazine, January, 1920, Horace Kephart says that the pounding-mill is a most wonderful machine, and that it represents a long step in human progress. His description and comments are quoted as follows:

"Fifteen years ago, when I first came into the Southern mountains, I heard at times of a mysterious machine whereby a pestle was worked up and down by water-power. This was called a pounding-mill or, facetiously, a "lazy-John" or "tri-weekly." The descriptions given by the old settlers were certainly genuine; and yet I could not get through my head how such a thing would work.

"Then, last summer, I found a real pounding-mill, within six miles of my residence, Bryson City. It is at the home of Telitha Bumgarner, on a branch of Deep Creek, and was made by her son, Jim.

"The photographs here printed are, so far as I know, the first ones of an American pounding-mill that have ever been published.

19

A similar but ruder and less efficient contrivance, found in the wilds of northern Korea, was described and illustrated in the National Geographic Magazine for July, 1919.

"I consider the pounding-mill one of the most remarkable machines ever made by man; for it is the simplest possible application of power. It is not a gradual development but a *leap* in human progress, directly from hand labor to power machinery, without any intermediate stage.

"Every one who sees it stands amazed at the thing's simplicity and originality of design. I have watched expert machinists and engineers gazing at Jim Bumgarner's pounding-mill for minute after minute, as though entranced. Old Talitha told me: "Two o' them woods surveyors cum and hung over yan fence for a long spell; and then one o' them said to the other, "Bill, thar's perfectual motion. The darned thing works!.""

"In making the mill, a post is planted. To its upper part, a horizontal pole about ten feet long is pivoted at the center, so that the ends are free to work up and down, like the walking-beam, of an old fashioned steamboat engine.

"At one end of the beam is similarly pivoted a pestle about five feet long and ten inches thick. The lower end of the pestle is shaved down to about two-inch diameter, where a narrow iron band keeps it from burring.

"The mortar is nothing but a stump hollowed out to funnel-shape and boxed at the top to keep the grain from flying out. A hole is cut through the bottom of the mortar, from which the meal is spooned out. The hole is closed by a little shutter at other times.

"At the other end of the beam, and on top of it, is a box serving as water bucket, which holds about six or seven gallons. This box is attached to the beam underneath by a wooden hinge, formed by a V-shaped withe on either side of the box, the lower part of which goes around a wooden pin stuck through the beam. Thus the bucket is pivoted and free to tilt when it descends. To keep it from tilting too far, another withe, like the bow of an ox-yoke, is attached to the end nearest to the post, the U thus formed going down and around the beam.

"It will be observed that there are only three bearing surfaces in the whole machine, and there is no rotary motion at all.

"A trough from the brook carries water to the bucket. The gate for turning on and cutting off the water is simplicity itself. A few feet back from the mouth is a square hole cut through one side of the trough. A bit of shingle about six inches square closes this aperture when water is to be turned on. To cut off the stream, the shingle is merely set on end, diamond-shape, athwart the trough, against a pair of cleats just forward of the hole.

"When the pestle goes down in the mortar to pound the corn, and the bucket is up under the spout, water is turned on. As the bucket fills, its weight overbalances that of the pestle. Down goes the bucket, up goes the pestle. The water being now mostly against the far end, the pivoted bucket has to tilt, and so all the water spills out. Then

20

again down goes the pestle with a hard thump! So, on and on it goes—the wonderful pounding-mill!

"When I timed this machine it pounded every five seconds. Sometimes a greedy chipmunk or a red squirrel hops into the mortar and stays too long. In such case the descending pestle makes mincemeat of him and the corn.

"Everything in this water-engine is made from trees and bushes that grew near the spot, except the box boards, the nails, and the iron band on the pestle. It could have been made just as well without any sawed boards or nails at all, the bucket being hewn out of solid timber.

"Jim's mill is now only used to pound up stock feed, and so requires no attention until the job is done. To make meal fit for bread, someone would have to go there every now and then to remove the pounded grain, sift out the finer particles, and return the coarser ones. Of course the process was slow; but time was no consideration in the backwoods".

The inventor and the place where the Pounding-mill was first used has, so far evaded research. That it was in common use in earlier days in the mountains here, is evidenced by the fact that there are in Swain County three, or more "pounding-mill branches"; and equally as many in Haywood County.

Note: The time of the pounding-mill strokes ("5 seconds"), is too fast — it pounded about every 15 seconds!   —W.C.M.

In October, 1927, while going with a field party up Deep Creek to begin surveys of Bryson Place, I "discovered" the same pounding-mill visited and described by Kephart. At that time I had never heard of such a thing as pounding-mill. My attention was attracted by an unusual noise in the bush-shrouded branch near the trail we were following. K'splash, K'splash! K'thud!! repeated four or five times per minute. Investigation revealed the contrivance in operation as described by Mr. Kephart.

A threatening storm cloud was about to break, so we hurried away. But on a later visit, I talked with Jim Bumgarner, and questioned him about his pounding-mill and its use. He said that in the morning before going away to work he would put in about half gallon of corn, and start the mill. At evening when he would return there would be about enough fine meal for bread a day. The remainder would be too coarse, and generally used for chicken feed. This was some years after Kephart's visit. Jim said his mill had been in operation a good many years, and different parts of it had been replaced from time to time.

A year or two later than my "discovery", Mr. Reuben Robinson of Champion Fibre Company purchased the pounding-mill from Jim Bumgarner, and had it installed at his summer camp, "Timber-Top", near Old Indian Gap in the Smokies. It remained there until 1939, when he signified his willingness to donate it to the park for possible museum display. It was then "collected", dismantled, and the different parts carefully numbered for identification purposes, and stored at Park Headquarters near Gatlinburg. Detailed and dimensioned drawings were made, and full description prepared, duplicates of which were filed in the Congressional Library, Washington, D. C.

Douglas Grant's pen drawing was sketched from photographs and descriptions, and correctly represents Jim Bumgarner's pounding-mill as it was in 1927. Both the apparatus itself, and the rail fence in the background, are correctly represented as being bound together, in part with vines and hickory or whiteoak withes.

The Pounding Mill

POUNDING MILL.—This pen drawing of the Talitha, or Jim Bumgarner pounding mill, was developed in part from a photograph by the late Horace Kephart about 1920. It is described in his article in Old *Outing Magazine* January, 1920. The same pounding mill, or its successor in the same location was observed by the author in 1927. Notes were taken of its description and operation. The pestle made about 3 three strokes per minute. The owner, Jim Bumgarner, stated that he would put in about one gallon of corn early in the morning before going away to work. On his return at the end of the day enough fine meal to supply the needs of the family the next day might be taken out. The remaining coarse grist would be run the next day, or could be used for chicken feed.

In an effort to encourage and to secure the preservation and restoration of the Mingus Mill, the subject of this article, and the subject

22

of Douglas Grant's modified pen drawing, the following memorandum was submitted to National Park Service.

Mingus Mill

"The Mingus Mill has always impressed me as being a very valuable American relic that the Service can not afford to overlook.

The process of reducing grain to flour to supply the elemental needs of the human species from the very earliest time is a matter of importance, and has played a major role in the development and progress of civilization.

"The development of mills, milling and milling practices in America, from the crudest beginnings in colonial times to the giant industries of today is not an uninterestng story. Prior to the Revolutionary War mills and milling was largely a community customs enterprise, in which every community had one or more mills to supply the local needs.

"Like many other American enterprises and industries, in the period following the war of Independence, mills and milling, both in its customs and industrial phases, began to take on new life, and with this new life, inventions, new methods, and new processes appeared.

As the country developed different areas became leading milling centers.

"About the time of the Revolutionary War, Delaware was such a leading center. Then, successively, Richmond, Baltimore, the Genesee Valley of New York, in the 1840's; thence further westward; St. Louis, Cincinnati, Milwaukee, and finally, the Minneapolis-St. Paul area.

"Likewise each of these areas, as they developed, had their great millers and industrialists who pushed their business to the limit of success in milling and marketing. Of no less importance; but perhaps, less well known, there were a number of inventors and appliers of new and better methods and processes.

"In 1787, one Oliver Evans invented and introduced into Baltimore area a system of elevators and conveyors that made flour milling an automatic process from the sack in the wagon to the finished product in the barrel. This system became universal, and was continued till the invention and introduction of the roller-type of mills in the 1870s and 1880s.

"John Stevens of Wisconsin invented a roller type of mill in 1870, and was granted patents in 1880. In 1868-70, one, N. E. Lacroix, invented and installed in the Minneapolis area, a type of roller mill similar to those then being used in Hungary. The American inventions, however, are said to have been independent of those of Europe, being used about the same time.

"Introduction of the roller mills rapidly displaced the old rotary-stone process of grinding, and before the year 1890, practically all the commercial mills were using them. The use of rotary-stone mills for small unit and customs milling, however, continued to some extent into the twentieth century. In America this old process of milling, through its progressive stages, was in use from colonial times down to the introduction of roller mills, roughly a period of one hundred and fifty years.

"The production of flour consists essentially of two operations; first the crushing of the grain; second, the separation of the grist into its different grades, such as fine flour, middlings, shorts, bran. The bottom or "bed stone" was stationary. The top stone or "runner" was rotated at proper speed by water power or other mechanical means. These stones were almost universally of French buhrstone, quarried only in southern France. The grist was then separated by means of a bolting reel and silk cloth, both inclosed in a bolting chest.

"In the roller process the grain is crushed by being passed between a series of steel rollers. The grist in this case is separated by various types of shaker sieves.

The Mingus Mill is of the old type; it has a fine set of French buhrstones that were shipped from France, and hauled on a wagon from Charleston, S. C., about 1875. The Oliver Evans system of elevator and conveyor is well represented here; the bolting reel and bolting chest is in perfect condition; and all appliances are in, more or less, good condition.

24

"Briefly, Mingus Mill is representative of about one hundred and fifty years of prevailing types of mills and milling practices in America as related to small unit and customs operations; and, as such, constitutes a valuable American relic, and should be preserved. In addition to these interesting features there is represented here a fine, old type of finish carpentry, both in the building itself and in the mechanical appliances, most of which were made on the spot.

"This mill was constructed and put into operation in 1878, just about the time of the turning point from the old to the new process, by a "Master-Mechanic" (millwright), with his Journeyman and Apprentices. The lumber that went into the construction of this plant was sawed by a sash-saw mill near the site. Shortly after the building of the mill a turbine water wheel was installed in place of the old over-shot wheel that had formerly been in use here. I think an over-shot wheel should be constructed and turbine removed.

"It is my belief that the restoration of the Mingus Mill and its proper exhibition to the public would add much of "color" and interest to the park, and should become a vital part of the cultural and interpretative program.

"There is reason to believe that some of the large milling companies could be induced to sponsor the restoration and exhibition of this old relic of the milling industry."

It remains to be said that in addition to the flouring mill described above, there was also a corn-grinding unit powered from the same main shaft; both could be operated at the same time, or separately. The corn mill had been improved from time to time. At the time of its acquisition by the North Carolina Park Commission about 1930, it was rated as one of the best and most modern mills, certainly within the bounds of the park. It would turn out forty to fifty bushels of meal per day.

Tradition, and some records indicate that a mill had been in operation here, near the mouth of Mingus Creek, long before the war between the states. The site is in the immediate vicinity where John Jacob Mingus, believed to be the first white settler on lands now included in the Great Smoky Mountains National Park, built his log cabin, quite probably as early as 1792. A well built log structure, said to have been the old Mingus home, was still standing nearby only a few years prior to the time when surveys for the park were commenced in 1927. Also a rock-walled spring that supplied these pioneers is nearby, which, however, was covered up by a road and landscaping construction about 1938.

The Mingus Mill is still standing, but is in a poor state of repair.

Chapter V

Soco An Important Gap,
Where History Was Made

"The name of Soco, as applied to Soco Gap and Soco Creek, derives from the Cherokee word "Sa-gwa", meaning "one place" — *H. C. Wilburn*

By common usage the name, as corrupted by the whites, became fixed to the gap, near which the stream rises, and flowing westward joins the Oconaluftee one mile below Cherokee.

An interesting side light on Soco Creek is contained in a deed of transfer from Felix Walker, bearing date, January 1, 1818, to one Julia Madame Plantore of Philadelphia, Pa. The consideration that Walker received in exchange for his tract of land was: "Three small likenesses, one for himself, one for Felix Walter Baird, and one for Miss Plancey Maddox, made by the said Julia Madame Plantore, and also one plate painting of small size, the representation of the peace of Ghent".

The four hundred and twenty acre tract of land conveyed in this transaction is described as: "A parcel of Mountain land, whereon is good timber, excellent good water, and good range in summer, lying and being in the County of Haywood, beginning near the fork of So-cah Creek, where the great road crosses at the foot of the mountain, lying on both sides of the creek and on both sides of the Big Road.

The location of this tract of land is thought to be at the mouth of Lost Cove Branch, one and three-fourths miles down from Soco Gap. It would include three small streams, as well as nearly a mile from Soco Creek, and would also fulfill the specifications, "Good timber, excellent good water and Summer Range". Part of it would lie on both sides of the creek, and on both sides of the Great Road. The Great Road referred to being the Ancient Indian trail that passed this way.

The correct Cherokee designation for what is now known as Soco Gap is, A-ha-lu-na (Ah-hah-law-nah, in Cherokee characters), meaning "ambushed", or U-ni-ha-lu-na (in Cherokee characters) meaning, "where they watched". The trail from the Pigeon River area crosses at this gap, and in the old times the Cherokees were accustomed to keep a lookout here for the approach of enemies from the North. On the occasion which gave it the name, they ambushed here, just below the gap on the Haywood side, a large party of invading Shaw-

26

anos, and killed all but one, whose ears they cut off, after which, according to a common custom, they released him to carry the news to his people.

It is also to be noted that, according to tradition, both Indian and white, and recorded many years ago, the Cherokees were called in council at Soco (A-ha-lu-na) Gap to meet the great Tecumseh when he came South, in the year of 1812, in efforts to recruit all Southern tribes he could to repel white recroachments on Indian lands north of the Ohio River. It was here at this council that, after hearing the eloquent appeals of the "Great Shooting Star", as Tecumseh was called by the Cherokees, and a number of them had given the war whoop, signifying their willingness to go to war, Junaluska, the great peace Chief, calmly and wisely advised his people against going to war against the white people.

Soco Gap is one of the four notable depressions or gaps in the great Balsam range as it winds its thirty-six miles from Tri-corner Knob of the Great Smokies to Tennessee Bald at the junction of the Pisgah Ridge. The other three are, Balsam Gap, Black Camp Gap, and Pin Oak Gap. All four of these gaps have served as gateways across the Balsams at different periods of settlement and economic development. Before the coming of the white man, Soco Gap seemed to be, by far, the most important passage way for aboriginal travel.

About the year 1700, when the Long Hunters, the mineral prospectors, and other adventurers, began to break through the passes of Blue Ridge and penetrate the intra-mountain region, now known as Western North Carolina, the Cherokees in the French Broad and Pigeon River Valleys took fright and also took refuge behind the great Balsam range. It is thought that this explains why, in recorded historic times, no Indians are reported to have been living in these areas. Numerous Indian mounds, village sites, burial places, and the country side strewn with arrow heads, pottery, and other evidences, attest a comparatively dense population in the recent past. This applies especially to the Pigeon River Valley. (See note below)

In view of this situation it is not strange that the Cherokees, esconced as they were behind the great Balsam range, should maintain a "lookout" or a "watch" at A-ha-lu-na, the main portal to their security from both the whites and their hereditary enemies, the Iriquois of New York, the Shawanoes of the Ohio Valley, and the Catawbas of the Piedmont region of North Carolina and South Carolina.

A large beech tree with the date, 1706, rudely carved in its bark, once stood beside the ancient Indian trail three-fourths mile east of Davis Gap, now erroneously called Pigeon Gap, and four and one-half miles south-east of Waynesville. It was observed there by a "young private" of General Rutherford's army as he marched with his twenty-four hundred soldiers against the Cherokee Indians in September, 1776. Many years later, Judge Samuel Lowry who was the young private in Rutherford's army, held a court in Waynesville. He again visited the site "marked" beech tree, and verified the date, 1706, as indicated above.

27

This "marked" tree, at this early date, is evidence of the visitation of hunters or adventurers in the Pigeon Valley at that surprisingly early time. Such visitations were inimical to Indian peace and tranquility, and lends support to the statement above, to the effect that they abandoned the area around the year 1700.

'THREE CHEERS FOR THE RED, WHITE AND BLUE' — IN WAYNESVILLE (1828)

AUTHOR'S NOTE: The following is the *Western Carolinian's* (Asheville) report of a July 4th Celebration at Waynesville in 1828. By way of explanation, the Jeffersonian Democratic party at that time was known as the Republican party.

Whatever happens here this 1866 Fourth of July will be nothing compared to what they once did on the day, when perhaps the memory of the freedom fight was fresher.

Back in 1828, according to The Western Carolinian, the following took place at Waynesville:

"At a meeting of a respectable number of the citizens of Haywood County assembled in the courthouse at Waynesville, Col. Robert Love was appointed president and Elijah Deaver, vice-president. The Declaration of Independence was read by Felix Axley Esq., of Murphy, N. C., who made a few appropriate remarks. After this, the company repaired to Mr. B. Chambers' tavern and partook of a dinner provided for the occasion. The cloth being removed, the following toasts were drunk:

"To The Day we celebrate"; "To The Constitution of the United States", "To The memory of Gen. George Washington."

"To The Constitution of North Carolina"; "To The Framers of the Declaration of Independence"; "To Charles Carroll, the only survivor among the signers of the Declaration of Independence".

"To The memory of Thomas Jefferson"; "To The ex-presidents; "To Marquis de LaFayette, the foreigner who, in 1776 espoused the cause of bleeding liberty".

"To The memory of Marion DeKalb, who watered the tree of liberty with his blood on the plains of ill-fated Camden"; To The American Navy; "To The American Fair"; "To the Navy."

"It is significant," the newspaper continued, "that the American Navy was singled out for a toast where the Army was not mentioned at all."

(It is highly likely, considering 13 toasts drunk up to that point, that nobody was aware the Army had been slighted).

However, the stalwarts of Haywood County were not through.

"Reuben Deaver," the newspaper records, "gave the following toast: 'May every Republican principled gentleman live to see the good effects of the tariff and rejoice to see the fair sex of our nation wearing the manufactures of their own hands.' "

"Felix Alley gave this toast: 'May domestic manufactures and internal improvements be joined in the holy bonds of matrimony until the Union produce the fair daughter of commerce.' "

And not to be outdone, the faithful newspaper reporter noted, "William Johnson, a native of Ireland, gave a toast to Christopher Columbus: "While we are toasting the heads of these people, here's a health to the discoverer of America.' "

They were men in those days. Not only could they swallow 16 toasts, but they knew what the Republican Party stood for.

(The bottom of the page of the old newspaper may have been torn off. It does not say whether they ever finished the dinner).

TSALI'S CAVE

The photograph of the Rock-shelter (not a cave) accompanying this article is believed to have been the hide-out of Tsali at the time of the forced removal of the main body of the Cherokee people by the United States Army under General Winfield Scott in the year of 1838. It is by traditional here-say that it has come to be called "Tsali's Cave."

A study of the current records of the removal period does not in any instance reveal any reference to a cave. In an official letter to General Winfield Scott, Commander-in-Chief of the United States Army, bearing date March 7, 1846, William H. Thomas gives a description of Tsali's camp and hiding place. In this letter Mr. Thomas was endeavoring to qualify his claim against the Federal Government for the cost of some five hundred bushels of corn that he had furnished the refugee Indians following the removal. In the course of his letter he gives the details of his services rendered in the rounding up of the recalcitrant Indians, and his part in the capture and bringing in of Tsali. He was not making any claim for his services which he rendered entirely on a volunteer basis; but he was trying to show the reasonableness of his outlay for the corn.

First, Mr. Thomas states in his letter that he employed an Indian guide who told him — quote "Charley (Tsali) and his company were concealed remote from the settlements on the Smoky Mountain. We were informed by the Guide that they (Tsali and party) would, as they told him, resist any attempt to capture them. When we came in sight of the camp on the top of a cliff too steep to be ascended except by a circuitous route round the precipice by holding on to some small bushes."

Further on in the same letter Mr. Thomas says — quote: "I met with an Indian that informed me that the murderers (Tsali and his party) were concealed in a large head of laurel and hemlock near the top of the Smoky Mountain." Again he says — quote: "When we reached the camp my being foremost, no doubt, prevented them from firing upon us, and by speaking to them in their own language, Etc."

The three descriptive terms used are: "Concealed remote from the settlements on the Smoky Mountain": "Camp on top of a cliff too steep to ascend": and "Concealed in a large head of laurel and hemlock". None of these descriptions can be construed as being, or referring to a "cave".

The rock shelter and camping place discovered by Ranger Noland, and photographed by Mr. Mills may well be conceived as meeting the descriptions of Mr. Thomas. Its location is on a very steep slope or cliff, overlooking the main left fork of Deep Creek, and about one-half mile above the south of Keg Drive Creek. This spot, till this day, is quite remote and inaccessible. It is near five miles through the "roughs", going up Deep Creek and about the same distance if approached from the sky line road by going down Fork Ridge.

Accumulation of ashes, and burnt, broken rocks under the shelter; and the smoke surface above evidences occupation by campers for many years. A small drain or trickle of water only a few feet away would supply water for campers. There is evidence too, that the sides of the shelter have been walled up, which in that case, would provide shelter for five or six persons.

Considered from the standpoint of strategy on the part of Tsali and his comrades, to be hidden in a deep cave would be folly. It is much more reasonable to assume that they would select a high, commanding position from which they could easily see the approach, and have the advantage of soldiers, or any one seeking to take them. This location and shelter meets these strategical requirements in a full measure, and is in accord with Mr. Thomas's several descriptive statements.

Inquiry among the Cherokee Indians reveals that Keg Drive Creek near the Tsali Rock derived its name from the fact that Jim Keg who lived at Birdtown for many years frequently hunted bear in that area. It could be that he and his hunting companions camped under this same rock shelter.

Chapter VI

Miscellaneous Stories

CASHIERS VALLEY

No less an authority than Felix E. Alley of Waynesville, a judge of the Superior Courts of North Carolina, who was born and bred in the Whiteside Cove section of Cashiers Township, states as an irrefutable fact, in a letter, that the valley was named for an old hermit-hunter who lived in the valley for years before any other white man came into the valley, and was well known to many of the early settlers. This man's name says Judge Alley, was Cashiers, and the settlement was known from the beginning as Cashiers Valley.

All other versions of the naming of Cashiers Valley are, indeed, traditional, as Judge Alley says, and there are at least a half dozen different ones, all however centering around the exploits of a horse, or a mule or a bull.

As a matter of historical fact the valley was known as Cashiers valley long before the Hamptons set up their estate here about 1838.

The persistence of these stories about a horse, a mule or maybe a bull, with a name from which "Cashiers" might easily be derived cannot be entirely brushed off as not having some foundation. One thing they do establish beyond question is that the grass of Cashiers Valley in the early days was a most remarkable grass.

This fact brought in many settlers in the 1830s. The Zacharys, McKinneys, Nortons, Allisons, McCalls and others came into the valley in that period. The Zachary family records are quite clear.

The head of the family, Col. John A. Zachary, had been a captain of the Surry County, (N. C.) militia in the war of 1812. Surry County, of which Mt. Airy is now the county seat, lies to the northwest of Winston-Salem and was settled some years before the American Revolution.

William Zachary, of a family originally from London, which had settled in Virginia, established a home in Surry County about 1775. He was a Quaker and opposed to warfare, but his son, John A. Zachary, helped organize the local militia in the War of 1812, served as a captain and later Colonel or ranking commander of the Surry County Militia.

Colonel Zachary prospered but unfortunately signed the bond of a man who thereupon fled the jurisdiction of the court. In an attempt to produce the fugitive and thus save the bond, Colonel Zachary made a search for him in north Georgia, but lost the trail in Alabama, and returned home to pay the bond. On his way back he came through the mountains, passing through Cashiers Valley.

The fertility of the land, evident from the remarkable grass, attracted his attention, and the next year 1833, he came back to the valley with one of his sons, Alexander — always known, however, as Andy — built two cabins, put up the walls of a two-story loghouse, cleared 20 acres and made a crop, and then returned in the fall of 1834 to Surry County.

In January 1835, the family started from Surry County on the long trip to Cashiers Valley, traveling in a six-horse wagon and a "carriage", down the eastern and southeastern side of the mountains until they reached the vicinity of Pickens, S. C., where they turned northward and entered Cashiers Valley along the course of Chatooga River, coming in just to the east of Whiteside Mountain.

Colonel Zachary and members of the family — there were 14 children — took up grants of State land and located around and comprising what is now the site of much of the village and the environs.

State Grant No. 124 for 640 acres was entered by Colonel Zachary in 1835. This grant has been located and mapped by the U.S. Forest Service and is identified by the Service as the land on which High Hampton Inn now stands, including the lake site and the adjacent section of the golf course.

The grant extended toward the present village site, but did not cover the original Zachary homestead site, though the two Zachary cemeteries may have been reserved.

'BIG MUSTER', COURT DAYS AND RALLIES

The old muster militia companies were active in this country in the early days and on up until the outbreak of the Civil War. There were four or five such organizations within what would be the present bounds of Haywood County, and located by precincts as follows: Beaverdam, Crabtree (including Fines Creek), Waynesville, Pigeon and probably Jonathan's Creek. Then there were two or three west of the Balsams.

These companies were commanded by captains, same as our present National Guards; and had from about seventy-five or 80 men up to maybe a hundred in each company. They had their own local drill grounds, where they met regularly about once a month for practice-drill.

'BIG MUSTER'

Then once a year, on the second Saturday in October, all the companies gathered at Waynesville for drill, inspection and a parade. This day, called 'Big Muster', was a gala occasion. Usually there would be a speech—and always music, hard cider and gingerbread. Also in those days, when they had the local distiller-ies and the open rum shop, there were always more potent drinks on hand than hard cider. So, 'Big Muster' would be whooped up in a fight or two.

Superior Court days also drew large crowds. Two terms, generally, were held each year, a spring and a fall term. The political parties would time their speakings so as to fall on court weeks in the different counties as much as possible, in order to have bigger crowds.

THE SPEAKINGS

In those days, it was nearly always joint campaigns that were carried on between the parties—Democrats, Whigs or Populists, whichever might be opposed at the time. (The Republican party, as it is known today, had not been born then). And the term 'stump-speaking' was sometimes literally true. The candidates often spoke out in the open—even from the ground, box, crude platform, or maybe a stump.

But whenever the speaking was scheduled to be held on a court day, the judge would yield something like an hour of court-time thus giving about two hours at the 'dinner recess' period for the speaking.

Note: Haywood's first courthouse was probably built of hewn logs. (It is not definitely known). It could have been of sash-sawed frame material.

"With All the Coloring"

So, we can imagine something of the picture on such occasions: Maybe they are filing into the courtroom, or the crowd might be gathering around the speakers stand out in the courthouse yard. Nearly all are men — perhaps there are a few women. (The women seldom attended court as mere spectators).

The men are dressed in coarse, loose homespun; soft, coarsely-woven felt, fur or skin hats and caps; and probably many of them are in their worn, soiled and slick hunting shirts. Some have brought their hunting rifles along (as was customary on such occasions, and here and there we see a man with his trusted coon dog by his side.

People were perhaps more partisan in those days than they are now. The speakers would explain the issues of the campaign (each one for his side) in rough-and-tumble fashion, and in no uncertain terms. And out from the vociferious crowd would occasionally come a loud — "Hurrah!" (for So-and-So).

For, we repeat, they whooped it up in those days at the political gatherings, etc. There would often be a fist fight or two before the speakings ended; and then again, they might go off all right.

Hard Cider, Gingerbread, Etc.

To add to the coloring of these occasions, of course, there were the stands of hard cider, gingerbread, apples, etc. Then, it is said a glass of cider with a piece of gingerbread was only a nickel. At "Houses of Public Entertainment (in the village of Waynesville and elsewhere, brandy, rum, beer and other "spiritous liquers", could be had at correspondingly cheap prices. Of course, this all added to the hilarity of these public gatherings.

33

RECONSTRUCTING THE OLD SQUARE AND VILLAGE

By 1813, Haywood's first jail — with whipping post and stocks in the yard — had been erected. Also the courthouse was finished in 1814. The jail stood near present intersection of Church and Montgomery Streets; the courthouse nearby on the old 'Square'. Here our first 'Public Square' was laid off, after Robert Love had given the land.

Waynesville's present brightly lighted, bustling Main Street was then (and for many years later) nothing but a somewhat crooked clay road, running along the crest of the ridge. At first there was only about three blocks of it, with the old square being the focal point. Present Church Street (then one of the main entrance roads) wound down the hill, the course being about as at present, and intersected with the main roads) wound down the hill; the old main (east-west) road then ran up to Richland Creek.

East Street was, for many years, only about one block long. From there on was nothing but a trail leading along the fence row up and cross Johnston Hill — the dividing line between William Johnston on the north and the Welch lands (mostly) on the south. Also John Smathers owned up on the square, northeast corner.

Leading along present South Main was the 'Mt. Prospect' — Green Hill Cemetery road; Pigeon (Bethel) Road led off at its present intersection with Main.

The first post office (that we have any record of) was also near the Church Street by the (later) Milas Davis house; a store stood on the front, later Smathers building. The John Smathers store was directly across on Main. There was an office (later Squire Faucett's) at the time on the old post office lot, there being the ravine depression lying just back of it, with woods.

Colonel Robert Love owned most of the remaining land and vacant lots on the west and southwest side, excepting that owned by Wayne Battle, the Welches, J. M. Tate, Herrens, John Howell, the Hyatts, and probably two or three others.

All else around the old square and sparsely settled little village was woodland and — or cultivated, fenced-in fields. Cattle and hogs, with bells tinkling, roamed all about.

Down near the foot of present Church Street (later John Cabe residence) was the old Love's Camping Spring — place, where travelers (with wagons, carts and on horseback) drew up, camped for the night, and watered their stock. (This continued up until in the 1880's, when the railroad came). The first (log) Baptist 'Meetin' House stood nearby. Green Hill Academy was away up on the hill at present Green Hill Cemetery.

COPY OF A PART OF THE JOURNAL OF COL. WM. H. THOMAS IN AUGUST, 1829

Aug. 11th, 1829: Staid all night at Levi Pondexter's. Next morning after breakfast went with L. Pondexter to where he and Joseph Welch were digging a ridge, which is a considerable curiosity; from thence I went to Little Will's, on the Stokeah; from thence in company with

Little Will, I proceeded on my way to Cheoah where I attended a dance at the townhouse near Big George's, and spent the remainder of the night at Big George's. Next morning I made some experiments which appeared to show that there were gold near that place. About 10 o'clock I proceeded on my way to Valley River and reached Chunaluska (Junaluska's) a little before dark.

14th:

Next morning, 14th I went to a place thought to contain gold, and made some experiments, but found no gold, but remarkably furnished with signs. From here went to where Chunaluska's first wife lived, and from there in company with Chunaluska I went to the mine below John Welch's, and spent some time in examining it, and from there proceeded on to New Echota in company with said Cherokee, and just before dark we took up at an Indian's by the name of Wilnota, who informed us there was a lead mine not far from his house on the other side of the river (2words illegible), and a silver mine also in the same Neighborhood. Early next morning we started on our journey and stopped at Mr. Raper's and took breakfast, who informed us that there had been something like silver run out of some ore not far from his house, and that his father had found something like gold, and he agreed to give me some of the ore as I came back. After we had taken breakfast we proceeded on our way and staid all night at an Indian's. Early next morning we started and after a tolerable hard day's ride, we, a little after dark, arrived at New Echota. On Friday, 15th we put up at Mr. Alexander McCoy's.

Next day I went to the court of the Cherokee Nation where I heard a young attorney speak, by the name of Rogers, and another by the name of Wix. The former appeared to me as a man of education, and also of considerable eloquence; the other appeared to speak the English language imperfectly. On Saturday I attended Divine worship at the Council house where I heard two of the natives sing and preach in their own language. One by the name of Husk of the Presbyterian profession, and the other by the name of Gunter, of the Methodist Society. Both appeared to be men of good nature as well as ability, and possessed of that which distinguishes a Christian. The congregation appeared to be very much affected under the preaching, and what added to the Solemnity of the same was a criminal seated close to the preacher, bound with a rope and handcuffed, which had been condemned for murder, and was expected to be put to death on Monday. He sat with one of their hymn books in his hand and appeared to be lamenting his case., while nearly all classes of the Cherokees joined in praising the Lord from gray hairs down to youths, and each countenance appeared to speak Solemnity, and whilst the preacher dwelt on the terrible affects of intemperance and sin, and on the other hand with the apparent deepest anxiety to promote their good, he reasoned on the necessity of being temperate, and the practising of virtue in order to be happy here and hereafter, and with a heart apparently flowing with that love which is unspeakable and full of glory. The love of God and the happiness of Heaven, I perceived brought the briny tears to trickle down the furrowed faces of many gray-headed natives.

After two sermons were preached I retired to my lodgings at Mr. McCoy's. On Sunday morning at 10 o'clock the congregation attended the Council house, and after some singing in the Indians' language the Reverend Mr. Jones, a native of Wales, delivered a sermon in the English language, and as soon as it was finished one of the Natives repeated it in the Cherokee language, so that the congregation all might understand.

The prisoner was still brought in in time of the worship, and after a short intermission at mid-day the native preachers continued their religious exercises in ther own language until night. Next day I attended the Council and Supreme Court of the nation, the Council and the Committee to enter into the subject of reprieving the criminal, and the young Mr. Rogers presented a petition with a considerable number of names affixed to it setting forth the aggravating circumstances which occasioned the criminal to do the murder and supported with a concise and beautiful argument. Afterwards Mr. Jones was admitted to speak on the subject, who spoke tolerably lengthy and much to the purpose. Then Mr. Boudenot, a native, addressed the Committee and Council in the Cherokee language, and appeared to be possessed of considerable eloquence; and afterwards the said Mr. Gunter spoke very lengthy on the subject, who is a gentleman of undisputed eloquence, and afterwards several of the natives spoke on the subject, but in a concise manner. In a short time the majority was found to be for reprieving him, and in a short time afterwards he was set at liberty.

On Tuesday I attended the Council, and read the laws of the nation which I found framed pretty much on the same principles of the laws of the United States. I also found to my great astonishment that their law respecting minerals was different from what I had heard, and instead of each individual being entitled to work two years at any mine he might find, all mines were considered as property of the nation and no individual had any right to work at any of them. therefore found that unless the law was annulled which had been passed relative to minerals, the nation nor I could have any encouragement to hunt mines in the limits of the Cherokee nation, and in order to remove that difficulty I formed an acquaintance with several of the leading Committeemen and Councilors who I found to possess a spirit of enterprising in no less degree than to most enterprising run in the United States, and needed only to know where there was mines in their country to desire to have an interest in them, in order to conceive them, there was, I showed them several things and told them several more. I also reasoned on the individual benefit, as well as that of the nation, should the Committee and Council make suitable amendments to the law. I continued in this employment, adding to the anticipations of enterprise and prosperity of the nation until Thursday, 22nd. When after taking dinner at 12 o'clock I left town in order to go to Hightown in company of a young lawyer by the name of Adair, but not until I had procured a petition to be presented to the Committee by a gentleman who had found some particles of gold & by showing his particles to several of the Committee it caused the gold fever like contagion & in a short time gold was the only thing to afford a subject of conversation for gentlemen.

On my way to Mr. Adair's on the height and about 20 miles I traveled until I came to the neighborhood of Hightown through a plane almost uninhabited, and for the most part a barren wilderness."

NOTE: Here Wilburn adds:

No literature that I have access to gives any definite dates as to just when Col. Thomas actually became Chief of The Cherokees; nor when he ceased to be their Chief. Chief Yonaguska, who adopted him as his son when Col. Thomas was about 15 years old, later at the time of the old Chief's death in April 1839, designated him as his successor, and the Cherokee people recognized no other as their Chief as long as Col. Thomas was able to go among them. James Mooney says that shortly after the year 1866 Mr. Thomas lost his health, and became mentally ill.

But it seems that Col. Thomas, by the time he was 21 years old, which was 1826, had become recognized as a wise friend and adviser to the Cherokee people generally, and also an adviser and helper of the Chief at this early age.

James Mooney, who is the best authority on Cherokee affairs, knew Col. Thomas well and frequently talked with him. In fact he gives Col. Thomas credit for much of his information contained in his extensive writings on the Cherokee Indians. In his government report Mooney has this to say about Col. Thomas:—

"Shortly after 1866 Col. Thomas was compelled by physical and mental infirmity to retire from further active participation in the affairs of the East Cherokee Indians, *after more than half a century spent in intimate connection with them,* during the greater portion of which time, he had been their most trusted friend and advisor."

Note: Col. Thomas was acting Chief of the Cherokee for a round 30 years, and prior to becoming Chief, as a very young man, he assisted Chief Yonaguska. James Mooney and H. C. Wilburn have this to say about Col. W. H. Thomas: —

Mooney lived amongst the Cherokees in the 1880s and 1890s and got his information from Col. Thomas, Major Stringfield, Captain James W. Terrell, who took over the management of the Cherokee matters after Col. Thomas retired; and from a number of the older Cherokee people who knew and loved Col. Thomas.

So, it seems that his connection as Chief, can not be definitely limited as to time, but seemingly from about 1826 to 1866.

"THE JONATHAN'S CREEK AND TENNESSEE MOUNTAIN TURNPIKE"

"Jonathan's Creek and Tennessee Mountain Turnpike" — yes, that was a long name. But it was a long road; and it was a long, long time a-building (twelve years to be exact).

All considered, this was one of the boldest road-building movements to be launched here in that day. Not only so because of length of road and the very steep and rough terrain it traversed, but also because of the limited means and very poor road-building equipment the people had.

At an organization meeting here in October, 1851, William H. Thomas of Jackson County was elected president of the company, with R. G. A. Love, secretary, John Moody, David Howell, Robert Boyd, and W. G. B. Garrett (all of Haywood) were named directors. James Baxter of Cosby, Tennessee, and William Green of Big Creek were added later. Thomas Welch of Cherokee was selected to grade the road.

The organization was a stock company, working under a charter obtained the same year. Prior to this (in 1847) a charter had been obtained but no active organization, it seems, had been effected.

From October, 1851, till December, 1855, when actual construction work on the road was begun, a period of more than four years had elapsed with little accomplished.

Idea 100 Years Old

During this time the old Minute Book (to be found in the office of the clerk of Superior Court here) reveals the fact that meeting after meeting was held: Some of the officials had resigned and replacements made, one or two complete reorganizations had been effected and there had been periods when nothing, seemingly, was accomplished.

Also a "Committee of View" was appointed to "look out a Pigeon River route." This committee returned with a report that "the Pigeon River route is entirely beyond the means of the company to build."

Across Smokies Route

After the mountain route had been decided upon, Welch was ordered to begin the survey. As at first designated this was to begin "at a point near Boyd's on Jonathan's Creek" (the Robert Boyd place) "and continue to the Tennessee line" (at Cosby). (Except in a few places, Highway 284 today practically follows this old survey)| Up Cove Creek mountain and through the gap, at more than 4,500 feet altitude it went; then from Cove Creek Gap "making a thousand turns" to Cataloochee Creek. Thence down this creek, and the road is soon turning (after crossing Little Cataloochee) in the direction of Mt. Sterling Gap. This gap is reached after again making so many turns that one, on going up, gets dizzy. Winding down from the gap to Big Creek — more turns.

'Take the Turns with Ease'

Surveyor Welch reported to the company that he made this survey "with a grade of one foot in fourteen, with the exception of a short distance on the Jonathan's Creek side of Cove Creek Mountain. From Cataloochee Creek through the gap of Mt. Sterling to the Tennessee line where George Grooms lives," Welch said, (this) "was made with a grade of one foot in twelve."

Morever, this old surveyor, with nothing but an old-fashioned surveyor's compass and chain, and with probably only two or three helpers, had only three weeks in which to make his survey and bring in a report. It seems unbelievable, but that is the record.

The road was to be made fourteen feet wide, generally. But specifications were that "on sharp turns the road is to be made eighteen feet wide, so that wagons can take the turns with ease."

Contracts Are Let

Approximately $22,000 in stock was taken by public subscriptions, including $5,000 taken by the state, there being more than 100 individual subscribers. So, finally on December 3, 1855, the road was ready to be let.

Contracts were let in sections of one-half mile each to the lowest bidders, although a contractor could take more than one section. It is said there were, all told first and last, about 30 or 35 individual contractors for the road; the contracts ran all the way from $39.50 up to $500. William Ramsey bid off the Big Creek bridge January 1, 1858, for $139. Much of this labor was paid for in Cherokee bonds.

See them at Work

To better visualize the 'bigness' of this undertaking, we must remember that this 28 miles of grade traversed generally some of the "wildest" and most rugged terrain in Western North Carolina, all covered with dense growths of "the forest primeval." Felling trees and clearing out the rights-of-way was the first work to be done. Imagine these working crews stretched out (at intervals of a half mile or more) along the entire distance of 28 miles, all at work!

"Axes ringing, saws a-singing, hammers swinging" — all hands bringing every effort to bear upon the work of getting the road made.

But there were many interruptions, delays and lay-offs. Severe winter weather, stopping work to make crops, and lay-offs for lack of funds were some of them. For grading work they had little more than the ordinary farm implements of that day — picks, mattocks, shovels, small plows, sledge-hammers, etc. They didn't even have blasting powder. Instead, they heated the big rocks that couldn't be moved by building big fires on them; and then they shattered the rock with sledge-hammer. In grading around mountainsides, they would often construct log retaining walls on the lower side of the road in very sloping places, then fill in with dirt, rocks, etc.

The Finish

Finally, however, and in spite of all these handicaps, the Jonathan's Creek and Tennessee Mountain Turnpike was finished — late in October 1860. It had been five years (nearly) under actual construction, and twelve years since promotion of it was started.

Although the road was built just before the Civil War, the stock company had no thought of a military road. The organizers, mostly Jonathan's Creek and Waynesville citizens, had the idea of capitalizing on the stock-drive business at that time — mostly East Tennesseeans, driving through to South Carolina and Augusta markets. That's why it was made a toll road.

39

The road was opened as a toll road, but as such it wasn't profitable. After some twenty years of operation, the toll system were discontinued.

LAWLESSNESS GENERALLY WENT WITH ISOLATION

In the northern part of Haywood county in the Pigeon River gorge, and extending up the river from Waterville Hydro-Electric plant for a distance of about fifteen miles, lies the roughest, most isolated and inaccessible section of the county. For nearly all of this distance the gorge on both sides is too narrow, steep and inaccessible for habitation.

Period of Isolation

The family or two which first settled here just a few years before the Civil War were, we have been told, probably "squatters" on what was then Love speculation land. Sam McGaha was the first of record, February 1857. McGaha doubtless settled in good faith since he obtained a deed for his 100 acre tract on that date.

Years later a few other settlers ventured in from time to time until the Big Bend settlement numbered probably 35 to 40 people at the close of the century. By the time the Carolina Power and Light Company began construction of their plant in 1925, the number had increased to an estimated 50 to 65, population of about 12 families. At that time there were Browns, McGahas, Packetts, Groomses, Prices, Hendersons, Gateses and others besides the Hickses.

The settlement was reached by traveling on foot or horseback along two rough, steep winding trails, one leading across the mountain from the Big Creek side, the other leading, generally, down a ravine from the upper Hurricane.

Disregard for Law

Isolated in here as they were, about 25 miles from Newport, Tenn., and about 35 miles from Waynesville, many of these people seemingly grew up with little regard for law and order. They had no roads, no store, no schools (not more than two or three schools were ever taught there), no church or Sunday School services, except for the periods that Miss Odum, a missionary and the Salvation Army had services held, seldom had any mail or reading matter—and little Sabbath as it is generally kept. But be it said, in fairness to the Big Bend folks, that such lawlessness was not confined to that section alone during the years of 1920-1934; for that was the period of the crime wave — in Haywood, and elsewhere.

First Execution

Sol Grooms, the first person executed in this county, was from the nearby Sterling Creek section, just over on the Big Creek side of the mountain. He was convicted of the axe-slaying of a Townsend boy at the Grooms home. The execution — and our first one by hanging, occurred in the 1870's (we have not yet found the trial-record). People flocked from far and near, we have been told, to Waynesville and Cobb hill to see the grim spectacle of execution by hanging. The poor man, Grooms, it is said, when asked if he had anything to say before the trap was sprung, calmly requested a "chaw of t'backer". Some thought Grooms, who was of Indian extraction, was unbalanced and should have been sent to a mental institution instead, but that was long before the day of psychiatrists.

THE SCOTT BROWN-MIMS WHITE CASE

Now, the public works, lumber manufacturing and all the work connected with the building of the power plant, in the Big Creek section had been closed out in the early '30's. Consequently some of the lawless, floating element employed here, and which had made the Big Bend very much a rendezvous, left also. This helped some as a quieting-down influence. Crime and lawlessness, however, which had not only been going on here, but was general, continued until its awful culmination in the Scott Brown-Mims White dual slaying at the "Restin' Log", in August, 1930.

After the disappearance of Brown and White this case remained an unsolved mystery for something like seven months. During this time Mrs. Brown, mother of Scott, made many trips to Waynesville, Newport and elsewhere trying to get the law, prosecutors, officials — somebody to really get busy and solve the mystery if possible. (The writer happened to have his magistrate's office in the old Court House at the time and knows about this poor woman's great anxiety and solicitude.)

But seemingly no clues to the whereabouts of Brown and White could be found — as time went relentlessly on!

Finally the assistance of J. J. O'Malley (a young detective visiting in Waynesville some five or six months after the crime happened) was enlisted, and the solution and final closing of the case was, briefly, as follows:

The perpetrators of the crime were — by smart maneuvering, found out, and confessions were obtained. Detective O'Malley and Deputy A. P. Ledbetter were given a rehearsal of the crime by the confessor, and were led to the place under the roots of an upturned tree (on the mountain-top overlooking Big Bend) where the bodies of Brown and White had been buried. This was in the last days of February, 1931, and the first week in March.

Then followed, in reasonably quick succession, the sensational trial of the four men implicated, their conviction and sentences — of from 2 to 30 years in State's prison.

HAYWOOD'S OLD COURTHOUSE DATES FROM 1867, IS STILL IN OTHER USE

The second Haywood County courthouse, built shortly after the Civil War, is one of the oldest structures still in use in the County.

The first floor of this old brick structure is now occupied by the Town of Waynesville's Light and Water Department. The town recently tore off the top, or second story which was the court room many years ago.

This second courthouse, part of which is still standing at the corner of Main and East Streets, was built of rough home-made brick and was used up until 1884. In that year the third "Temple of Justice" was finished. It stood two blocks, farther north on Main, practically on the site of our present modern building.

The ceiling joists, 32 feet long, are all one-piece timbers hewn from yellow pine with a broad axe — and "straight as a gun barrel". The broad thick floor boards, said to be the original, are still sound and firm.

The lower floor was for county offices. The courtroom was kept covered with sawdust and ground tan bark. This was to protect from the quids of tobacco and the "juice of the filthy weed" — as Judge Merrimon is said to have termed it on one occasion. It also served as a muffler for the clap, clap of heavy brogans of that day. Then, too, the janitor's work was lessened perhaps five-fold!

The late Dr. Eugene Gudger remembered, as a boy, he said, going there to court with his father. Whenever the covering of sawdust became well saturated with tobacco, the janitor would remove and renew with a fresh supply from the sawmills.

This was after the time when Judge Merrimon 'rode the circuit'. As the story goes:

Merrimon on one occasion found the courtroom just "too dirty and filthy" for public use as such — and he promptly told the county officials so. On this round he also found conditions elsewhere — at "Old Webster", Marshall, and to some extent all over the judicial district, about the same.

Well, it is said, the judge made it plain that there must be a cleaning this up before his next round — and it was done.

"Old man Bill Brock" was the court officer. He would come out on the little 'porch' to the upstairs courtroom and begin "cryin' for the Court". He had a loud voice anyway, so he'd bellow out —

"Oh, yes—Oh, yes! (So-and-so), come into court as you're bound t' do, 'r yore bond'll for-fetid."

Dr. Gudger said (sometime before he passed away several years ago) he well remembered how the court crowds gathered about-long before court-time, jesting and laughing, much like they do today. Some few would bring their dog and long-barreled rifle guns along; and would vie with one another in telling of their hunting tales. In case political speakings were set during court week as, was often done, the judge would yield about an hour of court time for the speaking. The court crier would also announce the hour set for the speaking.

CAMPMEETINGS WERE MAJOR PART OF LIFE IN MOUNTAINS IN 1870's, 80's.

The last-of-the-century camp meetings offered rich experiences for the old-timers; and they also left a rich heritage, full of traditions.

42

These annual meetings, which were held in a few established places throughout this Western N. C. section, were often spoken of as "seasons of refreshing from the Lord."

The main period of these meetings in this section, was about two score years, or from the early 1870's up until about 1890.

So, as such "refreshing seasons", they were eagerly looked forward to by the communities for which they were held.

These meetings usually lasted from two to three weeks; they were held at the most convenient time of the year best suited for farm folks. That was generally from about the middle of July into the first week of August.

Preparation For The Meeting

The arrangement and cleaning up of the camp grounds, as well as the killing of beeves and preparation of other foods began about a week in advance.

Of course, there were the 'camp followers' in those days, same as now, some of whom were poor and knew of the hospitality at the tables on such occasions. Knowing this, the well-to-do families always went prepared — that no one should go hungry. They killed beeves, muttons, and chickens; baked loaf and biscuit, gingerbread and cake, also brought out jars of preserves and canned goods a plenty!

The character and faith of the preachers and laymen of that day, measured up. At the Iron Duff camp ground there were such men as: John M. Queen, Sr., Frank M. Davis, Riley Ferguson, Preacher Towles, Thomas Ferguson, James Murray, Joe McCracken, Davy McCracken, William Haynes, Lawson Messer, Uncle Hosey Mauney, Eldridge Medford, the Howells on Jonathan Creek, James Crawford and others, perhaps equally as faithful. At Shook's camp ground: Humphrey Haynes, Dave Shook, Mills Shook, Cansier Haynes, Mark Killian, Preacher Towles, the Byerses, Smathers and others.

Significance of Mourner's Bench

The mourner's bench played an important and significant part in most of the churches of this entire mountain region of the South for many generations past. Past, we say, because it now has almost disappeared; a few of the so-called fundamentalist, or old-style churches, still use it. It signified not only an attitude of repentance, but a resolve to "pray through" to forgiveness. It was the place where the penitents or "mourners" were supposed to wrestle Jacob-like until they got heart-felt religion — then to let the church and congregation know it by shouting. If a person who "got through" by his own seeking (or together with the prayers of others in his behalf) and was not the demonstrative, shouting type, he was supposed to at least be able to stand up, tell the Church about it and shake hands, as a sign of his repentance.

Alley McCracken and others used to tell a story illustrative of the times: At one of these meetings Uncle Bill Haynes went to Aunt Adeline Messer and said "Adeline, I want you to pray for my son, John."

"Pray for him yourself," she replied, "I've got my own younguns to pray for."

The Meeting Begins

Now, let us imagine that the meeting under this old brush arbor is already to begin, either the 11 o'clock or the "early candlelight" service. The preacher or, maybe, the song-leader picks up the old Christian Harmony and "hists" for the hymn, perhaps "Amazing Grace" or "Come Thou Fount —". This is the signal for all outside activity and noise to cease and for the people to assemble.

We gave you an idea of the kind of messages they delivered in those days and the style or manner of most preaching. It was not only unusually loud and long, but was also characteristic of the Jonathan Edwards fire and brimstone days. Those were the days when, it is said, God's wrath, rather than Christ's love, was preached and sinners were "shaken over the pit". (But with all this, there was often fine fundamental interpretations of the Scriptures and good, sincere preaching.) Toward the close of the sermon the preacher usually departed from his text altogether — to warn, exhort and to entreat "sinners" to come forward. Then they would often step down from the pulpit and get in the aisle — and now the —

Altar Call Is Made

This was the signal for the "workers" to go out into the congregation and "talk to sinners". (This was the term used.) In the good meetings often several persons would go up for prayer; and in the "awful meetings" fifteen or twenty at the mourner's bench together was not unusual. So it is on this particular night — as we are trying to picture for you an "awful meetin' ". An appropriate hymn — like, we'll say, "Nothing But the Blood of Jesus," resounds in this crude "temple of the Lord", the singing and praying all intermingled. Now someone is shouting — now another — Yes, it's the voice of a new convert, and some of the congregation are straining to see.

Thus it goes on until near midnight, when the service closes, more because of almost complete exhaustion, perhaps, than anything else.

At last the meeting closes for the year, and the candidates for baptism are received. Then the crude seats are stacked up for another year — and the hogs and cattle come in and take over in the meantime.

THE STORY OF MAJOR REDMOND
(He Quit His Career of Crime — Uncaptured and —— Unscathed) ——

There was a man who in the early part of this 20th century, stood up in many different pulpits of this mountain country and proclaimed the Gospel — earnestly and powerfully, calling 'sinners' to repentance.

He told them that sin did'nt pay — that he had tried it; and that furthermore, one had to repent of sin in order to get right with God.

And in Oconee and Pickins counties of South Carolina, Rabun County, Georgia; Jackson and Transylvania Counties in North Carolina and maybe in other places, folks flocked in to hear him.

We first see this man, now an orphan boy of 16 years, working for a family by the name of Gillespie on East Fork of Pigeon River in Haywood County. Probably he was just working for his board, lodging and the clothes he wore.

Next we find him at a Mr. Grasty's over in Transylvania County, just across the mountain from Haywood. Here he was also working in the Grasty farm-home, probably as before; but he is a year older, now 17.

On this fall day young Redmond was hauling in a wagon load of corn tops, and was sitting up on the tops driving, when he saw a man approaching on horse back. The man drew up to the wagon, holding a pistol on young Redmond, and, as it was said, meanwhile cursing him. This was a deputy U. S. Marshall by the name of Duckworth, who lived in the county just below Rosman. He told Redmond he was putting him under arrest, charged with liquor violations of some sort. He now began to talk more calmly. And for some reason the Marshall either lowered his pistol or looked off—when instantly young Redmond whipped out his pistol—bang! There was only one shot. The boy had the 22 Derringer in his bosom pocket. The bullet entered the Marshal's neck at the collar button, drilling clean thru, collar button and all!

Leaving the now dying (or dead) Marshal where he lay, Major Redmond was now getting a few of his belongings together at the Grasty home—and was soon on his way to—nobody knew where!

Of course, the news of the tragedy was soon known. The particulars right at this point are not known; but certainly search was being made. Also it is known that the Duckworth family, being right substantial and prominent folks, had soon put out a reward for the capture of Redmond, stipulating that he was to be returned "alive" in order to get the reward.

It is said that Redmond, in making his quick get-a-way, saddled a big claybank horse and went mostly, it is thought, thru the mountains and wood lands. It is not known for sure that he stole out the horse; but presumably he did not get permission from the Grastys to take the horse.

Redmond was next heard from as being on Scott's Creek in Jackson County, where supposedly he was living with a rather notorious character of that section by the name of Sutton. Sutton who it seems, was himself in trouble with the law — for the same such liquor violations as Redmond, only worse, was now helping to conceal and keep Redmond in hiding.

Now a year or more had elapsed, when three deputy sheriffs of Jackson County closed in on Redmond at the Sutton place on Scott's Creek to arrest him. Same as Duckworth had done, they called out for him to "halt!"—that he was under arrest. They did not get any further. (Redmond now had at all times, it was said, two or three pistols in holsters on his belt). As before, he was too quick for the deputies; instantly whipping out a pistol, he fired — once, twice — three times, maybe. One of the officers fell dead where he stood, the other two making their get-a-way.

45

Soon he had made his escape again. So another warrant, charging the capital crime of murder, was issued for him. But they could find no trace or clues whatsoever of him this time. He had, of course, now been declared an outlaw, giving any citizen the right to arrest him—dead or alive. Also the Duckworth reward was still in good standing; but it had not been changed, ie, Redmond must still be brought in *Alive,* in order to get their reward. (We do not know if the county had offered any.)

Now, some three years had passed—with still no workable clues or knowledge of Redmond's whereabouts. But soon afterwards, news came to the officials of Jackson and Transylvania Counties that the sheriffs' officers of Rabun County, Georgia had found him. And not only so, but that they had closed in on him at his rural home there, and an awful slaughter had taken place.

The details—as much as could be obtained, are as follows:

Major Redmond, after fleeing Scott's Creek, had gone to Rabun County, Georgia. Here he had married a "nice, beautiful girl" in this rural (and then lawless) county; and they had settled down on his father-in-law's farm. Also at this time, Redmond and his wife had one child.

The four officers from the Raybun County Sheriff's department, the high sheriff himself, and three deputies, learning just where Major Redmond lived, slipped in and surrounded him (back and front) in the mid-morning darkness. Here they lay in wait until about daylight—when Redmond awakened and kindled up his fire. Still they waited for him to come out, which he soon did, and started toward his barn. (Now it was said by Redmond's neighbors that he was going, at all times, more heavily armed than ever before.) As soon as he stepped from his house into the yard, the officers closed in. "Halt!" they commanded, "hands up!" Instead of his hands going up, he instantly turned and began firing with his high-powered rifle which he already had in his hand. There also came shots, two or three, from the officers. But it was too late; for alas! incredible as it may seem, the high sheriff and two of his deputies had already been shot down. They were either all three dead or fatally wounded. Only one of the deputies escaped with his life.

NOTE: This is the version of the lamentable affair, as it has been generally given down thru the years. Redmond was not even hit. It seems almost incredible indeed. Was it because the officers were such bad shots? We would not think so. Or was it because knowing Redmond to be the sure-shot-and also quick, (which he was) they were unnerved and too quick? This is probably the better conclusion.

It was said that Redmond now, besides his rifle, also had six pistols in holsters, all strapped to his belt, which he carried buckled around his waist. This we do not believe—it was probably doubled or tripled, because of the traditions that usually build up around such a character.

No officers came again for some time. Meanwhile, Redmond continued to stay at his home, continuing with his work of farming. It seems strange that no posse nor reinforcements of any kind whatsoever were organized to take this now, seemingly, super-man, or maybe as they considered Redmond, man with a charmed life.

The next officers to come for him were a sheriff and one deputy; these, it was said, were from the same office, the sheriff's department at Raybun County seat.

They found Redmond in a woodland with his father-in-law, cutting and hauling timber. They also failed to arrest him—because dead men can't do those things. As the sheriff and his deputy approached, their guns having not yet drawn, (but each one with hand on his gun, as was supposed), Redmond once again was determined to not be taken—neither dead nor alive. As always before, he quickly opened fire; and when the smoke had cleared it was seen that both officers were on the ground—they had been mortally wounded. But Redmond was still unscathed—probably neither one of the officers having gotten in a single shot, strange at it may seem.

The Old Marshal Comes Alone.

Now there is only one more episode to recount insofar as the number of attempts there were made to arrest Redmond are concerned. About seven years had now elapsed, not much over, since deputy Marshall Duckworth was killed, he being the first victim of this young desperados gun. And since then six more officers had, by him, been slain, making a total of seven—an average of one each year of his crime career.

In view of this long-standing record of failure to capture Redmond and get him in prison for trial, a veteran officer of Asheville, Deputy U. S. Marshal Hersh Harkins, decided on a different plan or scheme to get him:

He would go alone; he would go seemingly unarmed; and would go to Redmond's home disguised as a salesman or peddler — with a large case — such as peddlers carried.

Arriving on horse back late in the afternoon at Redmond's house, Marshall Harkins announced his business. Redmond readily told him to alight, and that they would hitch his horse out at the barn. (It has been stated that Redmond right then knew it was Harkins). "Mr. Harkins," he said, "I know who you are, you are no peddler." Then he told the officer to "give me your gun; where is it? I'll take it. I have already killed too many men — more than I wanted to kill." So saying, he took the marshall on back to the house, where he spent the night — not as Redmond's captor, but as his prisoner-guest.

The next morning he handed the pistol back to Mr. Harkins — empty of course, and sent him on his way back to Asheville, empty-handed.

"I was never treated better", the officer is reported to have told folks.

Soon after this, Redmond, still a young man of around 25, moved again, this time to Oconee County, South Carolina.

Redmond Becomes A Minister

Here, folks said, a great change was made in his life. Redmond now telling his friends (of whom, it was said, he had many) that he

47

was — had already, quit his career as a hunted murderer and moving here and there, a restless, wanted man. Now he was going to church and take part in community affairs. And on profession of faith in Christ (at revival meeting, held in the community not long after he had settled down). he was soon given license to preach the Gospel — which he said he desired to do.

Now, after getting his pardon, by the help of many good people of the community, (with even County officials signing his petition to the Governor of South Carolina for pardon), Major Redmond was certainly a wonderfully changed man.

This is what folks who knew him in those parts, a few of whom are still living, like to say about him.

YARBORO'S STORY SYMBOLIZES TOBACCO HISTORY IN HAYWOOD

MORE THAN FOUR SCORE YEARS of growing tobacco in Haywood is the record of Tom Yarboro, of Haywood. Mr. Yarboro began his long career when a lad of 10, and now 94 years old, has just marketed his current crop — the 84th annual crop he has grown or helped produce. *NOTE: This was about 16 or 18 years ago.*

"I'm still over there", said Tom Yarboro to the writer — when he mentioned the subject of tobacco. He was referring to his standing as a contestant for the oldest tobacco grower in the 19 Western North Carolina counties.

"We feel pretty sure you'll win, Uncle Tom," we replied. "Anyway, we want to get your story for a writeup."

"I'll be 93 years old if I live to see next June 15th," continued Mr. Yarboro, "and I've been raisin' tobacco or helpin' raise it ever since I was eleven or twelve years old. I was about that age when I started helpin' my daddy in his tobacco at Panthers Creek."

"Have you raised it every year, Uncle Tom?" we asked.

"Yes, Sir, every year.'"

To give Tom Yarboro's experience in the growing of tobacco, both bright and burley, from an individual standpoint would be like writing the history of tobacco in Haywood since 1871 or '72. That's about the time the industry was started here — and that's about the time Tom Yarboro, as a boy, went into the "nasty ol' 'backer' patch."

At first they shipped their bright tobacco to Danville or Lynchburg markets; then a little later when a market was opened up at Asheville, they hauled it through to that point. Uncle Tom says he well remembers when, as a lad of about twelve years, his first trip with his father to Asheville with a load of tobacco.

"We hauled it in an ox-wagon," he said. "The first day we got to Canton (then Ford of Pigeon), the second day to Sulphur Springs branch, then next morning into Asheville."

Since the return trip required about the same time, about five days must, therefore, be allotted for the round trip.

Bright tobacco, unless it was good, usually sold very cheap — sometimes not even bringing enough pay for fertilizer and warehouse

*The old Hemphill Mill,
(no longer standing)
was our earliest Mill.*

*Mr. Dock A. Howell, Waynesville Centenarian. He
will be one hundred years old in December 1966. See
story on page 56.*

Jacob Owen's Cove Creek Mill, built before The Civil War.

Haywood County's Second Court House.

The Edmonston House, built around 1830.

The old Edmonston Smoke House still stands.

charges. Uncle Tom chuckled when he recalled the year one Haywood man ("I don't recollect the name," he said), who after selling his tobacco lacked forty cents having enough money to pay all charges. "He offered to bring the warehouse man a big fat chicken to make it up." Mr. Yarboro said. However, bright tobacco averaged around eighteen or twenty cents until near the close of the century — when prices got so low nearly everybody quit growing it.

First Burley Growers

Now, the record of burley tobacco in this county is quite a different story.

The first man to make a crop in this County was William Morrow, of Lower Jonathan's Creek, in 1918. He got his seed (the Lockwood Variety) in Tennessee. This was "a great big ol' rough tobacco," Tom explained. "I got some seed from William and put me out a crop, 'bout an acre, next year", he continued: "also Billy Parkins on Panther Creek put some out the same year I did. So us three was the first to grow burley in this county, so far as I know," said Uncle Tom.

But the Lockwood variety didn't last long here, it seems. According to Tom it was "too big, rough and strong." Why, I growed it that had leaves over two feet wide and nearly four feet long."

Same Patch For 33 Years

But one of the most remarkable things in Mr. Yarboro's long burley experience is the fact that he has grown his crop on the same acre plot of land for 33 years.

"There's 'bout an acre of it, there by the creek at my old home," (Upper White Oak said he;) "and I've put that same patch in tobacco ever' year for 33 years." It usually brings him around a thousand dollars, he went on to say, but one year he remembered it was eleven hundred. *That was probably the year* the patch produced 2,400 lbs.

Mr. Yarboro, who stays most of the time with his daughter, Mrs. Jessie Noland, here in Waynesville, comes from old pioneer stock. He was born June 15th, 1861, just shortly after his father had been called (or joined) the Confederate service. His father, Wesley Yarboro, was one of the early settlers of Panther Creek, later moving to Lower Jonathan Creek. When White Oak was erected as a township (1895) having been cut off of Jonathan Creek, the Yarboro place came to be in Upper White Oak.

THE STRANGE DISAPPEARANCE — AND FINDING, OF COLONEL RAYMOND ROBINS

NOTE: On Friday, November 18, 1932, Col. Raymond Robins, formerly of New York, was found at Whittier, N. C., after a two and a half month nation-wide hunt. The search was finally almost given up as hopeless. It was by all odds the longest, also the most sensational and mysterious case of a missing person in which this mountain region (Asheville, Whittier, Balsam and Medford Farm) has ever figured.

Here is the story, slightly changed, as written by George McCoy, 20 years after the disappearance of Robins, after the sensational discovery of Robins.

* * *

Thirteen-year-old Carl Byrd Fisher of Whittier was looking at a copy of Grit, a newspaper, on November 11, 1932. In it he saw a picture of a man who looked familiar to him.

"Dad," the boy asked, "Have you ever seen this man?"

The father, J. O. Fisher, Whittier merchant, glanced at the photograph.

"I surely have," he replied.

"That's Mr. Rogers, Carl," he said.

Under the picture was the explanation that it was a photograph of the missing Col. Raymond Robins and a request to anyone seeing a man who looked like him to notify S. O. Levinson, a Chicago lawyer.

That night, Carl sent a letter to Levinson in Chicago. The latter's secretary forwarded it to the lawyer, who was in New York City, and he took it to the New York Office of Amos W. W. Woodcock, prohibition administrator. Two steps were taken, Levinson notified Robins' relatives in Brooklyn and a nephew, John C. Dreier, left for Whittier to meet prohibition officers who had been alerted by Woodcock's office.

J. Ed Kanipe of Asheville, deputy prohibition administrator, gathered all available information about Col. Robins and then went to Whittier to make a personal study of the man known as Reynolds H. Rogers. Kanipe was accompanied by M. A. White, another investigator.

After talking with Rogers and making other studies, Kanipe returned to Asheville and notified Dreier that he was firmly convinced Rogers was really Robins. On Friday November 18, Kanipe and Dreier went to Whittier where Dreier made positive identification.

Returning to Asheville, Dreier announced that Col. Robins had been found in Western North Carolina.

* * * * *

The finding of Col. Robins did not explain his disappearance, the subject which created much speculation and many theories.

On Friday, September 2, 1932, the 59-year-old social economist and dry crusader made an appointment to confer with President Hoover at the White House on the following Tuesday, September 6. On Saturday evening, September 3, at 7 o'clock, Col. Robins checked out of the City Club in New York City after dining with Dr. Daniel A. Poling, New York prohibition crusader. He left the Dodge Hotel in Washington as his forwarding address.

Instead, however, he came direct to Asheville, where he had visited on several occasions. Smooth shaved, garbed in blue overalls and wearing a gray cap, he boarded a west-bound bus at the Union Bus Terminal on Monday morning, September 5. Alighting at Balsam, he engaged lodgings at a boarding house operated by Mrs. W. E. Bryson giving his name as Reynolds H. Rogers of Harlan, Ky.

The next afternoon he boarded an Asheville-bound bus and stopped off at the Medford Farm Tourist Resort near Waynesville.

The next day, Thursday, September 8, he returned to the Medford Farm and spent the night there.

The following afternoon he boarded another bus and traveled as far as Whittier where he established himself in the McHan boarding house. There he remained until Friday, November 18, when his identity was established through enterprises of a 13 year-old boy.

While at Whittier, Rogers collected newspaper accounts of the hunt for Col. Robins, whose disappearance created a sensation. Announcement of his disappearance was made at the White House on Thursday, September 8, and President Hoover expressed concern for his safety. Concern deepened when Mrs. Robins, in Southwest Harbor, Maine, expressed fear her husband had been killed or kidnapped by Florida bootleggers, working with bootleggers in New York, since he had been active against liquor law violators in Orange County, Florida.

Federal investigatiors were placed on the case and the search spread to many parts of the country.

One theory, which proved to be correct, was that he might be wandering around,, suffering from amnesia. For nine months he had worked almost day and night in organizing the Allied Forces of Prohibition. His tour included 286 cities. When in Chicago at the time of the national political conventions, he looked drawn of face and obviously was under great strain.

* * * * *

As the search continued, Col. Robins, known at Whittier as Reynolds H. Rogers, was enjoying serene contentment and happiness in the mountain village.

Soon after he arrived in Whittier, he began taking long walks alone in the mountains, going most of the time to Battle Cove Knob where he had erected a lookout in a large dead oak tree. Near this lookout he erected a crude wooden altar surmounted by a cross. There he sought spiritual peace and comfort.

Was Rogers, in building his altar and cross, subconsciously harking back to the time when he, as Raymond Robins, a hot-blooded young adventurer scoffing at religion, was converted and led to dedicate his life to the service of humanity?

Robins, then a skillful young miner from the silver lodes of the West started out with two companions and a grubstake to prospect for gold in the Klondyke. The trio found gold and wrested it from the earth, but before they could carry it to civilization the Arctic cold swept down. For days they huddled in a little camp.

Robins then resolved to make a break for civilization. When he had traveled many weary miles and the warmth and lack of feeling that mark the beginning of the end were creeping into his almost exhausted body, he came upon a tree, gaunt and scarred, standing like a sentinel above the snow-covered storm-swept ground. The Arctic sun gave but a cold radiance. Robins stopped — transfixed. Upon the snow on the ground at his feet there appeared a shadow cast by the tree. It was the perfect shadow of a cross.

"It is hard for another person to fully realize," he said later, "but I was overwhelmed." Falling on his knees in the snow, he prayed to the God he had never known before and there in the Arctic storm he dedicated his life to the service of humanity.

Fighting with renewed spirit, he won against what seemed to be hopeless odds. He thereafter devoted himself to religious and social betterment work, being aided by his wife. Their work gained wide recognition.

At Whittier, when he visited the altar in the mountains, the people respected him and did not intrude. They liked him and enjoyed his company. He was friendly, but not intimate. He grew a beard and on his hikes, carried a long walking stick. Occasionally he prospected for minerals in the mountains, the same as he did for gold in the Klondyke.

On the trip alone in the mountains, he fell and injured his leg. He found shelter in the home of William Ross, a Cherokee Indian. When he returned to Whittier on Friday, November 18. Ed Kanipe was there, waiting to talk to him.

* * * * *

Announcement that Robins had been found created considerable excitement. Crowds gathered and reporters rushed to Whittier. Officers, in a car, escorted him to Norburn Hospital in Asheville and later he was taken to Appalachian Hall.

Bearded and stooped and wearing faded blue overalls, shirt and heavy brogans, Robins sat in a room at Norburn Hospital. Mrs. Robins, who had come to Asheville by train and auto, entered the room and spoke quietly.

"Hello, Raymond," she said.

Col. Robins looked at her without recognition.

On Sunday, November 20, after he had been transferred to Appalachian Hall, Mrs. Robins visited him a second time. He again failed to recognize her.

The next day, on a third visit, Mrs. Robins took his hand in hers, smiled and called his name.

Under terrible strain, the expression on his face changed suddenly and he looked totally different. Then he called Mrs. Robins' name, "Margaret," as he recognized her. His memory was restored.

Col. Robins, accompanied by his wife and his nephew, John C. Dreier, left Asheville on November 23 and returned to his home, Chinsegut Hill, near Brooksville, Florida, the estate of some 2,000 acres he and Mrs. Robins had presented to the Federal Government the previous April for a wildlife refuge, reserving it as a residence during their lifetimes.

* * * * *

Col. Robins was born on Staten Island, N. Y., September 17, 1873. He received his bachelor of laws degree from George Washington University, Washington, D. C.

He served many causes, including world peace and law enforcement, and was active politically, first in behalf of William Jennings Bryan and later Theodore Roosevelt. As head of the American Red

52

Cross mission to Russia in 1917 and 1918, he studied conditions there. His latter years have been spent on Chinsegut Hill plantation.

PLOTT HOUNDS, PICK OF BEAR HUNTERS

The Plott hounds are the most famous bear hunting dogs in all the land.

Their familiar cry—a spine-tingling, bulge-like call—has been ringing through these old hills for over 175 years.

For downright courage and persistence, they have been the pick of the mountain bear hunters since Henry Plott developed the breed back in 1780.

Their exploits are legion and the years have shaped them into a legend. A thousand tales testify to their talents which, naturally, have led those who never have trailed a pack of Plott hounds to argue they are a myth.

Actually, the Plott hounds trace their ancestry back to the Old World, back to a breed that must have been just about the best hunting dogs that ever lived.

How they came to America and how they grew up and survived in the wilderness is one of those stories that fits into the pattern of the empire builders.

They are part of the story of the settlement of the wilderness that is now Western North Carolina and of the age of the seekers of wingroom.

That story begins in Germany when, in 1750, two young brothers decided to pull up stakes and settle in America.

They took with them their cash earnings, a few possessions, and three large brindle dogs. Nobody knows what kind of dogs they were, but the brothers thought they would be useful in hunting bear, deer and buffalo on the frontier.

One of the brothers never saw the strange new country where he expected to carve out a home and hunt and farm. He died during the long voyage and was buried at sea.

But the other completed the journey and, the dogs as his only remaining companions from the homeland, struck out for the land of promise which was called the Southern Appalachians.

Eventually, he settled in a high valley in the promised land where the trees were bunched in squads on the ridges and where there was grass a-plenty.

His name was Jonathan Plott, and he built well and left a heritage that is greater than all the monuments in Germany.

His descendants still live in the Plott Valley, in the shadow of Balsam, a 6,000-foot peak near Waynesville, and on Jonathan's Creek.

Old Jonathan Plott probably would be a bit surprised to find a valley and a mountain and a creek all bearing the family name, and again he might not.

But he undoubtedly would be more than a little amazed to find that it has been the dogs he brought along from Germany that have made the name Plott a legend.

It matters not that the original stock has been outcrossed with other good hunting blood, the exact chosen strains known only to the Plotts themselves.

Here in the valley lives Henry Vaughn Plott, a fourth generation descendant of old Jonathan.

He is the master of the Plott hounds. He devotes his entire time to raising, training and hunting the descendants of the three dogs which made the long trip from Germany 215 years ago.

Already the bear hunting season is in full swing and the Plott hounds are baying and making it tough for the bears wherever they are running.

Henry Vaughn Plott keeps from 20 to 30 dogs in his kennels, half of which are in top hunting form and already initiated in the art of trailing a bear.

The remainder are pups, brood bitches, or young dogs just learning the technique of keeping a cold trail through the high balsam groves and thick rhododendron thickets.

They are a bundle of muscles and nerves.

Old time bear hunters who make it a prime requisite to have good dogs out front will tell you that Plott hounds are death on bears and really make a hunt a thing to be remembered as long as a man lives.

The Plott hounds, who can be as vicious as a wild cat, range in color from the original brindle to buckskin with a black "saddle." Some of the latter have a small marking on their chests.

A few have typically hound faces and ears. Others have a squarer head and short muzzle and ears, reminding you somewhat of the Grey Ghosts of Weimar.

And who knows, since they came from Germany originally, they just might have a strain of the Weirmaraner in them.

Plott hounds hunt in packs, and give tongue when they hit a good bear trail.

Many a hunter who has trailed a pack of Plott hounds will tell you it's more than worth a man's time and trouble and hardship just to hear their music even if you don't make a kill.

Ed Bumgarner, who is quite a bear hunter, says it's the sweetest music in the world, and Henry Vaughn Plott will tell you they make a sound "like no other that has ever floated through the hills."

Being the bear dog man he is, Plott can easily distinguish each voice in the pack.

The hounds rarely attack a cornered bear, but they see that the bear stays put until the hunters arrive.

The stamina of a Plott hound is boundless. Once he hits a trail he'll stay on it until he has his quarry cornered, even it it takes a couple of days.

Plott explained that their alertness and eagerness to please their master make them a good companion as well as good hunters.

For years the Plott hounds were little known outside the mountains, except by the tales carried out by folks who had been privileged to hunt with them.

But now their fame has spread and they have been hunted all across the land. Plott has hunted his pack in Michigan, Florida and Tennessee as well as in Eastern North Carolina.

They are the bear-huntin'est dogs ever to come out of the hills, and it's a cinch if the bear could speak their mind they would curse the day Jonathan Plott headed for America with his three dogs.

AUTHOR'S NOTE: The above is an article by John Parris, well known Western North Carolina columnist. The information about the Plott family was gotten together by Grace Plott, great, great granddaughter of Johannes Plott, who, at 16 year of age, survived the sea voyage across from Germany — and got here with the first "Plott dog".

WAYNESVILLE IN 1884

(*A Look at Our Old Town 82 Years Ago*)

The Waynesville News, established by W. S. Hemby about the beginning of 1884 has this to say in an April '84 issue:

"Jasper Smathers' big 4 horse bus is quite a convenience to and from the depot."

No doubt it was, with the old road (now partly Depot St.) often being a mirey clay lane.

The town at that time, numbering scarcely 400 souls, was limited almost to the area lying between two creeks of Richland and Sheldon's Branch, and extending from the Quinlan place on the South to the Ratcliffe house (now LeFaine Hotel) on the north. What is now Main Street, principally, was then an irregular dirt lane—at once dusty red clay, then sticky red mud, according to the weather. The center or town hall, that being the old court house (the '84 court house had not been built); and so, the main road leading to the depot ran down what is now Church St. to C. E. Ray's Sons, then down Haywood and to the depot.

The railroad had been finished to Waynesville in the summer or fall of 1883; but boxcars were used for a depot at first, until the depot was built.

"The Whistle Did Blow"

And here is an account of the celebration at the opening taken from the Biblical Recorder (from an old scrapbook of Dr. H. N. Wells'):

"The whistle did blow at Waynesville sure enough last Tuesday. Gov. Jarvis was there and Lieut Governor Robinson and many others who made up the 3000 present on the occasion of the 'first time the brakes were put on for Waynesville.' Now our summer visitors can have an all-rail route to the celebrated White Sulphur Springs — two degrees colder than the Greenbriar Sulphur Springs of Virginia, if our memory serves us."

And the following from Murphy Independent: "Now that trains are running between Asheville and Waynesville it is to be hoped the R. R. authorities will have a time table indicating the arrival and departure of trains, for the benefit of those living west of the present terminus of the road."

Whereupon the Waynesville News replied: "The passenger train is due here every 1:23 p.m., stays one hour and seven minutes, leaving for Asheville at 2:30.'"

And here's some selections from the news items; "T. G. Cobb at the News office, will pay cash for Indian relics, such as arrowheads, wedges, tomahawks, etc."

"Mr. H. G. West, wife and children are stopping at Brights Hotel."

"There is a fine dog in town owned by our druggist, Mr. McIntosh who (that) goes to the National Hotel with a note in his mouth . . . . which reads, "Mr. Norvell, I would like to get my dinner (or supper), and greatly oblige, your hungry servant, Nero' He waits till the note is read then looks very knowingly at Mr. Norvell for his repast."

* * * * *

We find the churches and pastors at that time were: Baptist, Rev. E. Allison; Episcopal, Rev. D. H. Buell; Methodist, Rev. T. R. Handy and Presbyterian, Rev. W. E. McIlwain.

* * * * *

Solicitor Garland S. Ferguson was being boomed for Congress (he continued serving as Judge instead), and Col. W. W. Stringfield was principal of Waynesville High, with W. L. Norwood as assistant.

An item told of the death of Mrs. Sophia Allison on Jonathan's Creek, in April '84.

Also the North Carolina Teachers' Assembly had been organized at the Springs hotel in 1883, their first meeting.

* * * * *

J. K. Boone was Clerk of Superior Court; Col. Stringfield was writing about (getting up) a Confederate reunion for the county and had made out the muster roll of Thomas' Legion; and C. M. Carpenter was correspondent at Tito—now Dellwood. (That's what Jim Boyd, Jr. means now when he sometimes asks a Dellwood man, "How's Tito?"

(Note: James Boyd, Jr. passed away several years ago.)

James M. Moody (later Congressman) had been admitted to the bar.

Town Ticket (?)

Then the following were being boosted for the Waynesville town ticket: Mayor J. K. Boone; Commissioners (Aldermen) R. Q. McCracken, C. W. Miller and Jno. A. Ferguson; Treasurer W. T. Crawford (then a young man, who later became Congressman).

REMINISCENCES OF A CENTENARIAN, D. A. HOWELL, OF WAYNESVILLE

Eighty years ago this fall (1886) four Haywood County boys, around 19 to 20 years old, decided to go to school—all on their own. They had heard about a good school in Maryville, Tennessee—cheap tuition, board and all that. But how to get there was the problem that bothered these four ambitious boys, but with little money to go on. This was their final solution:

In August of that year, Dock Howell, Jim Boyd, Tom Denton and John Owens, all of Jonathan Creek, started out—on foot! Yes, on foot; but they had packed some of their few belongings in "a big old suitcase", as Dock Howell put it — the only one of them still living. They sent the suit case by express around by Asheville. The rest of their things they packed along with them, including enough food (home-cooked 'grub') to last them two days, maybe. They were three days on the road.

The first day they reached Big Creek, where they slept out in the woods. "We were tired enough", said Mr. Howell, "to just eat a snack that nite and fall to sleep". There was a lumber camp near by, he said

After traveling all next day, they were out in the settlement not far from Sevierville, where they spent the nite "at a Little River, and were on the last lap of their long walk—they got close to Maryville that nite, where another family took them in.

Here they asked questions and got information about schools, the one at Maryville and also at Athens, Tennessee. Young Howell and Owens stopped at Maryville and entered — where young Owens, it seems, had attended school the spring before. But Jim Boyd and Tom Denton decided on Athens. "They said they wanted to try out that school," Mr. Howell remarked.

NOTE: D. A. Howell, now 100 years old, still talks interestingly about the old days. His mind is good; and he is also physically strong except for his eye sight.

"I stayed at the Maryville school four months, or up into December of that year (1886) when I decided to return home — and did not return. I left John Owens there," said Mr. Howell. He said that on quitting school, he was short on money — so he also returned home on foot — a total of 180 miles.

"That finished my schooling", he said. "The rest of my schooling was in the school of experience and 'hard knocks'."

Went to Work at Father's Mill

I then went to work at once with my daddy on Hemphill tending his mill. My daddy died in 1896. I stayed on after that with the family until 1898, when I left and came to Waynesville. We also had a store on Jonathan's Creek; this I moved on coming to Waynesville—where I went into business for myself that year (1898).

Trade back then was mostly by barter — money was hard to get. Corn sold at 25 to 30 cents a bushel, and eggs at 6 to 8 cents a dozen. So, my store business here at Waynesville fit in nicely with our family mill at Hemphill. I could still take corn in trade at my store here, have it ground at Hemphill, and the meal bagged and returned here for sale in the store. I also had a good business in eggs and chickens— as most general stores did. I had commissary and other work camps to supply which kept me, or someone in my store, busy — even into the night.

57

In this way I soon made enough to put up my own store. That building is still standing on Main Street — the Smith Drug Store.

Wages

Trade was mostly by barter in those days, because there was very little cash to be had. A cradler would work all day in the wheat field — 10 hours a day, for one dollar. That was the highest farm wages paid. And there wasn't many workers that expected to be paid off in money — not unless they had an understanding to that effect. They were generally paid off like this: In meat (bacon) at 10¢ a lb.; hams 12½¢; corn 30 to 35¢ per bu.; wheat 75c to $1.00 per bu.; molasses 25 to 40¢ per gallon.

Ordinary field labor was 50¢ per day for men; women, 30 to 35¢; children, 15 to 20¢.

Old Warehouses

Along in the middle 1880's and early '90's Waynesville had two tobacco warehouses. One was in the present Co-Op building, before it was ever used for a livery stable, and the other one was the present C. E. Rays Sons Store (the old part). Asheville men did nost of the financing and operating of this business. It did not last long.

At Bill Gaddy's shop on Main Street, shaves were 3 for 25¢, haircuts 20¢.

Jack Welch, colored, also had a barber shop on Main Street back before then. He, of course, only took white customers. Welch also shaved at 10¢ per, and 20 to 25 cents for a haircut. His shop was near present L. N. Davis' office, but it was first up above the old P. O. building.

* * * * *

"Times have changed wonderfully", said Uncle Dock. He went on to say that when he was tending the mill on Jonathan's Creek, his daddy would often be out buying up corn. After gathering time he would start out over the county, and would sometimes buy up over 500 bushels. At one farmer's place ('Big Riley' Ferguson's) Mr. Howell said his father would generally buy two or three hundred bushels. Mr. Ferguson, he said, was the largest corn-grower in the County.

We would store the corn at the mill; then come spring time — and corn got scarce, we would often grind corn all day — the meal, to be delivered to stores at Waynesville and elsewhere.

"This county raised more corn and hay then than it does now", Uncle Dock said — and we grew good wheat then — but there's none grown now.

"Captain Howell's bank, our first, stood right about where Curtis' Jewelry Shop now stands. That used to be a busy block along there, he said — "both sides." There were also tragedies — Dave Vaughn; a negro woman, and also Browning from Allens Creek, having been killed there. Browning in the bank and the colored woman just outside.

Other Recollections of 'Uncle Dock's':

George Miller kept the hardware store — which, I think, was the first in Waynesville, in the building (now enlarged) where Belk-Hudson is located. George Williams and his brother, Lockwood, succeeded George Miller. They were from Alabama; and before that they (as 'Williams Bros'.) were located up on the old Courthouse (corner of Main & East Sts., now Town Hall). That was after the 'old red brick court house' had been built (1883) down on the lot where our present court house stands.

Uncle Dock, resuming his story, now said, "A strange thing happened here".

"Where?", I asked.

"At the old Clyde Ray building, now Belk-Hudson", he replied. Then he went on:

"It seems that both George Miller (relative of W. E. (Big) Miller) and George Williams slept up stairs in this old building, but each occupying it at different times. They also had cooking arrangements; and so, they 'bached' here much of the time, both as a matter of convenience and also to better guard the store at night.

"Now," continued Uncle Dock, "George Miller died up there in this room — and some say that Williams, too died there, I don't know about that; but Miller was found dead up there."

After all these years, and after the remodeling, hammering and changing, we asked Uncle Dock if he thought there were any ghosts left. We decided that there were none left — especially since folks no longer believe in them.

THE HAYWOOD HOWELLS — LONG LIFERS

D. A. (Uncle Dock) Howell, of the foregoing story, comes from a family noted for longevity of life.

First of all, the mother of Joseph Howell (son of John Howell, the original) of Edgecombe County, North Carolina, lived to be nearly a hundred years old. And Jos. Howell, who lived in Cabarrus County prior to the Revolutionary War, is reported to have lived to be 123 years old.

Eli Howell, of the same family, who moved to Alabama, lived to be 90 years old; and Elizabeth, a daughter of Joseph Howell, also lived to be the same age. Margaret, another daughter of Joseph, went on to 95, and Evan, a brother, lived to be 86.

Next, Joseph Howell II, who moved from Edgecombe to Alabama, lived to be 102.

Now, as regards the Haywood branch of the same family of Howells, we find that the record for long life has been well maintained here:

Nelson Howell was a son of Henry Howell, one of the two pioneer brothers who came early to Haywood County. Nelson lived on Jonathan's Creek, where he died at age 97. Henry Howell lived near the 'Narrows' on the Crabtree side of the Pigeon River, while John, his brother, lived on Howell Mill Road, near Waynesville, They both lived to a ripe old age.

Evan, a brother of Nelson, lived to be 96 years old. Also, D. Collins Howell ("Doctor", the Minister) lived to be 93. Later came Kinsey Howell, of Cove Creek, who attained the ripe old age of 99 years — plus a few months.

But that is not all. In the late 1940's, Capt. Alden Howell (the first banker of the County), passed away at his daughter's home in California, while in his 106th year.

Now, this brings us down to D. A. (Uncle Dock") Howell of Waynesville, who, if he lives till this coming December (1966), will be 100 years old.

In this list alone we find five members of the Howell family who lived to be centenarians, or well over the mark, and several others who nearly reached that age.

CATALOOCHEE COMMUNITY IN HAYWOOD NOTED FOR EARLY ELECTION RETURNS

The community of Cataloochee has attracted much national attention in the past few years, particularly at election time.

The community itself, embracing a land area as large as some whole townships, has a total population of three families and only seven registered voters.

When the polls open at 6 o'clock on election morning, all seven voters, including the Republican judge, who incidentally, votes a Democratic ticket, are at their posts.

By 8 or 8:30, even though the community is 23 miles from the Courthouse in Waynesville, and has no telephone service, the returns go on the wires.

The radio station in Waynesville usually broadcasts the returns as soon as they are in and the return service picks it up for other stations throughout the nation.

By the time afternoon daily papers are on the street; every person in the country who is interested in the returns, sees that they have voted seven straight tickets.

For the past several general elections, Cataloochee has been the first precinct in the county to announce the results of the election.

Each time the community has made the headlines.

It is significant to note that the state usually follows the trend and sways heavily in favor of the Democratic party.

Cataloochee is located in the northwest portion of Haywood County, and according to many anglers, affords the best trout fishing in Western North Carolina.

Besides the main creek there are many tributaries, offering excellent breeding waters for the rainbow and mountain or "speckled" trout.

The streams, 26 miles of fishing waters in all, are swift and clear, and the water is always cold, even in the hot summer months, at the height of the trout season.

60

The entire area, from the Cove Creek Gap, north to the Tennessee border, was taken into the Great Smoky Mountains National Park in 1935. (NOTE: Nearly all).

At that time Cataloochee had a population of about 75 families, mostly farmers, who grazed fine cattle and sheep in the lush mountain pastures and the fertile fields in the valley.

All the property was bought by the state and donated to the government for the National Park and all but three families living in the valley moved outside.

These three remain as the only inhabitants of what was once a thriving community, with three post offices, one at Nellie, one at Cataloochee, the other at Ola.

There was also a school which is still in operation for eight months out of the year. It has one teacher and about 12 students, ranging from the first through the seventh grades. The school is at Big Creek.

During 1937-42, a CCC camp was located at Cataloochee. The hundred or more boys who were stationed there cleared foot trails and riding paths, about 35 miles in all, throughout the area.

The group constructed temporary camping grounds, complete with fireplaces and grills, for the convenience of fishermen and the campers from all parts of the country, who frequent the area during the summer months.

The paths pass through some of the most beautiful stands of virgin timber in Eastern America.

Giant poplars, oaks and many other varieties of hardwood trees line the paths for mile after mile.

It is not unusual to see hemlocks, with trunks five or six feet through, reaching more than 100 feet into the sky. And many of these forest giants have no branches for the first 75 feet, leaving the trunks unmarked for length of several saw logs.

It is a lumberman's paradise. But one thing is certain, unless it is necessary to satisfy the needs of this country in the time of national emergency, these stands of virgin timber will never be molested. The National Park Service is not in the lumber business.

Looking after this vast domain of wildlife and wilderness is one of the most widely known and best liked wardens in the Park Service, Mark Hannah.

Mark joined the Park Service many years ago. His first assignment was at Big Creek, about 14 miles from Cataloochee, across Mt. Sterling. In January, 1943, he was transferred to Cataloochee and is there yet.

He and his family live there the year around, and except for an occasional visit to Waynesville or Newport, Tenn., he sticks pretty close to his job.

He contacts other rangers and wardens and the Park Service headquarters, at Gatlinburg, Tenn., by radio. They have designated hours for checking schedules and for making routine reports.

During the five and one half months of the fire season, from the middle of February through May, and from the 16th of October through November, all wardens are in constant fear of fire.

61

Mark has two fire towers in his area, one at Spruce Mountain and the other, the highest in the park, at Mt. Sterling.

During the fire season, the Park Service keeps a lookout in each of the towers, and is in constant communication with the Park Service headquarters.

Since he came to Cataloochee 8 years ago, Hannah has had only three fires, and all three were caused by lightning. He attributes this to the fine cooperation he has had from both fishermen and campers.

One of Hannah's hobbies during the summer is killing rattle snakes. Last year he killed 38 rattlers and copperheads. The valley is well populated with both.

Many prominent Western Carolina men were born and raised on Cataloochee.

Among them are Professor Robert Hilliard Woody, born on Little Cataloochee, and is now teaching history at Duke University; Glenn Palmer, three times a representative from Haywood County in the state Legislature.

Jonathan Woody, Waynesville banker; Captain William J. Hannah, of Civil War fame, and one of Waynesville's best known lawyers, before his death in 1936.

W. G. B. Messer of Lenoir, one of Western Carolina's most outstanding farmers; and the Rev. B. B. Caldwell, who conducts a weekly religious program over nation-wide radio hook-up from Greenville, S. C.

NOTE: The above is taken from an article by Bob Winchester.

WHEN THE STAGE COACH RAN WEST FROM ASHEVILLE

The era of the spectacular old stagecoach began here about the year 1828. In that year a line was in operation between Greenville, S. C. and Greeneville, Tenn., via Asheville and Warm Spring (name later changed to Hot Springs).

Recollections of those days by the old-timers were vivid because the arrival and departure of the big, lumbering coaches was a spectacular sight. With drivers seated on a high seat behind four to six horse-teams, and with his long heralding horn by his side, it was no wonder that folks at the taverns or stopping places for the coaches ran out to witness the dashing arrivals.

Went to Georgia

By 1840 it is said that this line was even being operated to Augusta, Ga. (Arthur's History, p. 243). Different owners continued to operate this line, or a part of it at least, until the Spartanburg-Asheville railroad had reached Tryon, about 1876. The road from "Greenville to Greeneville" was in operation for many years, Asheville being the half way between the two terminals. When the railroad was completed to Greenville, S. C. in 1855, Colonel Ripley, who had bought the line and was living in Hendersonville, operated a daily schedule.

Dr. T. A. Allen, writing of his recollections of those days, says: "They ran Concord coaches, sometimes called Albany coaches, which were swung on leather braces, and carried nine passengers inside, with a boot behind for trunks. Then there was a space on top and beside the driver for several additional passengers.

Driver An Autocrat

"The driver was an autocrat." (He) Carried a long, tin horn, which he blew on approaching the stops, to warn the innkeepers of the number of passengers to be entertained. Nothing was lovelier on a moonlit, frosty night than these sweet notes echoing over the hill and dale:

"O. hark, O hear—low, thin and clear
And thinner, clearer, farther going!
O, sweet and far from cliff and scar
The horns of Elfland faintly blowing!"

When these stage lines had been discontinued in the early '80's on the approach of the railroad to Asheville, mail hacks alone (which also carried passengers) were operated on many roads. On one of these important routes—from Asheville to Murphy—the mails were being carried as early as 1870. A few years later, perhaps by the middle of the '70's, it had become a daily route.

The stopping places in 1871 were: Turnpike (or Smathers') for dinner; Waynesville for supper (where a stop was made till next day); then to Webster for dinner; and to Josh Frank's (two miles east of Franklin for supper and night stop. The third day with the mail to Franklin, to Aquone for dinner, and to Mrs. Walker's at Old Valley-town for supper. Next day the trip was made to Murphy where dinner was had and then back that night to Old Valleytown on the return trip.

As the railroad from Asheville progressed westward toward Canton, Waynesville, Sylva, and finally Murphy, the hack-route was shortened proportionately.

NOTE: The route of the stagecoach through Haywood in those days was, of course, the old eastwest "State Road".

There is very little of this old roadbed to be seen today. It has been changed up through Hominy Valley to Canton Hill. Leaying Canton, it followed (generally) old No. 19-23 to Clyde. Here it went through the Mingus Cut, following more nearly the present railroad to Long's store at Old Tuscola. From the Reeves place it ran, generally, with present 19A to Waynesville's Old Square. Here it led off down the hill to Richland Creek and up to the Welch place, by the Brendle place, and then generally with present 19A.

THE REMARKABLE JOHN F. ROGERS FAMILY

This family is remarkable not only from the fact that it is a large one for a family of today — seven boys and seven girls; but all are still living, the youngest, Elizabeth being 45 and Grady, the oldest 68 years old.

Furthermore, all fairly well and carrying on — teaching, farming, business, work as homemakers or at other jobs.

John F. Rogers, the father, shown in the picture, passed away three years ago (1963), and Mrs. Rogers several years before.

The combined life-years of this family of fourteen children totals so far 800 years, and, if we add to that the number of years the father and mother lived, we would have 957 — nearly the age of Methuselah.

But in this family of fourteen children, about half of them did not have children of their own — they did not keep up the tradition of the family, and one of them, Jessie Boone, remained single.

However, of the number who married and had children together with those who have grandchildren, the record stands presently at:

Fourteen children, 36 grandchildren and 23 great-grandchildren.

WATCHING THEM WORK

He came in from his hunting trip: First thing he did was to lay up his gun in the home-made gun rack on the wall. His rifle was probably a Gillespie, made by the gun-maker of that name in Rutherfordton. Also his cap was either a soft homemade felt by the village hatter or a coon skin he had probably made himself.

The hunter pulls up a home made split-bottom chair and sits down by the blazing wood fire to warm, probably pulling off a wet pair of home made brogan shoes to better warm his feet.

"Don't you want a dry pair of socks?" asked his wife—whereupon she goes and fetches a pair of home-knit woolen socks. (She had gone into the rough, boxed up clothes closet under the steps leading to the "loft"—where the children slept.)

The thrifty old pioneer then begins to look around, meditating while his brogans dry off—let's look with him.

We see that not only his chairs are home made; but also the bed-steads, the cupboard and dining table (he probably called it the "eatin' table"). Then there was the mantle ("fireboard"), and, in short, almost everything in the house, including the fire dogs, pot hooks, and baby's cradle, etc.

Farming Implements

Now, farmer John—after hunting in the woods that morning, is going to work some in the field. Let's follow him out to his log stable —where there is also a rail fence cow lot, and see what he does: He takes along with him a salt gourd; he says he is going to salt some cattle that he has running on the range. (The early settlers generally grew gourds, for their "drinkin' gourds", both at the spring house and for use in the kitchen, as well as for salt and soap gourds).

Before going to the range he helps his son to get ready for work in the field. A home made bull tongue plow and small wood-framed harrow of the same make, are placed on a "one-hoss" sled, that had been made at home, or nearly all of it at least.

Now look around in the stable: Forked sapling pieces from the woods fixed and nailed up on the wall for hanging gears on; home made boxes for feed troughs, etc.

"Made what they didn't have—and could not buy", is a saying that fit our early pioneers exactly. There were also mauls—made from white oak tree buts and iron and wooden gluts, axe handles — and

The remarkable John F. Rogers Family - Seated, left to right: Mrs. Steve Stowe, Gastonia, N.C.; Mrs. Weldon Willis, Asheville, N.C.; Mrs. Jack McCracken, Waynesville, Route 3; Father John F. Rogers, deceased; Miss Jessie Boone Rogers, Jacksonville, Fla.; Mrs. Paul Ford, Charlotte; Mrs. Charles Duckett, Clyde, Route 1; Mrs. Bob Rutledge, Jacksonville, Fla.; Standing: Grady Rogers, Canton, Route 3; Frank Rogers, Waynesville; Zeb Rogers, South Boston, Va.; Hugh Rogers, Canton, Route 3; Herschell Rogers, Waynesville; Jack Rogers, Orlando, Fla.; John Rogers, Glen Burnie, Md. (story on page 63).

The Asbury Rogers House, built before the Civil War.

The old Shook House at Clyde, built by Jacob Shook prior to 1810.

often the bit itself, door shutters and their string latches; home made coffins, and home made gallows, whipping-posts and stocks.

In good-sized communities there was generally to be found black-smiths, wood turners, shoe makers, harness makers, etc; but there were many of the pioneers who were not able to buy or have these things made.

So that was the underlying principle of the crude economy of those days—crude but ingeneously worked out and dependable. Because they could always, if they were forced to, *make it for themselves, or do without*. What a 'far cry' from today!

WHAT DID THEY WANT HERE?

But still those brave English, Scotch-Irish, Dutch and German pioneers came—knowing that they would probably have to brave the wilderness, in order to obtain what they wanted here. Perhaps that was just what many of them wanted most to do—make their modest, but free homes in the freedom of the wilderness of free America.

They were tired of being under the threat of imprisonment for debt. At a time too, the Irish had suffered from a severe drought—a near famine, when their potato crops failed. The English also wanted more freedom—the others too, more of the freedoms which they knew they would find here—freedom of speech, of assembly, etc.

The handicaps which they faced on settling down in this highland wilderness were many—perhaps they foresaw much of this. But, none the less, they accepted the challenge—and went to work, as above stated. But this region—this wilderness in which they elected to hew out their homes, was both a fair and a fortunate one. For here they found a goodly land—with all the untapped potentials of a fine soil (generally); good and abundant 'woods and waters', the best streams for power, range for their cattle—and a paradise in which to hunt for the wild game they would need so much for subsistence at first.

So, here they settled down and went to work with a will. They wrangled and wrestled the wilderness—Jacob-like. They harnessed the streams: and they wrought in every other way mentioned herein— *and they won!*

HOW OUR 'MOUNTAIN SPEECH' BECAME SO COLORFUL.

Our forebears, the pioneers of this mountain country, made things. It had to be so. They made plows, hoes, rakes and other farming implements; beds, looms, homespuns, and most of everything they used.

But they did not stop there. They also made words — nouns, verbs, adjectives, terms, and phrases. They gave place-names to most of our mountains, rivers and creeks, picturesque places, the roughs and gorges, glades, balds, roads, and the inhabited places or communities.

The mixture of English, Scotch-Irish, and Dutch peoples tended to an apt speech, to fitting descriptions. It stood them in good stead whenever they needed a new word for an object or one of their new appliances or gadgets, as well as for a word or phrase to describe actions, feelings or things.

These words, terms and phrases tended to make our mountain speech rich. They gave it expression, body and color — like the richness of our valleys where these localisms were born.

Examples — Not In The Dictionaries

No, they are not found in the dictionaries. Not many of them are — certainly not as accepted usage.

The pole-stunt called *"skinning the cat"* is one of them. *"Raw hide"*, meaning to carry on the shoulder, is perhaps seldom heard outside this mountain section.

"Brogued it" (to travel in brogans) is another. (Wid Medford, the master bear-hunter, said he brogued it through Hell's Half Acre", etc.).

"Speaking for Buncombe" might be heard elsewhere, but is also considered a localism. (Felix Walker, of Jonathan Creek, when representing this district in Congress, told the House he was "speaking for Buncombe".)

"Put him in Dobbins' graveyard", meaning to put a man out of politics or defeat politically, is perhaps heard only in Haywood County.

"Tan (or warm) *your hide"* is not heard so often as formerly, because corporal punishment of children by switching has become in disfavor.

"Beat the socks off him", also *"skunked him"* and *"eat him up alive"*, all meaning to beat a person badly in a game, race, etc., are heard generally throughout this region.

"Joshed him till he was hacked". They might "josh" (joke) a person until he was "hacked".

If a girl refused a young man's company or to walk with him, it was said that she *"kicked"* him.

To *"peter out"* or *"white-eye"* means to fail, fall out or quit. The latter is seldom heard outside this mountain region.

Whenever a person pretended to be asleep or dead, they had just *"possumed up"* — and when they were extremely stubborn in a matter they had *"muled up"*.

In Haywood the early settlers built a road down Pigeon River to where the mountains closed in on both sides. They stopped here and called the place *"Shet-In"* (Shut-In). What better name could be had?

The mountains with barren spots on top they called *"Balds"*. Example: Crabtree Bald, Old Bald.

How did the name *"bull-tongue"* for the plow by that name come about? It was probably so called because of its pointed shape — much like the tongue of an ox.

The*"crane-hook"* which was fastened in the wide fireplaces for hanging pots and kettles reminded one of the crane's neck.

"Too Big For His Britches"

One *"too big for his britches"* was a proud, boastful person. Or to have the *"big head"* was sometimes applied instead.

Some mountaineer many years ago watched the effects of a hard rain-storm on his mountain farm. As he saw the water rushing down, cutting channels, he came up with — "It's a plum *gully washer!*" (It's very easy to surmise this origin).

Thus, much of the speech peculiar to our mountains grew. Not by intercourse with other peoples did it grow, because this was an isolated section of our state. It grew from within our midst — right in "these hyar mount'ins" and under impulses and needs of the moment.

A thrifty Scotch-Irish, English or Dutch pioneer might "paw the air" a few seconds in search of a word, but not for long. And he would also come up with an apt one — if he had to coin or mold it on the spot.

Because our forebears were makers and builders, not only in wood, iron and stone — but also of words.

See here:

They followed the "'cow-trail"; a distillery became a "still"; the operator was a "moonshiner"; a person had "uppity ways" (above the common people); they invented the "go-devil" and the "log-grab"; they cleared the "new ground" and "warmed the hide" of the steer with a "blacksnake" whip. Also, a small grist mill was a "corn-cracker", and if the miller tolled rather heavy he was a "skin-flint".

Some words like spider (for a small frying pan), straw-tick, tizicky, tintsey-bit, glut, hell-spot, waddin', stillyards (steel yards), slanch-wise, purties (for flowers, etc.) agues an' fever, fly-bush, tee-totally, and some others, are seldom heard any more.

But we continue to "draw a bead"; we "size up" a person; they still "hit the tick" (in many homes); a big tale looks "fishy"; and a man sometimes gets "too big for his britches". Like all the other examples cited above, they are still in use.

No doubt many of them will continue to be — for many, many years to come.

WHEN THEY "PASSED THE HAT" AROUND AT CHURCH

Preaching was about over. (Maybe there would yet be a "good ol' hymn" — and handshaking around the altar). The pastor took his seat, mopping his brow, as he looked over at Brother Stand-by in the 'Amen Corner'.

Brother Stand-by arose, gave his "Sunday pants" a hitch and looked around over the little congregation. Three or four young fellows back on the "mens side" slyly got up and darted out the door.

"Now, don't anybody leave, please," began Brother Stand-by; "we want to take up a collection for our preacher. He's come a long ways . . ."

Here the good brother reached into his pocket and dropped a quarter in the hat which he had taken from its nail on the wall. (The joke was that they thought Brother Stand-by always took the quarter-"starter" back).

He had made it plain to the members that they were "railly two app'intments behind" with their pastor, and they "orter try and make it up" that day.

67

Then he started along the aisle, pausing as he reached out his hat at every slatted-bench seat that was occupied. Occasionally a coin would be dropped in the hat, but more often not.

This drama of church life and practice in so-called "good ol' days" was pitifully enacted over and over again — in hundreds of our rural churches, where the picture was substantially the same.

After all the years, it seems rather pathetic now, as we look back. Witnessing such as this, most church-goers of today would hardly know what was going on. Oh yes, there are still a few churches in this mountain country where the hat is passed around — but very few. As for that matter, they say there is no difference in the hat and collection plate — something to drop the money in. However, "the hat" probably symbolizes other church practices and beliefs now outmoded and objectionable.

Women Were "In Their Place"

The "women's side" of the congregation was almost ignored. Very few women ever dropped anything in the hat — if they wanted to do so, they would signal. Also, they took no prominent place in carrying on the work of the church whatsoever. And as for "speaking in the church" — that question had, over the years, been thrashed out and decided upon: Women were "to be seen, not heard."

This method of church collections, together with contributions of provisions, usually raised the pastor's starvation "salary". This would run all the way from about $75.00 to $200.00 per year for each church (one to two preaching services a month); so, if the preacher "pastored" two churches he could sorter live in those days; but if he had only one church, he'd "shore have to put out a good crop."

"Glad Salvation's Free"

The idea of taking up a collection for "'furin'" missions, especially, was not popular. I think Stanton's lines reflect the lack of "spirit" in giving to the church in those days:

"Brother Williams was a singer —
He could beat 'em all at that;
And he always sang the loudest
When they passed around the hat.
"It takes money", said the preacher,
"to send the gospel o'er the sea";
But Brother Williams didn't hear it —
As he sang "Salvation's Free'."

Bacon, corn, dried apples, chickens, molasses, etc. would be given by the members as the steward, deacon or other person drove around with his wagon "getherin' up for the preacher". This was a rather hard and unwelcome task, as was also the taking up of cash collections at the church. Often the ones whose duty it was to do this have been heard to remark that they'd "almost rather take a whoppin' than to do it". One could see the misgivings in the good brother's face and actions — as he slowly got up from his corner, pulled himself together and reached for his hat.

Measured with today's church collections — even in the same communities—those taken up in the hat and by giving provisions were, indeed, small. But many in those days cited the Biblical instance of the "widow's mite", and said there was more in the "sperit" of the gift than in the amount given. Maybe so. But those who really supported (?) the church were of the opinion that entirely too many got off on the widow's mite plea. Oh,! if the poor woman had only known how much her 'mite' was to be abused in the centuries to come!

No, it wasn't very long ago measured by years. But when today we see the trained ushers marching two abreast down the carpeted aisles to the strains of pipe-organ music, it seems like a long, long time.

PART II

Sun Over 'Ol' Starlin'
(Mt. Sterling)

Preface

A historical novelette of life and tragedy in the Great Smoky Mountains of Western North Carolina — factually based; colorful, tender-and true to life here in those days.

This is the revealing story of a Haywood community that was — but has now almost vanished from the face of the earth.

Of the people who lived on that marginal strip of rough land in Haywood County, N. C., adjoining Cocke County, Tennessee, and sometimes known as Haywood's 'Northern Frontier'.

Although in extreme isolation, they lived, labored and stinted for seventy-five years — with very little knowledge of the great outside world, and without any help or guidance from it.

They were generally without public schools and church services, one community having had none whatsoever for seventy or seventy-five years. Undertakers, doctors, teachers and preachers seldom ventured in, and officers of the law had only when they had to do so.

The people had no mail service, having to travel for miles to reach a mail point. Only one rough road entered in, and it could not be traveled by any loaded vehicle in times of considerable rain.

Yet these families, partly because of heritage and custom, perhaps and partly from circumstance, seemingly did not consider all this any deprivation. And folks who occasionally went into the community found the people contented. Here one also met a hospitable and kind hearted folk, and they were probably doing the best they could under such handicaps.

Also, the community did not stand alone in this respect. Although outstanding, it was only a fair sample of other communities in this western mountain country, living in those days under like handicaps.

W. Clark Medford
Waynesville, N. C.
July 8, 1966

A LONE CABIN IN THE WILDERNESS

"Whoa, Buck!" The driver had pulled no line. It was just the two spoken words and, like the recruit at his sergeant's command, the buff-colored steer stopped and stood still.

They had drawn up at a new, and yet hardly finished, log cabin in one of the roughest and most secluded places in the wilds of the great Smoky Mountains of Western North Carolina.

The man was six feet tall, lean, swarthy and well-weathered, and was now in his late forties. Silas McDirk, untaught and illiterate in the world of schools and books; but he was well acquainted with the mountain surroundings. He knew the woods and waters — with their wild animals and bird life; also, as a sometimes-fisherman, he knew the best places to fish in the lower Pigeon River — the muffled roar which he could now hear, a mile and half distant below. He had hunted and fished in here quite a few times, and this was where he had longed to live for some time.

It was on a sunny day late in March (1858); and the last rays of the sun lingered on top of Rich Mountain (to the east) like a loving benediction.

Nature had already awakened from its winter sleep; and the signs of spring — all of which Silas McDirk well knew, were plain to see. "We got here in a good time," he said to the other members of his little family, as they mometarily rested there before their new cabin. Silas had built it in a sunny little cove on the east side of Long Arm Mountain. He had cleared off a small patch, in which stood the one-room log structure.

The steer was resting, with eyes almost closed. "Buck, you are tired — and so am I. But we'll have to git busy," he said, turning to Eve, his wife, and Nancy, their daughter. The daughter was still looking toward the east and asking questions; but her father said, "We must hurry, Nancy, and git the things inside before dark."

This last load had consisted of two sacks of corn nubbins for the steer, a sack of corn meal, box of canned fruits, a chest of family clothes and a few bed quilts, bundle of chair splits, a jug if molasses, sack of dried apples, and a half middling of bacon.

"It looks mighty scanty," observed Silas, as he and Eve placed the food-stuff in one corner of the cabin. "But I'll be bringin' in wild meat from the woods in a few days. Maybe I can manage to buy a little corn at Newport."

"Now as for the steer," McDirk continued, 'there's 'nough nubbins to last 'bout two weeks, an' I noticed the grass is springin' up nicely down on the branch banks and' in the little meador — he'll make out, yes sir-ee!"

Nancy, who had been sent to fetch some pine knots to burn in the fireplace for lighting up the room, now returned. The rosin-rich knots were split into halves and quarters and laid on the fire as needed. The cheerful glow of the flames was reflected into the farthest corners of the room.

All the family were hurrying to get the things in proper place. The little cupboard had been nailed up in the "kitchen end" of the house near the fireplace — cooking was to be done on the wood fire. Silas had fixed up the bunkbed in the other end of the room, where also stood the corded bed. Silas and his wife (he often referred to her as "Mother Eve") would occupy this bed. Nancy and her 3-year old boy "Little Sile" were to sleep in the bunkbed.

Little Sile, named for his grandfather, had been given a "bite" to eat, and being tired out from the trip had gone fast asleep.

'Mother Eve' had already cooked a "hasty supper", as she called it. "Maybe we can make out till mornin'", she said.

"It all seems so strange here," Nancy remarked as she took her seat at the table.

"Yes, bound to be strange for a-while," returned her mother, "but I hope we all like it here — so we won't have to move any more."

"Oh, yes! You'll like it, I feel shore," Silas quickly replied. Then he turned to Eve and said: "But didn't we have a hard spell of it yesterday an' today movin' the seb'm (seven) miles across the mountain?" Then he said, smiling: "How could folks a-done without Mother Eve anyway — me 'specially?" Silas then launched in telling what had been done in the past few days.

"Why, jist think — trimmin' out the sled road most of the way — that took two days hard work. 'Course, you helped me at that, puttin' the cut bushes back out of the way as I worked." Then the moving had taken two days of some nine hours each, in which Eve had helped her husband. Nancy had not come until this last load was made ready; then she 'bundled up' Little Sile and the family pulled out. They had started early. Silas, driving the steer, was in the lead. He held his rifle in the left hand, while with the long 'blacksnake' whip in his right, he expertly guided Buck — with 'steer talk' and an occasional crack of the whip just where he wanted it to fall.

Silas, who had been sitting with his woolen-sock-clad feet stretched out before the fire, now got up: "Well, we must all be hittin' the tick," he said. "Hit must be 'bout nine o'clock — way past our reg'lar bedtime — an' we've got plenty of work t' do t'mor'."

Except for the occasional hoot of an owl and the distant howl of a wolf that had been heard, it was all quiet outside. Nancy got up and opened the little leather-hinged peep-hole door to look out. "Ooh! I'm sorter skeered," she exclaimed.

"Ah, shucks! Git t' bed, gal — hain't nothin' t' be skeered of."

The McDirk family were all soon asleep — on the first night at their new home in Big Bend.

MAKING THE ASH-CAKE; AND THE CATTLE CALL

Buck, the trusted old steer, was "a little sore and stiff" — as Silas put it the next morning when he took out feed to where Buck was tethered to a sapling near the house. That was because, he said, of the "twistin' an' strainin'" Buck had gone through the day before — "then havin' to stand out in the chill of night. I'll have you a stall made in a day or two, ol' feller," Silas promised in a low voice — just as if he had been speaking to a person. (Of course, he had given the steer rest stops). "It was jist too much for the ol' boy," he had told Eve. Nancy, too, was "still tired from totin' Little Sile so much," the day before, she said.

* * *

The new day had opened clear and fairly warm, and Silas McDirk " 'Lowed as how it was a-goin' to be a good day for toppin' off his chimley (chimney)."

"I knowed I didn't git it hardly high 'nough," he was telling Eve, "But 'course I could finish it up a'ter we got moved."

They were discussing this at the breakfast table, and Silas had asked his wife if she could take the steer down a little ways below the house and bring up a few more rock which he already had laid out. But Nancy ("smart as a cricket," as her mother liked to tell folks), said that she, herself, would like to sled up the rock if her mother would straighten up and clean the room, "because mother understands that work better than I do," said Nancy. Meanwhile Silas would make the mud to be used in laying the rock and daubing the chimney. Both Eve and Nancy would help him in this work after he had climbed up the ladder to the scaffold and was ready to be "waited on." By this was meant, they were to take more rock and mud up the ladder as needed and put both on the scaffold within Silas' reach.

After finishing the flue, Silas climbed down from the roof. "I can tell a difference — it draws better now," Eve told him. "I think I'll bake an ash cake on the hearth for dinner.

"Good!" Silas replied. "I think I'll wait till a'ter dinner 'fore beginnin' on the steer-stall. I need a little rest anyway."

Making The Ash Cake

After Eve had swept the smooth center hearth rock clean, she proceeded to pat out the stiff corn dough she had prepared into a cake, ready to place before the fire. Then the red-hot embers were placed on the hearth rock, and quickly the cake was placed on the hot embers. A sizzling of steam came up from the hearth for a minute while more hot embers, then live coals, were being spread on top of the cake. Then the ash-cake was left to bake for quite a while — until it was well browned. When it was taken up, the ash that had adhered to the cake was carefully brushed or scraped off. Then it was ready for the meal.

Silas worked on the steer stall that afternoon. 'I'm goin' to make quick work of this thing," he said to his wife who had come out to look on. Eve McDirk, somewhat shorter and more stockily built than her husband, had big hips and strong arms — "just as strong as Sile's," she sometimes told folks. Eve had always done an equal share in the moving. She had married young — as most mountain girls did.

Nancy, who was now only twenty-one, had "run off and got married too young," her mother thought. "But that was not the worst of it," Eve would say — "she married what I would call a sort of good-for-nothin' man. They say to not speak ill of the dead — maybe that's in the Bible, maybe not. Well, anyway, he was gone from home most of the time — off moonshinin', I reckon, because he was picked up more than once for that. Finally he was killed in a drinkin' fight — so folks claimed. That was when Nancy's Little Sile wasn't yet two years old. Ever since then we've been keepin' Nancy and the Little boy."

Silas and Eve McDirk had reared two children — Nancy and an older brother, Ned, who lived over the Mountain in the Big Creek Community.

The Cattle-Callers

Silas McDirk also had been a herder in his younger days; and was "one of the best cattle-callers in the country," folks said. He herded for the Allisons, or maybe it was Reuben Moody of Jonathan Creek, back years before they ranged over the Cataloochee side. But there were many good cattle callers in those ranging days, because they got plenty of practice. They would cup hands to mouth (we do not know if this helped or not, maybe so). Anyway, those old Scotch-Irish and English cattle and hog callers called like this: "Co' boss, co!" and "sookee-ee" for cattle; and "Pig-ee — pig-oo!" for hogs. They had the fetching power, all right.

"I was purty good caller," Silas would remark, "but I gess Ned McFalls could beat me." Then Silas would tell the tale about how Ned fetched the Davidson herd off Bunk Mountain. Ned, it seems, was herder for the Davidson family.

"McFalls was huntin' the cattle over below Bunk Mountain — an' hit was a-gettin' late, so late he was about ready to quit huntin'. Then Ned decided to go up higher on the side o' the ridge an' try a-g'in. He put his hands up an' called loud as he could — 'Co Jake, Co! Sook-ee — s-o-o-k!' Jake was the Davidson big bull, an' he led the herd. Well, Ned said he h-yeard Jake beller (bellow), an' the bells rattlin' — they was a-comin' from off of Bunk Mountain. An' I'm a-tellin' you, folks, that was full two miles from where Ned was a-standin' on the ridge."

Now, Silas had said to Eve, "I'm a-goin' to make quick work of this," meaning the steer's stall. But he added, "I must make it safe — don't want anything happen to ol' Buck, caze he's mos'ly our bread-winner."

76

He made good progress that afternoon, sledding in 8-foot and 12-foot length poles, the ends of which he would hew down flat and nail onto the four corner posts, making the stall 8 x 12 feet.

Nancy and her mother were now helping in the work — sledding in the poles which Silas had cut nearby. After coming in with a load, they were resting a "spell" while they watched Silas at his hewing. Just then the distant report of a rifle, seemingly so, was heard across on the far east side of Pigeon River.

"What you reckon that means, dad?" Nancy inquired.

"Jist some feller a-huntin', I guess," Silas replied. "They say," he continued, "a kind of strange, wild-like man roams through them parts."

"Well, I hope he don't take to roamin' around here," returned Eve. "He might be dangerous — and, remember, you're away from home a good deal."

"Oh, I don't think he'll try to git across the river — good huntin' over in thar, too. Besides, if I was to be gone with the gun, why you an' Nancy's got the tommyhawk an' a big butcher knife — ha, ha!"

"Well, dad, I'll be scared when you're gone, I certainly will be," Nancy spoke up pleadingly.

"Ah! Nancy! You needn't be skeered — I bet your mom's not. I guess I ortn't told you 'bout the man. I got a glimpse of him onst — I think it was him — an', sir, he jist up an' skee-daddled into the bushes."

"The sun's right now sinkin' behind Ol' Starlin'," said Eve McDirk, as she turned toward the house. "I must fix up a bite to eat — I've got bread already baked; then we'll have fried bacon and sorghum molasses."

"I think we can jist about finish this tomor' — I'm quittin' for today," Silas said, picking up his tools.

— 3 —

ALARM AT NIGHT

The second night had been quiet and uneventful for the McDirk family in their new home — save for the distant howling of a wolf. Nancy had looked up from where she was sitting by the fire and asked her father, "What's that?"

"Same as we h-yeard last night, Nancy — that's a wolf," her father replied without looking up from the fire. "If I could git him thar would be two dollars for his hide — paid by the county."

At supper (we would call it dinner now) the McDirk family had eaten the same rations as the night before, except for the addition of dried apple fruit. Indeed, there was little variation from this menu of bread, coffee, side meat and molasses for a week or so, or until Silas had time to spare from his work to go hunting in the deep woods, which were on all sides.

The new day dawned bright, and by or a little after sun-up Nancy and her mother had the wash water steaming in the big iron kettle. It was suspended on a pole which was placed in the forks of two stakes that were driven into the ground. Soon Nancy was lending her father what assistance she could give in the construction of the steer stall.

At the lunch-time meal, Silas would not be able to get the stall done that day. "You see, I'm havin' to make a little loft in it for feed stuff," he explained. "But I think I can git done today all -'cept the roof."

"Well, this will be a good afternoon for my wash to dry, so I can help you some. I think you ort not to work as hard as you do, Silas. You're not as young as you once was," said Eve.

"Well, how about you, Old Lady? I'm jist a little up in my fifties — ain't that right?

"If I git through my work in time, I might take the dog an' gun for a try at the squirrels t'mor' a'ternoon.

"But I'll have to be feelin' purty well, 'caze trampin' aroun' on these steep slopes is not so easy — jist about as hard as buildin' steer stalls."

Little more was said at the supper table that night. The fire was dying down and it was already their usual bedtime. Silas got up and barred the door of their little cabin. Then he sat down, pulled off his brogan shoes, and put his feet up before the fire to warm.

How long Silas sat he did not know, because he had dropped off into a doze. Now he suddenly awakened, realizing that he had momentarily dropped off to sleep.

Had he heard something outside, or was it just his imagination? He went to the door and listened — then he heard it again! "Oh-w-o-o-ah!" It was repeated — once, twice. The dog, Trail, had also gotten up from his place before the fire and was now standing by his master.

Less than a minute had passed, when again came the shrill cry — Oh-w-o-o-ah! — louder — it seemed to be nearby! The dog gave a low growl.

"Was that a woman's cry, or was it a panther?" Eve inquired. She had been awakened by the screaming. Nancy had not been disturbed.

"I'm plumb shore," replied Silas. "Hit sounded t' me more like a big cat; thar's nobody livin' in hearin' distance."

All was quiet for several minutes. There was no other family or person living near — for a distance of six miles, unless it was the "wild man" (so called) living across the river.

Silas McDirk had gone back to bed for the second time and was almost asleep when — listen! It was the same cry or scream again — somewhat like the loud cry or scream of a woman in agony or distress. It came from a distance, seemingly, of not more than a quarter of a mile from the house!

"What is it, you think?" asked Eve as Silas jumped out of bed.

"I don't know for shore," he replied. "But I'm a-goin' to find out this time if I can." With that he hurriedly pulled on pants and brogans and started for the door. Silas took his rifle from the rack over the door — just as he heard a rattling, a snorting and breaking of boards out at the stall he had fixed for the steer. He met the frightened Buck, snorting and blowing, on his way toward the house. Buck had broken out of the stall. Hurrying on, Silas saw what looked like a large, black dog run into the dense growth nearby. He fired toward the spot, realizing that it would be only an accident if he had hit. Returning to the house, Silas found Eve and Nancy both up at the door, Nancy holding old Buck by the horns.

"What was it, Sile?" asked Eve.

"A panther or mountain cat, I feel shore," replied her husband. "Old Buck wouldn't a-got skeered like that by a wolf. Well, he don't seem to be hurt anywhirs," said Silas, looking the steer over.

He secured Buck at the cabin door, reloaded his rifle, then returned again to his bed.

— 4 —

McDIRK, EXPERIENCED MOUNTAIN MAN

Morning came clear and mild; and soon "God's good sunshine" (as Eve McDirk liked to say) was glorying up over Rich Mountain and Haynes Top which loomed up majestically some ten miles to the east.

The McDirk family had arisen early, and had found the steer still standing where he had been tied at their cabin door.

"I'm a-goin' to put a makeshift roof on the stall till I can do better," Silas said. "Jist a slantin' pole an' green pine-brush roof, weighted down. Hit'll shade an' make purty good shelter from the rain; course hit will leak some on Buck, but won't hurt 'im, seein' as how it will be warm this summer. By fall time, I hope to be able to put a split board roof on — yes siree! Ye see, ol' woman," he concluded, "I've got to git a little crap started this spring — land claird an' broke up, also corn planted. An' meantime, I'm jist bound to git in some huntin'.'"

So saying, he went on to work. Eve would help — handing up the pine brush to Silas.

"Little Sile wants to watch you an' mom work, daddy," said Nancy, as she came up, "if he won't be in your way."

"No, no, he won't be in the way — will ye, son?"

And so the work went on.

Silas McDirk, like many of the mountaineers of this Western North Carolina section in those days, could not read nor write. But he had a strong, resourceful and independent mind, which was characteristic of the Scotch-Irish, English and German-Dutch pioneers who settled this section. In Silas' case, his mind had been whetted sharp by hard experience — reverses, overcomings, moving about, and by close observation.

He had, therefore, acquired a sort of homespun philosophy of life
— "i-dees of life", he called it. His travels had been confined to three
counties — Haywood in North Carolina and two others in adjacent
East Tennessee. Therefore, the great outside world, to Silas McDirk,
was a mixture of imaginary things and people. He hadn't even been
to Knoxville or Asheville, because for him there was no way of getting
there unless he had gone by horseback or ridden his steer.

Thousands of people in this isolated section before the Civil War
were in the same condition. Many hundreds of the soldiers who joined
up or were drafted into service had never been outside of their native
counties before.

Silas and Eve Talk Over Their Problems

"This feels like shore 'nough spring," cheerfully observed Eve as
she returned from the spring with two buckets of water.

"Yes, hit's mighty purty," replied her husband, pausing in his
work.

"Got t' rest my back," Eve said, straightening up and placing her
hands on her broad hips. "An' the same good sun's a-shinin' right here
over Starlin', as I've said, as shines ever'whir else — the good Lord's
blessed sunshine for all the world."

"Yes, I reckon so," returned Silas, intent upon his work. "You
know more Scripter than I do, seein' as I kain't read."

"Spring an' this good sunshine — a season for plantin' our seed
an' tendin' of crops — to give ever'body a chanst to yearn their meat
an' bread," continued Eve, lapsing into her philosophical mood.

"While you gals stir us up a bite o' dinner, I think I'll take my gun
an' go down about the river. I've done got the leaves burnt off around
the house, case o' fire; if hit was t' git out in here — burn up all
creation — yes, siree!"

Silas had now gotten down from the roof.

"You say hit's good for huntin' in here?" inquired Eve. We'll have
to have squirrel or some kind o' cookin' varmint for the pot purty soon,
to go with the pone. That little hunk o' bacon we've got won't last
long. We've prob'ly got 'nough meal to last two weeks, an' about
three bushels o' corn."

Silas was putting his ladder under the floor. "What did you ax
'bout huntin' — good? Why, ol' woman," he said, "looky here —
south, east and north, in pertickler," (he pointed in the three directions
toward the vast expanse of wilderness), "hits all good huntin' ground
— squirrel, coon, pheasants, an' all sitch.

"Guess you know that's Pigeon River down thar you hear a-
roarin'. Hit's about eight or nine miles to west'ards, then 'bout the
same up river south; further than that, I think, north'ards. Now,
across the river thar's a few settlers — incloodin' the wild man —
ha-ha! So you see, I orter do well huntin' an' trappin'. I'll have t' git
some land clurd up 'fore I can do much to'ards puttin' out a crap."

On his trip to the river, Silas had seen a man come out of the dense
growth on the opposite side, pause momentarily on the river bank, and
then slip back into hiding. The man appeared to be a mixture of white

and Cherokee, he had told Eve and Nancy. The dark-visaged stranger had evidently been surprised to find someone at the river, and had immediately darted back into the deep shadows of the spruces. But Silas thought he could see the almost motionless form of a man back in the shadows, gun in hand.

Silas had fired a shot — only in the direction — making sure that he would miss the form in the shadows.

"Don't shoot — don't shoot! Me mean no harm," immediately the voice came from the shadows. "Me lay gun down —eef you lay gun down; then we talk — be friends."

But McDirk had not agreed to the proposed terms for an armstice. "I don't know what mischief that half-breed's up to," he told Eve at the dinner table that day. "So, I hollered back to him, 'No — you stay on yore side an' I'll stay on mine.' We'll wait a-while — see what turns up," Silas concluded.

— 5 —

THE SHOT AT THE RIVER

The next day following, Silas told Eve he was "a-goin' to take my rifle an' mozy off about the river — might find some game," he said, smiling.

"Sile, don't git into any trouble with that man you spoke about — if anything bad was to happen to you, what would me an' Nancy do?"

"I'm not a-goin' to shoot anybody," Silas returned thoughtfully. "Not if I can help it; and I don't think I'll be bothered," he concluded as he left Eve standing in the door of their cabin.

*   *

An hour had passed since Silas McDirk had left his house. Eve had become uneasy. "I haint h-yeard a thing," she told Nancy as she came into the cabin from the yard.

Then instantly, they heard a shot from the direction of Pigeon River. Eve rushed out and ran down the mountain toward the river, crying out as she ran, "Oh, Lordy, Lordy! Sile — oh, Sile!" On she ran till out of hearing of her daughter, who had started to follow, but turned and went back.

On reaching the river, a distance of a mile or more from her home, Eve McDirk found her husband talking in plain language to a man on the opposite side —

"I could a-killed you when you fard at me," Silas was saying, "but I didn't. Seein' as how you missed me, I'm ready fer you. But if you want to come out o' yore hidin' place an' talk the matter over — whatever hit is — like men, all right."

"Iwarn't a-hidin," the man replied, stepping out into full view. "Well, le's put our guns down," he said, laying his on the ground. Silas did likewise.

"You fard the fust shot," retorted Silas. "An' as fer the huntin' groun' on this side, if that's what you're mad about, well hit's no more yourn than mine."

81

"I wuz a-thinkin' o' settlin' over 'thar," the man said, somewhat meekly. "An' I guess I hunted over thar 'fore you ever did."

"I wuz thinkin' the same," returned McDirk. "An' I've already done it — moved in last week. Now, if you ———"

But Silas did not finish. With a dextrous movement the dark, rather short and well-built man slipped the gun pouch off, dropped it to the ground, and stepped to the edge of the stream.

"I think I knows hones' man when I sees 'im — an' talks with 'im," the man said. "You can lay yore gun down or not; but I wants to come across an' talk this leetle matter over with you — an' yore 'oman, eef that's her with you."

"Come over," invited Silas, wondering just how the half-breed was going to make the crossing.

Picking up a stout pole nearby, he waded into the river. In the swiftest water he placed his feet carefully for firm footing, making doubly sure with the use of the pole. At the deepest place, which was about ten feet out between two rocks, a half-submerged drift log had caught on the rocks. Here the half-breed (for such he later admitted himself to be) threw down the pole and, holding to the log, propelled himself through. The rest of the way was shallow water, so he was soon across and had joined McDirk.

"I see you know how to git across purty well," observed Silas, as the man shook himself in somewhat the manner of a wet dog. "My name's McDirk — Silas McDirk; an' this is my ol' 'oman," he finished by way of introduction.

"Yees, I crossed here feefteen, maybe twenty times," the half-breed said. "My name ees Jim Boomer — after the leetle boomer, some peepul say. Mother, she Cherokee 'oman; her name Susie Boomer."

"Do you live with yore mammy?" asked Silas.

"No. She dead. Me live by meself on t' other side reever. Would like to have better home."

Boomer's courage and frankness had already appealed to Silas. Mrs. McDirk, leaving the two men to talk over their differences, was already on her way back to the cabin. She had suggested before leaving that she could bring some dry clothes to the man, but Boomer declined the offer. He said he was used to crossing streams in this fashion — and hadn't "been much seek yit."

When the conversation ended, the two men were on much better terms than they had been an hour before. This better knowledge and esteem had been so much enhanced that Silas had even intimated that he might take Jim Boomer into the McDirk cabin, provided it was all right with Eve — who he said had the "job o' cookin' the grub." They could build another room to the side, Silas explained. (They would talk over that later).

When Jim Boomer had re-crossed the river in the same manner as before, he shouldered his gun and pouch; then, waving a stout brown arm in the direction of McDirk, he quickly trotted into the surrounding dense forest.

SILAS McDIRK'S HOME-SPUN "I-DEES"

Silas had ideas of his own on the great outside world — of which he said he didn't know "skeecely nothin' about; havin' no book larnin' an' havin' been no more 'n 30 or 35 miles from home." But he expressed these "i-dees" freely. For instance:—

"Eve's got the best education of anyone in my family. She went to about three or four short schools, she says; I didn't go to none — not a single day. Nancy larned to read an' write a little, and Fred, our oldest, 'bout the same. Their mother teached them what little book larnin' they got; but she couldn't spend all her time at that — had to help me make the livin'. My wife got her schoolin' before I got her eye (she says she got mine Oh, ha-ha! Now haint that sump'm?"

"Anyway, we got married an' come into this section — cheap land, you know. Eve didn't like it at first; but to hear her talk now, 'bout the 'good ol Starlin' sun, as she calls it, a body would think this is the g-yarden spot o' the world.

"Eve says that her name comes down from way back to old Mother Eve, ol' Adam's wife, or help-meet, I beleeve she was called in the Bible. My wife Eve, reads all this ol' time doin's to me. Well, I'm a-tellin you if Adam's Eve was as good a help-meet as my Eve is, he shore had a spunk-up good'n. My wife says that they lived in what was then the g-yarden spot o' the world. Well, I'm shore hit was "whole lot better than 'round here, else God A'mighty wouldn't a had to run 'em out — theyed a-stayed out. Darned if we can git more'n twelve bushels o' corn to the acre 'round here.

"Eve's got three or four books besides her Bible — thars one tells about George Washington. She says he's the father of our Country. I told her if that was so he shore had a job on his hands, caze hit was 'bout all we could do to raise two. 'Cordin' to the book, Washington was awful good gen' ral an' jam-up smart man. But thar was one thing he done I don't think was so smart — that was a-throwin' that silver dollar across the river. Seems like he had money to throw away. I don't guess he had to make it a-dressin, and sellin' hides — darned if you ketch me throwin' one of my dollars 'cross the river.

"Listenin' when Eve reads her Bible, I decided that people was meaner 'way back in Bible times' than they are today. Cain kilt his brother, an' whole lot o' the ol' kings was mean as all git out, yes, siree! Then one man got drunk, and treated his daughter sump-m awful — all sitch things as that. Then thars that awful stout man, Sampson. I told Eve I didn't b'lieve sitch a cock-eyed story, as that. Shucks! Haint been no man could pull big pillars like that from under a house — an' let it down on his self an' all the people. But Eve said that I ort not to talk like that, caze we must b'lieve God Almighty's word. I told her I had tried my dog-on hardest, but still hadn't got round to it. Sampson mout a got his own word slipt in thar some how — an' course, he jist felt like he was strong 'nough to pull a big house down. Right at that time ol' Sampson mout a jist had 'bout half a pint o' good mathiglum under his belt — I've felt that way too in my young days; but 'course, I couldn't a pulled a chicken roost over!

"Oh, me an' Eve, we have it up an' down sometimes — guess I'm sorter of a bad nut."

— 7 —

WAR'S ALARMS

Jim Boomer did not return the next day nor the next — not even the next month nor year. He never did return to the vicinity in which he was last seen. His disappearance was an inexplicable and unsolved mystery up to now. The facts of the final solution will not be given here, because to do so would be premature — it does not belong here in the story.

Boomer had promised McDirk that he would be back in a few days. He did not — could not know what fate held in store for him. This no one knows. That it should be so ordered or predestined (if so it be) that an unkind and cruel fate should, seemingly, lie in wait for any unsuspecting human soul is not understandable. Or, that the hand of Destiny, as some think, should wait to strike down innocent persons — and spare those more sinful and vile, as is often the case, is certainly one of life's most baffling questions.

But such was life in that day and in that mountain country of which Big Bend was a part. Such has always been life in all places since the beginning of civilization. We live it one breath only at a time — by the slow tick of Time's clock, as it were, each breath bringing us one pulse-minute nearer to our unknown end. Man, God's highest creation, is in this respect, but little better off than the lower animals; and yet he is much better off because of this. Oh life! Alas! destiny . . . .

Came Wars Alarms!

It is now late February, 1861. Nearly three years have gone by since we saw Silas McDirk — as he stood on the rocky bank of Pigeon River below his cabin and waved the half-breed good bye.

Much has happened since then — much for what was then a one-family community. At that time McDirk had no near neighbors. Now we find that three or four new families have moved in.

Newton Hackett came first and settled down at first as a tenant of Silas McDirk. He was followed by Andy Grimes, who probably had just about as much Indian blood as Boomer. Grimes settled down near the river, mostly as a hunter.

Melvin Wicks had bought and built near Silas McDirk.

During the past year, clouds of the impending great Civil War had been gathering — with all their dark forebodings. Some said the signs could now be plainly seen. Silas had just returned from the village of Newport, where he had gone to sell furs. "They're a-tellin' war down thar like all tarnation", he said. He was telling Hackett about the talk he had listened to:

84

A man by the name of Aberham Lincoln had been elected to go to Washington, he said — wherever that is, and take his seat as president if the New-nited States. Well, this man Lincoln, Silas 'lowed was a-gainst slavery, an' some folks think he ort'not be allowed to take his seat. But others thought different, he had gathered from their arguments: "they said that the man, Buchanan, the Democrat, had made a mess o' things and orter have been onseated.

Thus the talk ran on — way into the night at McDirk's cabin. Andy Grimes said that he had decided to be on Lincoln's side; Silas and Newton Hackett did not exactly commit themselves.

However, sentiment as between North and South was clearly divided in all that Northern section of Haywood County — more so than any where else.

The Turnpike Comes

Silas McDirk had made good on his claim; and he had also bought another tract of fifty acres, adjoining his first. "I 'low as how me an' Eve can git it paid for — if huntin' keeps good and furs hold up; don't know what afec this here war — if it comes, will have on things. Some folks down at Newport think times will be better."

Neighbor Hackett and Eve McDirk mostly just listened as Silas continued. He reckoned as how he'd done purty well in his trappin' and fur business. The prices had been a mite better, and the season, which would soon be over, hadn't been bad at all.

"Well, I've always said, "Eve began — "an' I've told Sile that the same good sun's a-shinin' right here over Starlin' mountain as shines over all the worl'. Course, we're pore an' all that — not edgy-cated; but the good Lord gives His blessid sunshine, the rain an' good crop seasons here — same as to the big rich folks 'way from here. Trouble is, some folks 'round here don't 'preciate all this like they should — go off into makin' licker, gamblin' and carousin' around. They'll come to a bad end — jist wait an' see. The good book says the Lord won't bless folks like that." Here Eve McDirk finished, seemingly satisfied with her little "preachment", as Silas put it.

By the fall of 1860, the Turnpike road had been finished through that part of the 'Great Smokies' to Big Creek and opened up for traffic. Settlers were now moving in fairly rapidly; so that by now the number of families in the whole section had increased from some ten or twelve families to probably twice that number.

"We orter have a school in here somewhirs," Eve McDirk had stated time and time again. "Sile agrees with me but don't seem t' be interested 'nough. Yes, and we could have preachin' in some place or other," Eve continued. "Right down here's the little blind Wicks gal — she told me no longer than last week as how she'd like to go to school — a school for the blind, that is some whirs down in this state."

Eve McDirk, sometimes called the "woman preacher" of the community, had already warned the three or four "worst sinners" of Big Bend — as she judged, that they would come to a bad end." (She never lived — to see how true most of her prophecies had been).

85

McDIRK BRINGS NEWS OF WAR

Preparations for spring planting in the settlements were some-what interrupted in late April. Silas McDirk had been to Newport for supplies the day before his neighbors came to get the news. He had been gone nearly two days, having spent the night before in town. He had gone horse-back and had also taken along a pack horse belonging to Newton Hackett for his few table supplies, also some shoe leather and dress goods. This, together with a few necessities for other neighbors had made a full load for Hackett's pack horse.

When Silas got home about sun down some half a dozen of his neighbors were waiting — not only for the things they had sent for but also for news about the war situation. He felt his importance no little bit as they gathered around him, asking questions.

"Yes, war has already begun — shore thing!", he said, after laying down some packages. (The war had actually begun with the firing on Ft. Sumpter, April 12th, but the news had not reached this little community till now.)

"Yes-siree! that new president, Aberham Lincoln was a'sendin' s'plies to a place down thar in South Carolina, an' thar was a band of soldiers — the Confed'rites I reckon, that stopped the ship. Then they took the fort — Sumpter, I think they called it, for themselves, I golly! So, now both sides are a'callin' for men to jine up with the army. Some are already talkin' about jinnin' up down at Newport; but they seems t' be for the Union, most of 'em."

"That leave a man not knowin' jist what t' do, whuther t' plant his crop or not," said Hackett.

Silas laughed. "Oh, no — hits not that bad, Newt. I'm a-goin' t' put out a crop, jist like I've al'ys done. As my ol' woman says, the same sun's a-shinin' here; an' we've got the land here, an' stock t' plow with, children and women folks to help — pshaw! We mus'nt give up, war or no war!" They probably won't take you, Sile, 'cause of yore age.", said Hackett.

"No, an' they'll not take you — onless they raise the age; its eighteen up to thirty years now, but folks say they'll prob'ly be takin' men over thirty purty soon if the war goes on."

"Us Injuns has got vantage o' you folks there," said George Grimes; you know our squaws are used to doin' most hard work. Now, ef war come, I leave, maybe my wife she git long alright any-how!"

"Well, I don't think there's any rale Cherokee squaw what can beat my ol' 'oman a-workin' '", replied McDirk. "You know," he said smiling, "I married the fust woman God A'mighty created, Eve that was; an' I golly, she started right out 'tendin' the g-yarden — an' she's been a-doin' it ever since — ha-ha-".

Eve McDirk had heard this before; she only said, "O, Sile that's 'bout a hundred times you've told that joke — hit don't hack me a bit."

These words were barely spoken — when they plainly heard a woman's scream in the direction of Hackett's cabin just over the little hill. By the time they had run into Silas's yard the scream was followed by a rifle shot. The three men, Hackett, Silas and Grimes were now on their way; Hackett, in the lead, could now hear his wife calling his name. But, on reaching the house, and being admitted by Minnie Hackett, who had to first remove the bar from inside the door, they found that the brave mountain woman had already started to re-load the rifle.

"What on earth!" exclaimed her husband.

"You shouldn't a lef' me an' the young-uns here like this, Newt," she said. But whatever hit was, man or varmint, I think I skeerd it off".

"Whir was he — it, whatever it was?" asked her husband. "Did you git to see it plain?"

"No, not plain," Minnie Hackett answered. "Hit seemed t' be slippin' 'round the house — thought I h-yeard it workin' at the door; that was when the dog growled. Then when I opened the peep-winder, hit darted 'round the corner an' run off to'ards the river — that's when I fard the rifle a'ter it."

"Guess you'd better let yore wife jine up with the army, Newt," laughed Silas, "an' you stay home an' tend the crops."

And so the days came and went — exciting days, filled with rumors and reports from the war front. Also they were hard lonely days and weeks — even months, of toil in the little mountain fields and patches, mostly by the older men and women folks, the few younger men being in the armed services. There were reports of nearby community boys joining, of companies marching off from Newport and Waynesville, the county seat, and of battles on the front.

The settlers gathered and talked; and because of this unsettled and excited condition throughout the whole country, the little farm work was interrupted or somewhat neglected in the whole community and on Starlin' Creek across Long Arm Mountain and Big Creek.

Bob Bowen, a new-comer, and sort of drifter — so folks said, had come in and married in to the Melvin Wicks family. Eve McDirk who was a pretty good observer, and always frank in expressing her opinions, 'lowed as how, "Bob Bowen, I jist know, is already makin' liquor 'round here somewhirs purty close."

Bob wouldn't help Mr. Wicks with the work at home, folks said; and it was reported that he was lying out to escape the draft, now coming this summer of '62.

George Grimes was now with the Union army somewhere in east Tennessee, it was said. On the other hand, one or two on Starlin' Creek had joined up with the Confederacy.

On this day in early May, 1862, little patches of oats that had been sown in Big Bend were coming up. Also Minnie Hackett had come over to the McDirk home to bring some spring onions to Eve.

"I've got plenty," she said, " 'nough to spare you all some. I s'pose you h-yeard the shootin' last night?" she asked.

"Yes," Eve answered, — "waked me up. But Silas was gone huntin', an' we jist h-yeard little while ago — Nancy did, that it was over at Mr. Wicks' house."

"Jist what I've been expectin'", returned Eve; "was anybody hurt?"

"No, reckon not, not onless Bob was hurt, he might a-been hit. Mr. Wicks shore put Bob out from behine that small tree where he was standin'; Melvin fard with his shot gun, a'ter Bob had already fard at him with a pistol."

"What was it all about?", asked Eve.

"Well, you know, Mr. Wicks had ordered Bob to stay away, a'ter they had that trouble 'while back. Newt told me all about it — he went down there last night a'ter the shootin' was over.

"Newt told me that Mr. Wicks said Bob come back last night and called him to the door. Knowin' the voice was his son-in-laws (Bowen's) Mr. Wicks got his gun as he started to the door. Bob insisted on seein' Emmy, his wife; he was told he couldn't see Emmy,, that she'd gone to bed. Then Bob started away like he was a-goin' to leave; but he quickly jumped behind a small tree in the yard an' shot at Mr. Wicks just as he started back into the house. But Melvin Wicks is no coward, Newt says. He turned an' fard on Bob as he ran from behind the tree.

Here Minnie Hackett paused.

"Was Melvin not hurt?" asked Eve McDirk.

"No; but Newt said he showed him whir the bullet from Bob's pistol splintered the door-facin' jist four or five inches prob'ly over Mr. Wicks head. He thinks some of the shot from his gun must a hit Bob as he run."

"Well, I've been expectin' sump'm like this to take place for a year or two," Eve said. I tell you hit won't do — all this here evil conduct."

Now Minnie Hackett said she would have to hurry back; she had left Newt at home, and he would be wantin' a "bite to eat purty soon."

— 9 —

JIM BOOMER'S STRANGE 'RETURN'

Silas McDirk and his good wife, Eve, and others of the community had held a funeral on a wooded hill near their home on the afternoon of this day in early November. The McDirks had acted mostly as undertakers, officiators, pall-bearers, and chief mourners. Because there had been no known survivors of the "deceased."

It had been great news, the events of which had mostly culminated on this the fourth day at Silas' two-room log cabin in the rough and secluded Big Bend section.

Some ten or twelve persons — fully one third of the settlement, were gathered around the blazing wood fire rehearsing the things that had happened. Silas was taking the lead.

"Hit was a lucky streak, I reckon, I had — 'course onsuspected," Silas said. My dawg had treed in a big holler log. When I got to him he was still a-barkin' and a-crawlin' in an' out i' that big holler in the log. Trail — that's his name, would sometimes look up at me; seemed like he was a-tryin' to tell me sump'm. 'Course I thought hit was maybe jist a possum — too fur back to recht. I hissed the dog in a'gin; he stayed a-while, but didn't bark jist sorter sniffed a-bout.

"Then all at onct — what do you reckon? Well sir, out come ol' Trail with a bone in his teeth! I could see right off hit was a human bone. At first my mind didn't go back to Jim Boomer. But a'ter I had cut a big piece out o' the holler log, 'bout eight feet up, an' was a-findin' more bones, skull an' so on, I said to myself, out loud, 'I jist bet this mout to be Jim Boomer — all that's left o' him.' An' so hits turned out to be."

"He prob'ly froze t' death or starved," Mrs. Hackett added.

"Yes, that's what the Cor'nor give in," replied McDirk. "I knowed sump'm orter be done; so I goes over to the store at Big Creek an' ol' man Hobbins told me I orter notify the Cor'nor. That's the way hit all turned out."

Oliver Grimes (a cousin of Board and Andy Grimes, who were killed by Captain Taylor's 'rebel' scouts) hadn't said much so far; he was a reticent sort of fellow. But now he spoke up: "Well, I'd swear to that rifle, Sile, as bein' the very gun I al'ays saw Jim Boomer a-carryin'," Oliver said. "I hunted great deal on that east side o' Pigeon River, where Jim most al'ays hunted, like up an' down the river an' sometimes 'way back on Harrycane an' Cold Springs. Met up with him a whole lot an' we sometimes hunted t'gether. That gun was his'n alright. An' that dried up, half rotten rawhide coat was, too — I could tell by them little flint di-dos that had been sewed on an' them thar horn buttons you found with the bones. That's jist what I told that Cor'nor at the inquess — or whatever hits called."

"That's why I wanted 'em to turn over to me what was left of his body,", said Silas. "I told 'em I would give his bones a decent buryin', 'Course we didn't have any preacher to carry on, but me an' Eve done the best we could. Eve read a little Scripter (she can read some, I kain't); then they had a good church song, an' I let the box down into it's restin' place."

Here Silas paused, and was seemingly in deep thought. His wife took over. "You know," said Eve, "I felt better a'ter that. Ever since that day down there at the river, when him an' Silas had that little fracas — an' then made up, I sorter thought well of Jim Boomer. Least wise, I was sorry for him. 'Course he didn't pervide an' take keer of his self like he should a-done — jist lived in a hunter's old op'n shack in summer, folks said, an' in a little rock cave in winter time."

"That's right," agreed Oliver Grimes. "I see with my own eyes that cave back in under a over hangin' rock. Kep dry stuff in thar to kinnel with. He could cook in thar — what little he had to cook, al'ays jist a little wil' meat that's all I sees."

Here Eve McDirk, who had been mending a pair of her husbands wool socks, laid the socks down and looked over the little group,

89

slowly, and thoughtfully. She felt her "good thoughts," as she called them, coming on. "I want to tell you, folks, we can all do better — right here in this rough mountain country, where hit seems nobody but us wants t' live," she said. "We could have better houses to live in, better crops, an' so on — an' we orter 'tend meetin' 'casionally, whenever they have it over near Starlin' Creek. Then, too, maybe we could git somebody t' come here an' teach our children two or three months in the fall, if we'd try hard a-nough."

"I'de thought a little bit 'bout that myself," interrupted Newton Hackett. "I would help pay when I sell my hides; caze you see, I have more children than any of the other families over here."

"Well, the good Book says, "the Lord will pervide," continued Eve; "that means, I think, that He will pervide for them that tries to pervide for themselves. Jist think, His sun's a-shinin right here over Starlin' — same as hit does anywhirs else, eb'm over big fine folks and people larnin away from here."

Silas McDirk, who had been listening, along with the others, smiled when his wife concluded. "Well, folks, come to think on it, Eve orter know all about the sun an' sitch things, caze she's been here a long time — fust woman God A'mighty made, you know."

Most of the crowd had heard this joke of Silas' before. His wife only said, "Oh, I reckon my ol' man jist got to put in some foolishness along."

Now it was getting late in the night, and the visitors were saying to their host, "Well, we must be a-gittin' along home. You uns all come to see us, Sile."

"We will, an' y'all come back" — (the general form of leave — taking in the Southern Mountains. You uns means, *you ones;* Y'all is a contraction of, *you all.*)

— 10 —

EPISODE ON BIG CREEK

Our story now shifts to the larger Big-Creek Starlin' community where it will have to do with the two warring factions there.

In the early spring of 1865, Capt. Taylor's Confederate scouts raided Big Creek for the fourth or fifth time during the war. There had been reports of pro-Union activities, bushwhackings, etc., and also of open aid and encouragement being given Colonel Knight, the Federal Commander in adjoining east Tennessee.

So this time the small company of Taylor's scouts burst in entirely unexpected and with fury. Since the Johnny Rebs had been seemingly inactive lately, Dock Carroll and some of the Hobbinses, together with Board and Andy Grimes of the Bend section, and others, ventured to have a secret dance at the Carroll home. They had posted only one guard outside on this particular night; but after nearly an hour of revelry there had been no alarm.

It was a motly, stamping, clattering crowd, as they swung partners, promenaded and clogged over the puncheon-slab floor. Men in the rough, pegged brogans, heavy shirts and tight fitting trousers and women in long linsey dresses and wool stockings were on the dance floor. Some of the stockings were undyed; but there was no formality — nothing hindered the jollity on this night. Over all came the voice of the dance caller; and inside the stuffy room there was the permeating and almost nauseating mixed odor of sheep's wool, dirty sweat of human bodies and stale air. All the couples were now out again on the floor choosing their partners, and the fiddler, Board Grimes, and his banjo accompanist had just sounded the notes of 'Shortinin' Bread', when there came the loud report of a rifle shot from the front yard.

Aided by the noise inside, three or four of Taylor's men had almost reached the rear of the house and others were nearing the front yard when the alarm shot was fired. The scouts instantly closed in before the guard could reload. He was relieved of his gun and placed in custody. The front door had been barred; so the only exits were the rear door and two windows. There came a smashing of windows and a scramble for the back door — and over all, excited voices mingled with that of some crying children.

Most of the men —those who were wanted, made their escape. One of the Hobbins men, a Union sympathizer, was killed in the skirmish back of the house; Board and Andy Grimes, together with Dock Carroll, made their escape. Carroll, some said had a secret hiding place — probably so, for he was not found that night. Skirmishing had continued and gun-fire had been heard until near dawn. Carroll's house was watched; and when he was seen to slip into the house just before daylight, he was surprised and taken.

Also another detachment of the scouts, looking for Board and Andy Grimes, had concealed themselves in the woods at the Grimes home, being careful to not make any awakening noise. A little after sunup the two men came in, slowly and cautiously. The scouts waited for a while. Then, after smoke had started rising from the chimney, the scouts rapidly closed in. Being given no chance of escape, both men surrendered with but little resistance.

However, a great commotion had been raised in the rest of the Grimes household, of some nine or ten women and children. The two women, realizing what would perhaps be the fate of their husbands, cried and begged Taylor's men to spare their lives, while the children stood near weeping. "No, this is war," the scouts told Board and Andy and thtir wives. "This will sorter make up fir what that yankee, Colonel Knight, has been a-doin' to our people here in these mountains."

It *was* war — here in the great Smoky Mountains, as elsewhere over the nation, and often it was heartless, cruel war — both sides being guilty: Death without trial — as it was on this occasion. There was no relenting on the part of the scouts as the two doomed men were marched away . . .

91

NEW-COMERS AND EVIL OMENS

Now, quite a few years after the close of the war, more families were to be found in Big Bend — as well as in other surrounding communities. One was the Bowen family, father and mother of the outsider, Bob Bowen.

And, although the war had taken two or three of their boys, there had been an overall increase in the population of the little community. Newton Hackett and his wife, Minnie, had contributed another girl to this increase, making nine girls (no boys) for the Hacketts.

Folks often teased Newton about his big family of girls, but he took the jokes good-naturedly.

"I'se got jist 'bout as many boys as Min's got gals," Newton would say. — turned four of them into boys. They helps me in the field, an' can do any kind o' work I do."

So it was quite natural that Hackett decided to make a little crude grist mill — "for me-self mostly", as he said. It was hand-powered, the crank and pulley-belt type with small, rough stones.

"I've got jist 'bout all the power I needs," Newton remarked shortly after the mill went into operation. "Three of my gals 'splies the han'-power, seein' as how they air all big an' strong. An' thars not much else fur'm to do — nothing endurin winter time."

Well, we've been needin' a little gris' mill in here — since you're a-grindin' some for the families 'round here, too," replied Silas McDirk, whose home Hackett was now visiting.

"Yes, it's a good thing, I reckon," spoke up Eve McDirk; "but yore gals, like our gal, orter be in school some — seems like we'll never git one in here though."

There was a moments silence, then Eve continued, "I don't like what's been goin' on in our community here lately, Newt", she said, looking Hackett straight in the face, "I hope you're not mixed up in it in any way — this here makin' liquor, I means."

"Why, Eve, do you think I'd be mixed up in it?", Hackett asked.

"All I know is jist what I hear. We all know that Bob Bowen was guilty of it — arrested right at his own still about six months ago, an' he haint been a livin' here more than two years. He would a been sent up for a spell, folks say, if them thar big liquor-drinkers at Newport and at Waynesville too, hadn't a paid him out. I hear that the revinoors seem to think that you was a furnishin' Bowen with some o' his meal, Newt, ———"

"Now, look here, Eve," Hackett interrupted. "I'd like to see the one what can prove it," he said heatedly. "First place, I haint been a-grindin' awful long; then I's just a-grindin' mostly my own corn, an' for a few here in the community."

"Well, they'd better keep their ol' stills offen our land — I'd have the revnoors a'ter 'em shore as I'm born," concluded Eve.

"She's got one o' her preachin' spells on, Newt", Silas said.

Linda Wicks Goes Off To School

There was a knock at the door, and Minnie Hackett immediately opened and came on in. "Well they're a-goin' to take that little Wicks blin' gal off next week," Mrs. Hackett announced as she took her seat. "One o' my gals jist came from thar; an' she said the high shirf an' a fine dresst man had been thar a talkin' to Mr. and Miz Wicks, an' ———"

"Well, thank the Lord!", interrupted Eve; "Maybe we can have *one* person in this Bend section that'll have some learnin' — eb'm if she is jist a little blin' gal. I've been a-hearin that thar was some folks up at Waynesville what was a tryin' t' git her in school some wheres down 'bout Raleigh."

"Yes, they're a-goin' t' try t' git her ready, an' take her off nex' week," concluded Minnie Hackett, rising from her seat. She had already told her husband that Oliver Grimes' boy had just brought a turn of corn to be ground — "toted hit all the way up the mountain on his little shoulder."

"No, set back down a minute, Min," said Eve McDirk. She had been spinnin' walking back and forth before her wheel as she talked. (It was evident that Eve was still in one of her 'preachin spells', as Silas put it).

"Thar's one more thing I wants t' say", she continued, "then I have to stir up a bite o' dinner."

"Y'all remembers when Melvin Wicks come in here. Then little later Bob Bowen — an married his oldes' gal, Emer. Well, us folks 'round here helped build that house — didn't charge him a cent. Then Bob moved in too, him bein' Mr. Wicks son-in-law. Well, I've never been sorry for Bob, him bein' a big stout young man — loafin 'round half the time, that is, when not makin' liquor tother half. But I's sorter sorry fur Mr. Wicks, speshily their little blin' gal, Linda. Well, she's eleven or twelve years old I guess. I don't rightly know if Melvin Wicks is guilty of any o' this liquor business; but he shore 'nough knows all about it, an' I don't s'pose he tries t' stop it — drinks his self they say."

"We most all of us takes a swigger o' mountain dew sometimes, don't we Silas," spoke up Newton Hackett, winking slyly.

"Sile don't drink much," returned Eve, "and he don't mix much with the ones what does."

There was a pause — as the Hacketts got up to go. "Well, preachin's over fur today, I reckon," said Silas.

The following Sunday afternoon was leave-taking time at the Wicks home, since their blind daughter, Linda, was to leave the next day to attend the School For the Blind at Raleigh. The winding trail to the Wicks place led down the mountain a short distance from Silas McDirk's to a clearing of about two acres, where Melvin Wicks and his son-in-law lived. The McDirk family of four, some of the Hacketts — about a dozen persons in all were there.

The cleared patch, including the Wicks house and little barn were fenced in with split rails. Outside a few cattle, including a work-steer and a milk cow, were to be seen. Also there was one lone sheep running with the cattle.

"That's the blind girl's pet sheep," said young Nancy McDirk. "They go around together sometimes — when Linda's outside workin' with it; she holds to the wool of the sheep's back."

Linda Wicks received most of the attention that afternoon — as was her due. Her father explained that she would be taken to Waynesville the next day. From there she would go by mail coach much of the way, then by train; and it would require about five days in all to make the journey.

Linda Wicks was talkative; but she did not want to talk much about her affliction. She liked to talk about her pet sheep, 'Trudy'. "She comes whenever I jist call, 'Come Trudy!'" explained Linda. Trudy waits outside for me to come and feed 'er; then she's ready for me to go with 'er — to be put out with the cows to range. I'll certainly miss my pet when I go to school," she said. "But I wants t' go t' school — want t' learn more 'bout the things I cain't see. An' I'd like t' learn t' play good music — I can pick the banjer (banjo) some already," she concluded.

The little group of visitors was soon taking leave of the Wicks family — and Linda, in particular. Eve McDirk told Linda to "be a good little girl an' study hard," then kissed her good bye. "Seein' people will write for me Nancy; and come over to see how my dear pet Trudy's getting along, play with her, too, she likes it." Then Linda held up her brown arms toward Nancy, imploringly.

"How I wish I could see you," she said. Nancy went into her arms, hugging Linda up as she kissed her good bye.

"Ain't goin' to be long till our little gal will be in school," observed Mrs. McDirk, as tears welled up in her dark eyes. "Jist think what other young folks — *who can see how to learn, could do if they'd only try.*"

— 12 —

TRAGEDY AT THE WICKS HOME

Winter had almost passed, it now being the last of March.

Linda Wicks had sent four or five letters written by her teacher or advanced school mates. In her last letter she complained to her parents of being sick, and said she would like to be at home. She had been in school about six months.

Some two weeks later, Melvin Wicks had gotten a letter from the superintendent of the school saying that, although the spring term would not close for more than a month, Linda was not doing well physically — poor appetite, etc., and that she was also homesick. So, the letter went on to say, that the school made arrangements for her transportation to Waynesville — to arrive on a certain date. The day that the family had received the letter, Melvin Wicks noticed that the

94

date for Linda's arrival at Waynesville, was only five days off. So he would have to get busy.

He went to consult Silas and Eve McDirk, whereupon Silas said; "Melvin, you are not well 'nough to make the trip to Waynesville and back. I will take my nag and git Newt's pack-mule for Linda to ride. I'll start day a'ter t'mor — so's to be up thar when she 'rives."

It was now reported in Big Bend that Bob Bowen had made bond and had his trial put off. He was out of jail they said; but no one had seen anything of him in the little settlement.

Now the afternoon of the day (or night it may be) for the arrival of Linda Wicks was here. They would come to Silas' house first, and there Linda would be met by her parents. But before night fall, not only were Linda's parents there — at least a dozen others of the community had gathered in; so all the available space in the McDirk two-room cabin was taken when Silas and Linda were heard coming — just before good dark.

Nancy McDirk was first, along with Linda's parents, to reach her It was a joyous meeting. indeed!

Linda was "awful glad" to get home, she said. She hadn't been too well satisfied at school; but they were good to her, and she had made "five or six good friends", she said. Furthermore, she had been doing right well in school, her teacher had said.

Linda was soon asking about the welfare of her pet sheep. After about half an hour at the McDirk house, she said she was tired and wanted to go home —

"First thing, though, I want to get to my pet — feel of her and hug her up," she said.

Everything went along pleasantly for the next week or ten days. Of late, since Bob Bowen had not been allowed to come and hold parties at the Wicks home, they were usually being held about once a week at Newton Hackett's. Newt, jokingly would say that he had 'nough gals of his own to hold a purty good-sized 'hoe-down'." He would also remark that his little grist mill was not man-powered, it was gal-powered; and that he didn't know what he would do whenever his gals commenced marryin' off — have to shet it down, I guess — ha-ha!"

Linda Wicks had already attended one or two of the parties at Hacketts. She had returned with a cheap, second-hand banjo, which she said the school allowed her to practice on in her room at times. And she didn't think there was any harm in it, she had told Mrs. McDirk. "They let me keep it at school." Linda was now practicing at home, and she had already "picked a tune or two for the dance," she said.

The Tragedy

Bob Bowen, who, it was known, had a deep grudge against Melvin Wicks, his father-in-law, because he wouldn't let Bob come to see Emer, had been seen in the community again one Saturday afternoon. He had gotten some unknown man to promise to go with him late that night to the Wicks home. Bowen reasoned that if he himself

95

called at the house, Wicks would recognize the voice and probably refuse to come out. So the stranger (his identify was never known) was told to go near the door and call Mr. Wicks out; Bowen had planned to conceal himself near the door.

Melvin Wicks heard the call, "Mr. Wicks!"; he roused up and inquired who it was — he knew it was a strange voice. "It's (So and So) was the reply. Then he asked for Wicks to come to the door, that he wanted to see him. Melvin got up, pulled on his pants and started. He heard Linda ask, "Daddy, who is it?" On reaching the door he saw the man standing well out in the yard, and had taken a step or two outside toward the stranger — bang! bang! came the blast from the corner of the house, only six or eight feet away.

"Oh, Lordy! You've killed me!" Wicks cried out. That was all.

The rest of the family, Mrs. Wicks, Emer (Bowen's wife), Linda, the blind girl, (the other children being away) were all soon at the body — screaming and weeping. It was plain, even to them, that nothing could be done.

It wasn't long until nearly half of the neighbors had shown up — two or three of them had heard the shots and the cries of weeping that followed.

The family stated that no one had been seen around the house prior to the shooting that night, and that nothing had been heard — until the call, which Linda said she heard, as did also Mrs. Wicks.

Newton Hackett volunteered to ride to Waynesville, the county seat, — for the law and a coroner. There would be a matter of at least ten to twelve hours waiting. The round trip distance was about sixty miles, fourteen of which was over the roughest of terrain.

The coroner held the inquest shortly after the officials had finally reached Big Bend, about eleven o'clock the next day (Sunday). (The homocide had occurred around 12:30 on the night before). One of the pistol bullets was taken from the body of Wicks.

Of course, Bowen was suspicioned at first; therefore, all investigation by the sheriffs department was directed that way. Rumors were that Bob Bowen had made threats, in the presence of some two or three persons, against Melvin Wicks after his arrival in the community on Saturday afternoon. These rumors were run down by the Sheriff and found to be better evidence against Bowen that he at first suspected.

Bowen was charged with the crime. After some two weeks search he was captured and disarmed — of a 38 calibre army pistol. The ballistics expert matched the clean ball that had been recovered as belonging. Another witness would swear that he saw Bowen and another man turn into the Wicks lane about mid-night on the night in question.

Thus, evidence built up until the July term of court at Waynesville, when Bowen was arraigned for trial on charge of murder in the first degree. His attorney submitted him guilty of second degree murder, which plea was accepted by the state. Evidence was heard by the Court, after which the judge sentenced him to thirty years in the States prison.

Most folks in the Big Bend section and elsewhere were satisfied with both the plea and sentence.

A large crowd had attended the funeral. The Wicks family and Eve McDirk had sent for a preacher at Newport to come and "preach the funeral." "We wants to give your daddy a sort of decent buryin'," Eve told Linda Wicks. Hit's not like it was when me and Sile buried all that was left of pore Jim Boomer, although we orter a done better by him."

So, the little 'grave yard' started by Joe Wicks and Silas McDirk on the ridge near-by had commenced to fill up.

— 13 —

BIG BEND REVERTS TO NORMALCY

This had been a major shock to the Big Bend community. The suddenness of the murder, gruesomeness of it at the scene, together with the long, heart-breaking delay in getting the law in, was something never to be forgotten by those who experienced it, especially the family.

Yet we reckon that it is not intended for man to become eternally saddened, cast down and bereft by the sorrowful, the bitter and awful things which he must experience in life. So, we have the beautiful, the cheerful and humorous to bouy us on as well as Time, the healer, to soothe our wounds.

So, there wasn't much interruption in the music and dancing, "hoe-downs," as they were commonly called — they must go on in Big Bend, as they did elsewhere in those days. In most places it was their principal diversion and pastime. They were being held now, by harvest time, at every home in the community except at Silas and Eve McDirk's.

Linda had been practicin' up, she said, and now being taken to most of these 'parties' as one of the "musishnners". She was glad she said, to get back to her "home-life in the mountains." Like a bird or one of the lower animals that has been confined, the School For the Blind had become as a cage to Linda Wicks, and she was glad to get out and get back home.

Sallie McMahan, a cousin of Linda's had come to live with the family since Melvin Wicks' death. The family now consisted of Mrs. Wicks, Emer (Bob Bowen's wife). Linda and an older brother, George Wicks, together with Sallie McMahan.

Sallie was a strong, raw-boned root-digger and "yarb" (herb) gatherer. She roamed the mountain sides and deep coves for several miles around in season—digging and gathering, sorting, washing and curing, or drying the herbs and roots out in the sun. At marketing time, she might borrow Silas McDirk's mule for transportation of her sack of dried roots, etc. to Newport or send word to some rootbuyer to come.

"Mos' ginerally, if the price is right good," she would say, "I gits ten, twelve or maybe fifteen dollars for my roots and yarbs." Thus she helped out with the living in the Wicks household as well as by

hoeing in the fields. "Besides, me an' Linda has rale good times goin'
to parties," she would say.

Linda was now being known — at about fifteen years of age, as
the banjer-pickin' gal of Big Bend. She had somewhat dramatized
the tragic death of her father by "makin'-up a song," as she said about
it. She was now "a-pickin' it" (playing it) even at the dances. She
always sang the verses as she played the tune — all of which she told
folks, "I made it up in my own head." It ran about like this:

> I hear the sad winds blowin' —
> Hit's a low an' mournful sound;
> For pore Daddy is now a-lyin
> Out in the cold, cold ground.
> "Twas in the night when a sleepin'
> He was called outside his door,
> An' was killed by a man, Bob Bowen —
> Pore Daddy, he is now no more.
> I'm now so sad an' lonely —
> An' you know I am plumb blind;
> But I know that the Lord in heb'm
> Loves me an' all mankind.

> _____

> I hear the sad winds blowin'—
> Hits a low an' mournful sound;
> For pore Daddy is now a-lyin'
> Out in that cold, cold groun'."

"There's more to it, but that's all I usually sings when I pick it on
the banjer," she often explained.

It was a very sad song to the folks of Big Bend, especially because of its association with the death of Melvin Wicks. And whenever
Linda opened up — loud and stridently in the minor key, the hound
dog often joined in with his howling.

They would always "pass around the hat" for Linda Wicks at the
dances. The amount the revelers usually "chipped in" was around fifty
to seventy-five cents. . ..

("Full many a flower is born to blush unseen and waste its
sweetness on a desert air.")   —Gray

It was now a period of unusual calm, and of seemingly, law
observance for the community. Eve McDirk observed this, saying:
"Hit's jist the good Lord a-blessin' us."

Doubtless 'moonshining' was being carried on to some extent.
But there had been no raids nor anybody taken up. There had, of
course, been the usual 'parties', with some drinking, but no violence
done.

And still, there was no school, no church life — and no place to go.
The parties were all the diversion the little settlement had. They went
to Newport for supplies — it was usually Silas McDirk and Hackett.
Sometimes the McMahon woman went along with them to sell her
"yerbs." They usually got back the same day in summertime, but not
always—

"Now don't be oneasy, you an' Nancy", Silas would say to Eve. "If we don't git back t'night, we'll be back t'mor'."

"Shucks! I never bat an eye when I leave my family — my wife an' the grown gals could battle ol' Kirk's army, said Hackett. At spring time the same crude farm implements were gotten out, maybe repaired, and the "breakin up" of the little mountain side patches began.

The women went into the fields — same as the men and did the same kind of work. On hot summer days the tired plough-horse or oxen would sometimes be stopped at the "end of the fur"; it was the restin'-spell, when all hands would either "set down" or "lay down" on the ground and wait for a bucket of water to be brought.

"Restin'-spell is over. The "plow hoss" feels the lash of a rope line and hears, "Gee-haw—giddy up!" Yes, hard work, indeed — and dull, as was also life in general with these people.

They were kind and hospitable — to all whom they did not suspicion and took to be their friends. But the minor note of sadness was there — often in the spoken word and conversations, and in some of the snatches of a few simple songs and ballads they sang.

From a mountain side in Chestnut-hunting time, through the blue haze of a calm Indian Summer, I first heard some of this minor music. Like Barbra Allen, and "Bury Me Not on the Lone Prarie," etc. It all left the impression of evil forebodings on my mind.

But so was life — as it slowly dragged on in this little isolated community on the east side of Long Arm Mountain, a spur of the Great Smokies . . . .

Until one autumn night — when Newt Hackett, aroused from his sleep, rushed over to Silas McDirk's house and shouted: "Sile-Sile! All hell's broke loose!" . . .

— 14 —

THE DEATH OF EVE McDIRK

Eve McDirk, long beloved in the little community, was saying she had "spells of ringin' in the ears," which, "accordin' to the old sayin' means death," she thought.

Silas, her husband, would tell folks "She's bed fast jist about all the time — keeps punyin' away; an' thars nothin' much we can do for her, me an' Nancy. Course, if we could git her to a doctor; they're so fur away, and she's too weak t' be took out. I've tried to git one to come — told 'im I'd pay; but he said, 'no hits jist too hard t' git t' yore place, Silas." So he fixed her up a little medicine, after he axed me 'bout how she complained an' so on. It don't seem t' do her any good."

Silas went on to say that Eve, in her "preachments," always said that since the good Lord created the land there 'round Ol' Starlin — same as elsewhere, it must a been His will for folks to live on it, and enjoy life if they could, same as elsewhere. "But I tells Eve," he

99

said smiling, "I guess this was the Lord's will; but that the will of the county managers seemed to be for us to jist make the best of it we can."

Thus, time in this little isolated community of Big Bend went on relentlessly so, — as the winter nights grew longer and colder, and as the poor families piled more wood on the fire to try to keep warm.

Since last spring, Eve McDirk had been denied the privilege of being out in the "good sunshine," which she so much enjoyed.

Now, as the end drew near, the neighbors — a whole house full of them, stood and moved silently about. Some of them, mostly the women, hovered near the humble "sick-bed", on which Eve McDirk unconsciously lay,, gasping for breath. Nancy, her head buried in her lean — and already work worn hands, was audibly weeping, 'Little Sile' by her side . . . . . .

It was well into the night when a few people, mostly men folks, began slowly leaving the McDirk home — Mother Eve had passed away; and soon word of it would be all about in the community. But not any farther away — it would be mid-morning before news would reach the nearest community across Long Arm Mountain, eight or nine miles distant.

Eve Had Seen Some of Her Wishes Come to Pass

While the modest coffin was being made next morning out of native boards, by Newt Hackett — as "best he could", with some help by others, the neighbors gathered again at Silas McDirk's cabin. Indeed, several of them had not left; they stayed to "help out" — wash up, clean, cook, and also to eat and talk, at the bereaved home, as was the custom. To Silas they offered their simple condolences, most of them saying, "Well, Silas, Eve was a good woman — we'll shore miss her here", or words to that extent.

"Yes, fellers," Silas would return, "if I could have I'd a rather gone myself in her place — guess the settlement would a been better off that a-way."

The women folks, with Minnie Hackett taking the lead, had dressed the body — in her "best, purty new dress" that Silas had bought the cloth for the spring before.

"She was too good for this evil place, anyway," commented Mrs. Hackett, "she's better off now, yes indeedy."

"I never could understand life much less death — the hereafter," said the blind Wicks girl. "My lady teacher though, down at Raleigh School for the blind, said that life hereafter is a sort of spirit life, no body to it."

"Guess you'll sorter have to learn us about some things now Linda, even if you are blind in the eyes." replied some one, "You've been to school some, we hain't."

All agreed that 'Mother Eve' had lived to see some of her wishes come true: The finding of Jim Boomers' 'remains'; the prosecution and conviction of two or three of the lawless ones of the community, and also living to see one community child, Linda Wicks, go off to school and learn to read and write.

100

"Why, she's the only one in here that can railly read and write 'cept myself, I reckon," Mrs. McDirk often said; "and Linda can beat me. My girl Nancy, never had any chance — never took to learnin' no way; and little readin' and writin' she can do, she got from me."

Burial Procession Is Led By Hackett and Linda

By 10 o'clock on the morning of the next day all the people — so it seemed, of the Big Bend community, together with a number of outsiders, had gathered at the McDirk home for the funeral. The day was somewhat chilly — a slightly chilling wind, but clear and with a warming sun. It was just the kind of day some said that Mother Eve would liked — with "the Lord's good sunshine overhead," seemingly a smiling benediction on the day.

Linda Wicks thought that they "ougt to have a little burial service of some sort; so the folks told her to take charge.

Newt Hackett had pitched his mule to the farm sled, and it now stood just outside the McDirk cabin, since Linda was blind, it had been arranged for her to ride in front on the sled seat with Mr. Hackett. Hackett himself and three other men with the coffin were now coming out of the house, followed by Mr. McDirk with Linda, Nancy and 'Little Sile'. The plain pine-board box, holding the improvised casket, which Newton Hackett had kindly nailed up ("the best he could do"); and on the head of which the neighbor women had placed some "paper flowers" tied with a ribbon, was placed on the bed of the sled. In this order, the little congregation of mourners now slowly moved off up the rocky and narrow road to the little "graveyard".

At the grave side, Linda quoted two or three verses of Scripture — which she said that she knew Ma McDirk liked. Then she said they would sing a verse or two of "In The Sweet Bye and Bye"; Linda let off in a shrill, plaintive voice and two or three of the women joined in as best they knew the words. After some exclamations of mourning on the part of the bereaved family, the men lowered the coffin and began to fill the grave . . . .

Soon they were moving off back down the road, chatting more freshly now. "It will be some time before we'll git used to being without Ma McDirk, some 'lowed.

"Don't guess I ever can," said Silas; "but me and Nancy and our boy will jist have t' make out — best we can do."

After some two or three weeks of quiet attention to the everyday hum drum of their normal activities — without any of their regular mountain 'hoe-downs', the little community returned to their usual rounds of at least one party a week.

They said, at first how sadly they missed Ma McDirk — the bereaved family, especially. But now — "what's the use of grievin' ", they said, "we all have to go."

Newton Hackett was still grinding away — his three stoutest galls furnishing the muscle-power at the hand crank; Silas was looking after his trapping and hide business, and Linda had 'made up', she said, another song 'in her head' — and was already trying it out at the 'parties'.

Thus life went on in Big Bend — until the "great change" began to take place.

And that change finally ushered in the changes *taking place today — with more to come* . . . . . .

The Sequence

The time of the above story ended years ago. And with those, ended years, many of the people have either passed away or left the communities — all but just a very few. Because they could no longer live there in Big Bend, Hurricane Creek and Cold Springs.

Nature — as Eve McDirk thought of it — the "good sunshine" etc. had not dealt as kindly with them, perhaps, as she thought or hoped it would. Or was it fate, instead of Nature's designing? Ma McDirk (had she lived to see it, would have said it was a sinful people's own undoing.) But be that as it may, here's what fate seemingly had in store for them:

With the coming of the Great Smoky Mountain National Park (although this effected the people of Cataloochee and Big Creek most); the cutting off of most all the timber in the sections of Cold Springs, Hurricane and elsewhere, and the consequent moving out of the saw mills, there was nothing left for the natives to do, that was sufficient or adequate to give them even a frugal living.

And although the National Forest and Wild Life Preserve was extended into this section, that only tended to force more of the land owners and tenant farmers out.

However, aside from the main purpose — of the National interest, which was to conserve all this naturally adapted region (with all it's scenic wonders of mountains, gorges and remaining forests for further generations, it has been said that these very people, who had been living here, but now live elsewhere, are living better,-easier and more enjoyable lives than ever before.

But the greatest modern improvrment — as well as significant departure from the old, declining life and activity in this section began about ten years ago, as follows:

The decision of the 'powers that be' to build the Western North Carolina link of the great defence and scenic highway, I40, through Haywood County and down the Pigeon River Gorge, was made about that time. And on the actual beginning of work (bringing in of powerful road equipment, followed by the thunderous roar of blasting down in the gorge) made the remaining natives look and wonder. "They've acks'ly begun work on the road," they said, "What d'ye reckon's comin' next!"

But Oliver Hicks still affirmed he was "jist not a-goin' to sign — no, siree."

The Haywood link of this great East-West 4-lane highway is already perhaps 50% completed. Beginning on the Middle Atlantic Coast and running through most of Western North Carolina 'Vacation Land,' it bi-sects the Big Bend-Hurricane Creek-Cold Spring section completely; and thereby opens up — to the world, a picturesque mountain section adjacent to the Great Smoky Mountain National

102

Park, together with a deep river gorge, a section that has been almost completely isolated for 100 years..

Then, after all, is this not of Nature's designing — a better working out with Nature and Nature's laws? We think so.

PART III

Uncle Abe

Introduction

By request, we here reproduce quite a number of selections from the newspaper column which has been running periodically in the *Waynesville Mountaineer* for 32 years. The column had the heading shown above for about four years, regularly, and was then changed according to the subject matter.　　　　　—W.C.M.

JOHNNY SPEEKS OUT

Now, teecher's got a bran' new soot —
    An' her permanaint's made o'er;
Since the raze, ye see, in sala-ree
    She sez she's not so pore.
Then teecher's got rale purty shoos,
    With boze that air in fashun,
An' painted lips an' finger tips—
    Oh, aint our teecher dashin'!

———

But, say she's smokin' seggretts—
    I've seed her in the hall-way;
She holds 'em so—then, phoo-oo! she'll blow,
    And shet her eyes moast alway.

———

An' the "helps" she haz, my goodness me!
I don't know all by name—
    Grafs, stensils, rools an' other tools—
    She sez, "Save time's the aim."

———

But pa, he sez, with a little smile,
    "The aim, now I wood guess:
Them charts an' rools an' uther tools
    Saves time to paint an' dress."

PORE LITTLE MOUS

When Sis went out to milk one morn
    'Bout ate o'clock I guess,
While shuckin' corn out in the barn,
    A mous ran up her dress—
    "Oh-wow! Come help here—quick!"
With hands claspt titely at her thi—
    The milk upon the flore,
Sis did not seece to scream an cry,
    Till the pigs rusht throo the dore—
    "Come here! and bring a stick!"
Then chickens came, fifteen or more—
    The milk ran here an' thair;
But Sis still stood above the flore,
    Her screams still pierct the air—
    "Oh, mercy! mercy me!"
In ran her brother with a cry,
    "My, what's this all about?"
Then, as pigs an' chickens he did spy,
    He tride to git them out—
    "Here, Rover, shoo-soo-ee!"
"Oh, come to me!" big sister cride,
    Oh! a mous is in my dress!"

Then rusht her brother to her side,
  Sed he, "Aint this a mess?"
  Sed Sis, "Oh, mercy me!"
"Turn loose an' shake, I no it's ded,"
  Sed brother, standin' nigh her;
"Oh no," sed Sis to brother Ned,
  "If I do it will run up higher"—
  "Hold, Ned an' let me see."
"Aint no mous thar, you silly Sis,"
  Sed Ned an' turned away.
Sis shook her dress—"Look! what is this?"
  Thar a one ounce mousey lay—
  "Pore mousey, little thing!"

WHEN BARBERS TAKE A NAP

While passin' the City Barber Shop tuther day Unkle Abe wuz at tracked by a noize inside sumwhat like that of the "Moniter Alive" out at the Fair; but on steppin' inside I found it wuz a-comin' from one of the barber's cheers — the barber had took advantage of the noon our to ketch up sum sleep.

An' of all the snorin'! well, I told the boys I hadn't heerd sitch snorin' since brite t'backer curin' days. On the high notes it sounded like sawin' hick'ry wood with the bark on, an' on the low notes like sawin' goards.

Well, Unkle Abe an' all the little Abes had to make out on hen Thanksgivin' — I jist magined it wuz turkey an' called it turkey, so made out a purty good dinner. Oh, well, all this turkey stuff is moasly sentament enyway, an' like George White sed by shoutin', it's not what it's crackt up to be, no sir-ee.

A crowd wuz a-standin'a in front of Windy's place last week —
"Lot o' noize an' loud talkin' in thar," said Bill Lamkin.
"Well, what wood ye expect?" sed sum one, "don't ye see that sine on the winder, it sez—WINDY'S PLACE."

NOZES OUT OF PLUM

Heerd a new barbar-shop yarn tuther day — thars no end to em ye no.

One of our Waynesville barbers sed that thar wuz a sertin man in Waynesville T. S. whoze noze is an inch out of plum; sed he coodn't do a furst class job on the man fer lookin' at his noze an' thinkin' about it.

Now, if this man had a-bin a Waynesville politishhun or office-holder, it woodn't be so surprisin' nor sad to find hiz noze out o' plum . . . it wood a-bin kinder symbolick ye see. (I've also node sum of our preechers to git a little out o' plum, or rather off ballance). but, seein' that this is an innercent bizness man, Unkle Abe is rale sorry.

The barber also sed that thar is a woman here whoze rite yeer is higher than her left. Then sum fokes nozes, he sed, didn't tip egzackly strate; ockasionally you'de find a person whoze yeer lobes wuz not a like, an' uthers with one side of the mowth a little different from tuther. An' often he'de found persons with one eye squinted more than tuther.

Come to think of it, fokes, if it's this bad, looks like barbers mout fit their selves up for facial surg'ry, an' put out sump'm like this:
NOZES RE-SOT HERE
SQUINTS TOOK OUT
YEERS LEVELLED
WRINKLES ARND OUT, & SO FOARTH.

FAR CRACKER FUN

The fun of puttin' crackers in cars, attachin' em to a spark plug so as to go off when the car starts up, still kontinews here in Waynesville . . . . 2 of the latest victims bein' Doctor Kirk an' Hardy Medford.

Hardy sed that while the fuze wuz a-sizzin' he thawt it wuz a short sirkit that wuz a-goin' to burn all the wirin' out; but when the cracker went off — "I thawt the thing had blode up," sed Hardy.

The trick on Doc happened up about the Temple.

Doc jumped out an' jerkt up the hood,

"What's the matter Doc, can you tell?"

"Yes," sed Doc, "it looks jist like the carbyrater's blode all to hell!"

Well, Glory be!

TO MEMBERS OF THE DOLE

They say the dole haz ended, fokes —
    Doc Turpin's about sold out;
An' if we find this a fackt
    You'll haff to "do about."
Two years you've bin upon the dole —
    You've hardly workt at all
An' like the caff, weened from the tit,
    I guess you're shore to bawl.
Since most of you air weakly like,
    At furst I'de take it eezy —
We no, of korce, you want to work,
    So fokes won't think you lazy.
You mout begin by countin' holes
    Out in the cow barn shed;
Or, better still by dustin' socks
    When all have gone to bed.
Then you cood plant sum Xmas corn,
    Put sick kittens "on the spot,"

Or run down a mother snale an' pups
  An' dee-horn the whole durn lot.
When this is done, go dig red worms —
  If it won't hurt ye to stoop;
Put on the pot, then skin the worms
  An' make sum red worm soop
Go jine the kindegarten class
  An' help play hide an' peep,
Dig butter flys from 8:00 to 4:00 —
  Then sing the hens to sleep.
"Don't like this work?" well then see me;
  I'll need ten men rite soon
To dry a swamp out near my hous —
  You're to ditch it with a spoon.
Now, you who've lived on hand-me-outs,
  This work will help yore sole;
Don't laff an' call this foolish stuff —
  Or I mout call ye Dole.

MODERN KOLD METHOD

A boy came to Waynesville, lookt into a Bewty parlor an' saw a woman havin' her hair dride. At the supper table that nite he axt:

"Pa, what kind of a place is that at Waynesville on Mane St? I saw a woman a-settin' back in thar, an' she had a thing that lookt like a German helmet over her hed . . . an' it lookt like the heet wuz a-comin' out of it. Wuz she a-bakin' her hed, er sump'm?"

"No, I think that's whir they kyore colds," replide the father.

NUFF TO MAKE HIM SCRATCH

A sertin Waynesville lad wuz sent to the drug store for paregoric. On the way he forgot the name, but went on enyway, thinkin' I suppose, that he wood remember it. But he didn't.

"It's 'oric' sump'm," the boy tride to explane.

"Bout what's the price?" axt the druggist.

"Ten or fifteen cents, if ye don't want mutch," the boy replide . . . 'an' it's got 'oric' in it."

When the boy returned home to find out the name, he wuz axt what the drug store man sed an' did.

Nothin' mutch, he just set there an' scratched his hed," sed the boy.

A CLOCE CALL

When Bill Harris brawt in the delayed P. W. A. checks for the sewin' room here, the mistake he made wuz in comin' at the front dore; he orter a come in at the reer dore an' with an armed gyard, at that. As it wuz, them winmen stript Bill of his coat an' one pant lag before he cood git in an' bar the dore.

"METHODIST TRICKS"

One of our ex-County Commissioners tells a yarn that illustrates the unusual friendliness that exists between the Baptist and Methodist churches out in the rural sections.

It seems that Rev. S——, preacher in charge of a certain mission circuit in this county several years ago, was living pretty hard. The Baptists were in the majority in that particular community, and had just held a "big" revival adding several more members to their church. About this time Bro. S—— apparently began to look toward "greener pastures," and on meeting up with one of the Baptist deacons one day, decided to "feel him out."

"Well, you folks certainly had a good meetin'. Bro. Brown," began the Methodist parson.

"Yes, a very good meetin'," returned the deacon, "and why wasn't you out more than you were to help us roll the wheel? . . . then maybe you would a got some members for your church."

"Maybe so; but you see Bro. Brown, my churches are on the drag and so far behind in my salary I hardly know what to do."

"Well, perhaps you are in the wrong church," jokingly replied the deacon.

"Now, I've been thinkin' about that pretty seriously of late," said Bro. S——. "Say, Bro. Brown, had you been thinkin' that I might come over and join your church?"

"No, Bro. S——, I was just joking."

"Well, now it's no joking matter with me, and if you would talk just right I'de consider the matter. And if I was to come over, I'de make you a mighty good member," continued the parson, "because, you see, I know all the Methodist tricks."

UNCLE ABE HAZ 10 DAYS EXCITIN' TIME

Mr. Ed. an Enterprize Staff:

Seein' as how thar's bin sum hint for a little Uncle Abe fillosofy an yoomer to go along with theze excitin' times, les all let down our hair an put our feet up on the table for a spell. (Woodn't that be a pictur?)

The greatest thing in this old world is larnin to relax. I don't no who sed that fust; but whoever, he probly dide of a stroke a-chasin' his other haff around the cave with a club.

Yes, siree! Uncle Abe's had sum exctin' times endurin the past 10 days; bout as mutch so as I had in Floridy whir I had to hide out in the swamps to scape the consarned house-clippin planes.

Seein' as how I didn't want to git killed, I staid in on Labors Day. But I didn't hav enny more sence than the rest of that crowd what tore off to Bethel one mornin' when the Bryson City man broke his wing, I meen the plane-wing, a-landin.

So, I tuck off in my Plymouth — a head start. But as you no, me an my kyar both have about the limit on our speedn-meeters; tharfor, the rest o' that crowd a-hurryn up Piggen River kep a-tootin at us (me an Plymy) to let em pass. Well, we jist tooted back an waved em on by. That's why we got up thar at the tail eand of the crowd, stid of the head eand.

"Hit's all over now, Uncle Abe," sed some feller as I pulled up.

"Well, don't look like you erly burds are enny better off than I am," sez I. You jist got fooled quicker."

'Moon-Struck'

Good Peeple, hav you ever thawt, as times go by, how mutch more excitin' they git? Jist think, only a few days ago them thar Rooshian Reds sent a rocker plum to the moon! An that consarned thing was a-talkin back to us — I mean to the sine-tiffick men — all the time ontil it got to the moon. Uncle Abe was there when one of theze confoundin things went off in Floridy. Awfulest hare-raising noize I've hyeard. That's why I tuck off to the swamps.

An now sum peeple's all eckcited, an a-sayin, "Look at the Reds. They got thar fust with the most; what are we a-goin to do? Are they wizer than us?" — an so foarth. Well maybe so — an maby not. Thar could be sitch a thing as gittin too allfard wize — an struck on the moon. Also the worm could turn, you no. Maby we'd better wate a-while an see — before we try to reach the moon. Caze if them Reds was to all start gittin moon-eyed an a-cryin for the moon, hit would be a warnin to us.

What Next?

Well, to a feller like Uncle Abe who has come all the way up from the ash hopper — bulltung plow days, all this sertinly is a wunder. Jist what it all means, only the Great Marster knows — don't you readers think so?

But thar was a woman come to my door last week, an she seemed to think she onderstood —

"Uncle Abe, don't you think it means the world's soon-comin to the eand?"

"No," I replide, "not nessary so."

"Why not?" she axt. "An the Bible warns us to be reddy."

"Well, hit's allrite to be reddy," sez I, "but thars no use a-gittin all eck-cited an go to shoutin from the hous-tops; les jist keep our shurts on, young lady — then we'll be better drest to go when our time comes."

Fishin' Wuz Fine

Also, Mr. Editur, I've had one good day's fishin'. Rite when I thawt they'de bout kwit bitin', I sumhow *felt* jist like they (the fish) wanted me to come down to the lake an' try em out.

Well, hit wuzn't long ontil I'de landed 2 — an one I called a 'whopper'. Course I had to stretch my 'majinashun to do this; but for a fisherman to stretch aint hard ye know. Also, breakin' my cane pole in landin' that fish lent a lot of colorin' — an stimmylated the majinashun.

Now what am I to do?, thinks I to myself. You see, I didn't have another pole. An no nife wo'th anything. Finely I found a pole — a little smaller than a stackpole. But it wuz the only thing, seemed like

111

— that is, if I had strenth a-nuff to use it. So, when I'd fastened the line an all to this small stackpole, I looked aroun' to see if thar was ennybody a-watchin'. No, nobody in site; so I kast out. But that was a purty good pole, arter all. Course, I had to heeve an set, set an heeve to kast out. I jist hope nobody got my pictur down thar — a-usin' that stackpole for a fishin rod.

NOW THIS IS THE LIMIT

"What's the price of this peece? axt a woman shopper in one of our lokal stores last week.
"Fifty cents a yard," replide the clerk.
"Oh, I can buy that for 49 cents," objected the woman.
"Well, take it at 49 then," agreed the clerk.
"Well, I bleeve I'll take ½ a yard," she sed.
Mr. Editur, sitch as this gits my dander up . . . an' I bet 5 cents that woman wuz in the habit of tradin' out of town.

I'm glad our Chamber of Kommerce haz started a Trade At Home Campane, 'cauze thars a few of our Waynesville wimmen what still think it looks big an' smart to go out of town to trade, then come back home an' parade the fackt before their naybors. Thar yooce to be a few ol' dames here who had a habit of goin' over thar to trade, then "rub it in' on our lokal murchants by havin' it put in the paper, sump'm like this:
"Mrs. Trade-away wuz shoppin' in Asheville Monday."
Well, I'm durn glad the Mountaineer haz cut out the rubbin in part.
Kovince one of theze wimmen that she lost 50 cents by goin' away from home to trade, an' she'll reply that the trip wuz worth a dollar.

ADVICE TO PREECHERS

When Unkle Abe wuz on the Cow Paster sirkit he had it fine the furst yeer, jist middlin' the 2nd, pore pickins' the 3rd, an' Starvashun fare the 4th yeer.
Ye see it wuz like this:
The furst yeer I had indigeschun, coodn't preech an' took advice instid of givin' it. The 2nd yeer I kommenct givin' advice. 3rd yeer I give more advice, also startid buyin' cattle. 4th yeer I jist about kwit preechin' an' bawt more cattle.
An' fokes, I want to tell ye it wuz shore a hard game what me an' my members plade that fourth yeer. The less they pade, the more time I spent tradin' in cattle . . . ontil 'bout all I had left wuz my cattle bizness.
So, my advice to Methodis' preechers is this: Don't go into the cattle bizness even tho ye air on a 'Cow Paster' sirkit. Of korce you'll be allowed to go into the chicken bizness if yore members don'r furnish a plenty. Now sum denominashuns allow their preechers to farm, sell goods, toom stomes, raze rabbits an' fish to splice out, on kondishun

112

that they repent ever Sunday; but since none of theze air fer the good of the order, I'de advize ye to stick to preechin' so long as ye don't haff to take up more than 3 notches on yore belt. Also—

Don't Sell Specks,
Don't be a Depty Shurf,
Jestice of The Peace,
Carry A Plan Book,
Run a Medicin Show.

As all theze shood be beneath the dignity of a preecher.

ATTENDS BALL GAME

Well, Unkle Abe went to the ball game at Canton Friday — an' like to a froze to deth. I kickt off a while aiter the furst ½, an wuz a-comin' down the rode all bent up like I had a busted pendix when a man hollered at me an' sed, sez he —

"Hello, Unkle Abe — what's the matter?"

"Matter, hell," sez I "kaint ye see when a man's froze dubble?"

What wuz the yooce of me a-stayin' when I didn't no a nuff bout football to tell who wuz a-beatin'. I hollered at the rong place onct an' a Waynesville man lookt like he cood bite my hed off, so aiter that I waited ontil the Waynesville crowd hollered.

I Feel 2 Ways At The Same Time

Now, if you've ever felt 2 ways at the same time you no what it meens woman or man. Thar aint no yooce a-beatin' round the bush, when a feller slips on froze ground an' 1 lag goze East an' tuther west, like mine did yisterday, it neerly tares him in 2.

Ye see, if I hadn't a told my trubble I'de a bin axt a thonsan' queschuns — now maybe I can git by on 500.

S'long,
Unkle Abe

"SHE'S NEVER FAILED YIT"

A fidgety little business woman, a farmer and an old lady with a cane — just these three, were all talking at the bus terminal a few days ago while waiting for the bus.

The little business woman would jump up about every minute and run out to see if the "Plague-take-id bus" was ever coming.

"Left my business, which I hardly ever do," she said, "and I just know they're needing me; always when I leave some one's bound to call and want to see ME. Nobody can look after the business just like I can . . . guess I ought not to a left."

"Well, you're prob'ly right," agreed the farmer. "I've been all along thar an' I know jist how you feel." (Pulls out his big watch as if to see the time and looks at it fully a minute). "Well accordin' to my time, it's due" said he, easing the big watch back into his pocket.

"Bound to be late, of course, and me a-waitin' to get back to the store," snapped the little business woman.

113

"Well, I wouldn't worry, I guess things will go along allright," replied the old lady.

The little business woman looks at her watch.

"Bout what time is it by yore watch lady?" asked the farmer.

"Six minutes past," she replied.

"Well, I mout be about two or three minutes slow," the farmer said, "then you COULD be fast.'"

"Don't think so, I set with the electric clock in the office before I left, and it's always right — unless the power goes off."

"Yes, that's what ruins em, that'll fix em." drawled the farmer.

"No, it doesn't hurt the clock, just has to be reset," she replied.

"Well, for my bizness I'll take the old clock that stands upon the far-board every time . . . jist like mine does at home, never fails me," rejoined the farmer.

For a brief minute there was silence except for the shuffling of feet on the outside . . . and someone came in to inquire about the bus.

"Goin' over about Asheville, air ye?" asked the farmer lookin at the old lady.

"Yes, going over to see my sister; I usually go over on Thanksgiving."

"Well, I don't guess you could go in a better time that is, to git sump'm good to eat," he replied.

The little business woman looked at her watch again, fidgeted on her seat, got up and went to the door.

"Oh, my! I do wish that bus would come on if it's ever agoin' to," she said with a little sigh.

"Hit'll be here purty soon now," said the farmer, pulling out his big watch again. "I've never knowd hit to fail yit."

"Well, I reckon when a person is SO anxious to get back to their business it just seems longer —."

"Now you're a-gitten to the pint," interrupted the farmer, "jist *seems* longer."

A moment's silence . . . then the bus blows. The little woman hurried toward the door —

"I told ye she wuz a-comin' . . . she's never failed yit, not to my knowin'," concluded the farmer, smiling.

UNCLE ABE ON VAKASHUN

Yes sir-ee, I went to see Uncle Dave Makun — moastly to see, of coars, jist like the kids. As jokers them two Delmire boys went flat, but they make harmoany alrite when it kums to the musick. Now, Uncle Dave is a purty good joker, an' better banjer player still. Sum of hiz jokes air a little smutty — moast too mutch fer a S.S. class, but jist rite to make a thee-ater crowd roar. I don't no whuther my 2 Kontemporary Kolyumists on this paper wur thar on the look out fer frash jokes or not . . . If so, of coars they woodn't kum out an' admit it like Uncle Abe haz.

114

Last Wed. nite wuzn't a good time fer preechers an' S.S. teachers to atten' the show, becaus all thur memburs an' studints wood a seed 'em. Now, it wuz alrite fer an Ex-Serkit ridur turned yoomerist to be thar.

Buf gitten back to the show, it wuz the awfulest mob I've ever seed, Mr. Editur, not expectin' Al Kapone an' Shurley Temple nites — not even expectin' the crowds that atten' Wed. nite prayer meetins. (I'm boun to menshun this, even tho he mout slip me a free ticket ackazunally.)

Well, aiter me an' Jim Plott an' Walt Massey had fit our way throo the krowd to the ticket winder (we yoozed one o' Walter's krutches to beet em back with) —

Then aiter I pushed an elbowd my way in,
An' waited thurty minits the show did begin.

Deer Editer,

I'm havin' the time of my life, Yes sir-ee! I'm writin sum of my stuff on the way home frum Flat Rock, N. C. whir I spent about 2 days of my Vakashun . . . that's why I'm heddin' this Artikle Flat Rock, it's been the source of moast of the Inspirashun fer this letter. Besides, Flat Rock needs pullin' out of the dumps by gitten well advertized, an' I thawt this letter, bein from Uncle Abe, wood do the trick.

Well, I wuz on my way thar to see my bruther an' befoar gitten off I told the konducktor I wood like to stop off at East Flat Rock an' then walk over to Flat Rock (the Sitty proper) so as to see mutch of the Sitty as possible endurin' my short stay; but the konducktor sed it wuz vs. rools to stop the trane out in an open feald to let fokes off. "Besides", sed he, "I've bin a passin throo here now nigh onto 30 yeers an' I kain't sware thar is enny Flat Rock cept the stashun by that name."

"Well, don't peeple git off an on thar, board yore trane?" sez I.

"Sumtimes," sed he, "an on Sundays they crowd up here ta see the trane go by . . . they kum from down thar in the woods sumwhir. You mout go down throo thar an' hunt fer the town," sed he, pintin' in the direckshun.

Well, I dun so, an as I wuz a-goin' along I hyeerd my name called out from behind. I turned an it wuz my bruther a-moashinin fer me to kum back.

Flat Rock is a purty bloo place; that's becawz the town wuz laid out on this here crawfish bloo-clay flat land. I yoozed the term "laid out" fer the simple reezun that the town haz never yit bin built. But if they ever git to makin' bloo brick out of that clay the town ought to prosper.

Turns To Hitch-Hikin

I've made mighty good time hitch-hikin' today, Mr. Editur. I've found out that raleroad an bus skedyools air intirely too slow when a man's in a hurry . . . hitch-hikin' is the thing. Besides, it's grate fun changin' cars an' eangineers so offtin like this: Ford to Shivvy, and' visa versy. Plymouth-Ford, Shivvy, sumtimes-Buick, Chrysler or

115

DeSoto, acid wood truck, cattle an' laundry trucks (moast ginerally). The only thing I hated about changin' so much was that I found it nessysary to reepeet my "fine wether" an' "good crops" line o' gab ever time by way of interdoocin' the konversashun . . . gits sorter monottynus, ye no.

But after all, I think hitch-hikin' is about the moast plezant occypashun I no of . . . then it reequires so little capitul. All that's reequired in tangible things is a soot case with 2 or 3 collige pennants paisted on. Now of the intangible things a man requars more. Of nurve an' brass he needs $2000. worth; pleezing smiles, $500. worth (that wuz the hardest fur Uncle Abe); tackt, $800.; sycology $1000.; gab, $200.; good will (on the other man's part), $3000.

So, summin' it all up, ye see that a feller arter have about $7500. in intangible assets to make a sucksessful hitch-hiker (I meen these things wood be wurth that mutch to him in legittymate bizness); so, if ye think that ye have the qualities menshuned abov, it ain't absolootly nessysary that ye have the soot case an' pennants to go on it.

An' here's a-wishin ye success, from one who is beginnin' ta lurn a better yooce of the thumb.

Yores trooly,
Uncle Abe

P. S. — Mr. Editur, I've done hich-hiked throo Brevard, Rossman, Cashurs Valley, Highlands, Wallholler, Senaker, Greenville, Sparklinburg, Flat Rock, Hendersonville, Biltmore, Old Fort, Morganton, Canton, an' I ain't dun yit . . . becaws my Vakashun's not over yit.

ADVICE FER THE COARTS

Thar wuz a good 'tendance at the meetin' of the Frog Level Wize Klub a few weeks ago, which I fergot to report. Unkel Jim, Talkin' Boy, Natty Joe, Big Slim . . . an' other lesser lites — who coodn't git in a wurd.

By appintment the meetin' wuz at Lowry Lee's — Lowry haz a good hot stove, too, ye no, seein' that he's in the coal bizness. The mane topik fer konsiderashun wuz the Coart, which had jist klozed a few days befoar . . . an Unkle Jim led out —

"It-ud be a hole lot better if they'd jist bolish lawyers an joories," sed he, "cauze then peeple wood come neer a-gittin justice."

"Well, how wood they hold Coart, then?" axt Natty Joe.

"Jist let 3 Judges set in the Joory box," replide Unkel Jim . . . 'coarse they no a lot more law than a feel full o' joory men; why ⅔ of them thar men what set in the box don't no what the lawyers an' ol' Judge is a-talkin' about — ½ the time an' —"

"Now, don-cha git that into yore hed ol' man," interrupted Talkin' Boy, "Theze here ol' mountaineers no moar than ye think they do . . . besides don't the Bible say we have a rite to be tride by men of our kind, edg-gykashun, breedin' an' like that?"

"Well, I've red the Bible throo 4 times, an' I ain't never foun' that in it yit." sed Unkel Jim with a wry smile.

"Maby it's bin put in the noo Bibles since ye quit readin' em, Unkel Jim" — this from Big Slim who hadn't spoke befoar.

116

WIMMIN HAVE THEIR DAY

"Well, I can tell ye one thing, fellers, thar's more wimmen a bein' hauled into Coart now than ever befoar . . . don't no what's the cawz uvit onless it's becauze they're a-tryin' to do like men —"

"Why, cert'nly that's the cawz uvit," interrupted Natty Joe, "didn't we giv 'em the ballet, an' ain't we bin a-givin the wimmen the same chances with men . . . makin' pollytishuns out uv-em, polecemen, airplain flyers an' sitch like? But, we're t' blame fer it — us men fokes air . . . me an' you an' ever other man — now how did-ge all vote?"

(Thar wuz a minit's silence.) "Don't rekollect ever votin' t' giv em the ballet," spoke up Natty Joe.

"Ye don't? Well, then if ye don't I gess you wuz so drunk ye didn't no what-cha wuz a-doin'," sed Talkin' Boy.

"That's not the only thing that's ruint the wimmen fokes," spoke up Unkle Jim, decidin' to chang the subjick, "I'de lay it more to all this here paintin' an stile-ish dressin' — speshly showin' so mutch o' ther boddies . . . nakidness my ol' woman calls it, an' that's jist about what it is sumtimes. Course, I never had enny gals of my own . . . took one of my gran'children, tho, aiter its' daddy dide an' raized it up. An' I'm here to tell ye that me an' my wife never did let that gal git the upper hand on us . . . she never did no what paint wuz, an' she sekeercely ever yoozed enny talkum powder . . . maby a little sumtimes on meetin' days an' —"

"Don't see why enny boddy wood object if a gal er woman wants her skin to look sof' an' purty —" ("Throw in sum more coal thar," boys," interrupted Lowry, "if yer goin' to set aroun' my stove an' talk all day, durn ye, ye've got to keep a far.")

"As I started to say," kontinued Talkin' Boy, "wimmen they're differnt from us men fokes, I reckon . . . good Lord made em differnt, ever since De-liler charmed ol' Sampson in the Scripters, ye no, an back befoar that, I gess."

"Kain't see it that way," finisht Unkle Jim, "I think wimmen orter be natcherl, jist like the good Lord intended fer'm to be . . . if her hide is rozy, soft an frash lookin' — then cource, she'll be satisfide with it; but if it's not she orter be satisfide. Now, take my ole woman . . . she wuz as purty as a peech in her day, lookt jist like a pickter —"

"Look here now, cut that out!" stormed Joe Gaddis, "we can sorter stand fer ye braggin' on your auty-mobeels, cows an' so foarth, but on the ol' woman — never!"

"Fact is, ye don't keer enny thing 'bout the ol' woman," added Lowry Lee "or you'de all be home a-gitten her sum wood — its' alreddy 6 o'clock."

"I'de like Unkle Abe better if you'de make it jist a little eezier t' reed," sed Nath Rogers tuther day.

"How about yore wife?" I axt.

117

"Oh, she can reed it jist like a dawg a-trottin'," replide the surveyor.

"Well, jist git her to reed it to ye then — she's got the most sense enny way," sez I.

UNKLE GEO. AN' AINT IDE TIE

Unkle Geo. Garrett an Aaint Ide Mullis tide in the dancin' kontest at the Safety Bankwit tuther nite . . . jist about what ever boddy thawt they'de do.

Say, fokes, that wuz the fancyist dancin' I've seed in a long time . . . an I've seed Fred Astaire, Ginger Rogers, Bill Robinson an' others on the skreen.

Unkle George sed when he got up on the flore that he coodnt see, heer nor talk, but we all thawt he made out mitely well fer a man in that kondishun . . . fact is, he got more plauze than enny of the speekers. I thawt the best part of Uncle George's speech wuz whar he sed:

"Now, I want to tell this meetin' that I've razed 18 children — all in the same hous, or ruther my wife haz . . . an' now — well, I think we orter be more keerful 'bout far."

He towered o'er hiz little wife —
　　She wuz so awful skeerd;
He swore he'de beat her then an' there
　　Yit no one interferrd.
A kruel klub wuz in hiz hand —
　　Alas! what cood she do?
The children dared not say a word —
　　For he had beat them, too.
The klub comes down — we hear a skreem —
　　How savage, mean an' base!
"You kruel thing," we hear her say,
　　You allus' hold the ace!"

Now, this is not spring poitry, Mr. Editur . . . it's the kine that's bin a-happenin' aroun' here all winter, jist took spring wether to thaw it out.

Sines Of Spring

Now the ground hawg sine mout sumtimes fale, fokes . . . but here air a few sines of Spring that never fale: Little boys git out their marbles — an giv the dare . . . the speckle hen lays a shore 'nuff aig . . . junk piles grow by leeps an' bouns . . . the wimmen giv their hair the annyal wash an' dry it in the sun . . . ing-urn sets on ever hand . . . plan-book an' gyarden seed agents git bizzy . . . "Sons of Rest" kongregate on the sunny sides . . . an' las but not leest, Homer Davis flys hiz kite.

Yes, Sir-ee, whenever we see theze sines around Waynesville we no that Spring is at hand — no matter what the Almanick or groun' hawg say.

And Hiz Name Wuz Paul

In re-gyards to the Hooly-hooly Show, jist want to say that Paul Camel had better keep quite . . . trooth is Paul wuz the one t' git most eck-sited, while Unkle Abe acks'ly felt sorter ashamed . . . ye see, me an' Paul got in late an' had to take a seet rite in the frunt row with the kids — an' rite in winkin' distance o' them thar gals! I wuzn't quite shore but what sum or that laffin' behine went fer me an' Paul.

Enny way, if my name had a bin Paul, you'de a never kotch me at a show like that . . . nuff to make the sperit of the grate Apossel greeve fer hiz wayward namesake.

Mr. J. H. Trantham, of Shee-cawgo, informs Unkle Abe that there wuz 2 mis-spelled wurds in this kolyum week before last. Thank ye, Joe; but I gess that wuz jist what we newspaper fokes call a ty-pergraffical eror.

Puts Hoss Collars On 'Em

"Gess you'll have sump'm t' say 'bout this enny way, Unkle Abe," sed Perfessor Safford few days ago when I kotch him a-puttin' hoss collars in the back of his cyar as he wuz leevin' fer the Fines Creek-Mars Hill game." So, I'll jist tell ye theze collars air fer our Fines Cr. boys."

"What-cha meen, Perfessor?" sez I — "don't put hoss collars on 'em, do ye?"

"Shore thing; an' when Joe Rathbone gits this 'un on," he sed pintin' to the biggest collar, "nuthin' can stop him."

Fokes, did-ya heer 'bout Peerce Kinsland's acksident? 'Cordin' to the story, Peerce had the Yaller Jackit, Rip-Saw an' a Asheville paper all wrappt up in hiz pockit together. Well, this cawzed so mutch frickshun in Peerce's pockit — The Yaller Jackit bein' hot enny way, that they all kotch on fire . . . an' Peerce had to jerk off hiz coat an' stomp out the blaze.

"Well, I see ye've bin havin' a lot uv trubble this winter . . . chickens a-freezin' t' deth, you a-fallin' down an' so foarth," sed Dock Rogers.

"Yes, Unkle Dock, . . . an' thar's more trooth in it than most peeple think. Ye see, Unkle Abe lives in a awful kold place ennyway . . . I've become so well klimatized I think I'll jist jine admural Byrd on hiz nex' South Pole Trip."

UNCLE ABE GITS KICKT BY HIZ COW

"Yes, she'll kick 'casionaly,' sed the man I bawt her from. "'Rindy's sorter nervus sumtimes not mutch."

"Well, you've done tole me, so I'll watch out," sez I — jist got t' have a milk cow, me an the kids; an o' coarse Mrs. Abe, too, but she can drink coffy better'n we can."

Two or 3 days had past when I walkt up to Rindy down in the stall.

I set her feed down an she commenct lickin'. "So, Rindy, so," sez I, a-strokin' her on the little stool an' commenct milkin. She seemed to be a little nervus, an wuz eatin' awful fast — still I wuz hopeful. I had milkt a quart or more an by that time had sorter drifted off to dreemin' I gess — thinkin' bout fishin', writin' er sump'm —

Then biff-bing! like an ecksplozun! What on erth! I thawt.

The buckit wuz out o' my hand an over ginst the wall, now smasht about flat. The bigger porshun of the milk wuz down my frunt-coat, shurt an pants. An thar stood 'So Rindy' — now the objeck of my rath, a-lookin at me, as if to say: Jiss take what I giv an like it. (She had finished up her feed.)

"Oh yeah — think ye'll git by with it, do ye?" sez I. Then I lit in — ye see it wuz my time t' do sum kickin'. I think I giv her bout 10 kicks fer the one she giv me — I kickt ontill my rite big toe sed — quit it wuz gittin sore!

Jiss then I heerd a voice at the barn dore: "What's all the rackit bout down here?" she axt.

"Looky here at this — an me, too!," sez I, holdin' up the buckit fer Mrs. Abe to see. "Gess you'd a-fit too, woodn't ye?," I replide. "Ye bet I laid it on, too," I conclooded. (I didn't say enny thing bout my sore toe).

"Well, it didn't do enny good — only made matters worse," sed Mrs. Abe. "Caze now the cow won't giv rest of her milk down. Git me some more feed — while I go an git another buckit, an I'll see if she'll giv it down."

"I'de like to go an change — I'm a-gittin cold," sez I.

"Well, go on an change then — I'll git the feed. An' look at the biskits — don't let 'em burn," she added.

Purty soon Mrs. Abe returned from the barn —

"She woodn't giv it down — not mutch," she sed, "look — bout a tea cup full. See, ye didn't gain enny thing from yore big kickin', did ye? The cow got the best of it a'ter all — knockt you out o' yore supper milk. We've got to save what there is on hand for the children."

"Yes," I sed sorter repentent like, as I got up an went to the dore, limpin' a little from the big toe.

Uncle Abe pauzed at the dore — "You an the children can hav the milk at dinner time," I sed; "I'll jist take coffy."

UNCLE ABE DOES SOME HOSS-TRADIN'

I never was mutch of a hoss-trader — as ye'll soon see. Caze I simply didn't kno a-nuff 'bout hosses. O'korce I node which end of the hoss to feed and water, but that was 'bout all. Somebody started a joke on me — maybe it was Silas Jolly, the kommunity wag, sayin' that I wonst hitcht the rong end o' the hoss to the plow. If so, I kaint hardly see how I dun it. Ennyway, I never did discuver

120

my mistake. An' if plowin' in reverce — the hoss pullin backards instid o' forards — workt that well, why I orter a had a lot o' kredit fer this wunderful plowin'!

Now the fust hoss trade I made was in Williamsburg, Va., whir I was in the furniture bizness. It was like this:

Instid o' hirin' a hoss, I thawt I wood jist by one — to make collekshuns with out in the kuntry.

"Thars sort of a twisted-foot little feller livin' out neer the river who mout have a hoss t' sell," some one told me, "he neerly all ways duz." So one mornin I went out thru the sticks — to whir a sort of slew-footed little hoss trader lived.

"Yes, sir," he sed, "I think I've got the very hoss ye need, mister — whatch yer name?"

I told him.

"Seems like I've hearn that name — is hit in the Bible?"

"Yes, sertinly, Abraham's in the Bible — one o' the biggest names in it," sez I.

"Enny kin to Aberham Linken?" he axt.

"Yes, Abraham Lincoln too," I replide — thar's whir I got my name."

"Well, I'm a son-of-a-gun!" he exclamed, "Yuve shore bin aroun',"

"Well, I've not got enny little name," he sed, "Jackson's a purty big name in theze parts — Stonewall Jackson, I reckon I'm kin to him."

So, a'ter theze interduckshuns, korce we wuz all set fer bizness. I lookt hiz ole hoss over:

"Awful bony!" sez I — when did he eat last?"

"Jist got 'im in," sed the little man, "day before yisterday — looks better alreddy. The man what oaned this hoss sed he had more hosses than he cood feed."

"He didn't feed this'n enny then, I reckon," sez I.

"I gyarantee I can feed this hoss up 'bout a week, curry 'im good an' so foarth . . ." (Slappin' the old hoss on the back) — Stan' aroun' here ole boy! Mister Aberham woodn't kno ye wood he?"

The hoss moved a little — not mutch.

"What's yore best price?" I axt.

"Fifty dollers," he replide, "I'de sell my wife fust — 'fore I'de take less — she's out o' the house."

"Well, I'm not interested in buyin' a wife rite now," I told Jackson, "I wuz jist thinkin' bout a hoss."

"But I *will* feed 'im up fer ye, curry an' treet 'im good till next Monday — that's five days — then fetch the hoss out to ye."

"I'll give ye forty," I countered. He sed no, coodn't do that. I turned to go — but I had only made a few steps —

"Wait!' he sed, "I jist bleeve I'll take ye up; korce hits too cheep,, but I' a-needin' a little money rite now; so, you pay me five dollers now, t' bind the trade, an' I'll bring ye the hoss nex Monday."

It was done. He was at my place of bizness erly Monday. The old hoss did look an ackt sum better (I didn't kno what the little man had done to the nag); so I paid the ballence — an' he seemed well pleezed.

121

He had a rite to be pleezed. A week has gone by — an the old hoss slowd up on me till I kaint make my rouns, kaint git him into a trot a'tall, not even a fast walk.

I sent fer Jackson — told 'im to come at onct, an see what's the matter (Rado Banks, a hoss fancyer frend of mine had alreddy told me what he thawt was the matter: "He's at least 20 yrs. old," sed Banks. "I don't think you'll have 'im on yore hands mutch longer.")

Enny way, Jackson — the little slew-footed lire, come — with a grately koncerned-lookin' face on him —

"Oh. the ole feller's cistern has jist got rong," he sed.

"I'll give ye a few of theze to give him." (Here he shook out into my hands some haff a dozen tablets neerly big as checkers. They lookt lik wheet doe tablets).

But my ole Jonah never got enny of his ol' master's doe tablets — for his "cistern." (I told Jackson I didn't kno that hosses had cisterns; "Oh, yes," he sed, "all animals have cisterns so they can digess what they eet.")

After that the time was short . . . One day . . . two days . . . three days, I think — he was lyin' down in the ol' stall back o' the store — an' coodn't git up . . .

But what a releaf to both Jonah an' myself — when the end did come; an' when I saw my frend Banks "snake" the karkas off down into the woods to its grave. I remember the mornin' was bright — Banks sed that eb'm the birds seemed t' be happy down at the grave-side.

I TOLD YOU THAT HOSS WOULDN'T WORK

Looks like the $40 loss Uncle Abe took by tradin' with Mr. Slew-foot wood a-larnt him; but no, a'ter a few years I took a no-shun t' try hoss tradin' onst more.

Here's what happened this time:

I was marrid then; so I thawt a marrid man orter be able t' cope with most enny thing.

"I bleeve I'll go over to the Hoss Sale an' bye me a hoss 't plow the gyarden with," I tole Mrs. Abe.

"Well, I hope you'll come out better'n you did with that slew-footed little hoss trader you tole me about — whir was that?"

"Oh, now don't go t' throwin' that man up t' me — I've bin tryin' t' fergit it."

Well I went on over to the sale-barn an' thar I saw a bay pony, 'bout 800 lbs, that I thawt mout jist soot me —

"No. I won't gyarantee 'im," sed the man' "theze ar Western hosses. But I do kno he's a good traveler; also the oaner tole me this pony wood work dubble, but he didn't kno 'bout hiz workin' singel."

The upshot of it waz: I bid $75. — an' got the hoss. An' jist think — he waz good 'nough t' throw in an ole bridel with a grass-rope rane! I rode the hoss on home an' waz pleezed with hiz walkin' gate. I tride wonst t' poot my lef' lag up on the pony's neck an' ride sorter one-sided — but I neerly fell off.

I rode in, an jumpin' off sorter proud-like, sed to Mrs. Abe: "Well, what d'ye think uv 'im?"

"Well, he looks rite well, but he shows good deel o' white in hiz ize."

"What d'ye want 'im t' show?," I axt — "red, er yaller ize — bloo maybe."

But I node you coodn't git Mrs. Abe t' change her 'pinyen, not mutch.

"I'll take an poot 'im up, feed 'im good," I sed, "then iffen I can git Mr. Grale t' help me a little I'll try 'im out in a single-foot plow in the mornin'."

"Well, I hope he works, she replide; "but if the man woodn't gyarntee 'im I'm afrade he wont."

She turned an went into the hous' — an started singin, "Thar's A Grate Day A-comin'".

WHAT ON ERTH DUZ SHE MEEN, THAWT I.

"Hold 'im, Will — Hold 'im!

Nex mornin' I led the pony down to the gyarden-strip nex t' house, an Grale cum over t' help me. The pony lookt roun' at furst — an then, Sur, he shode the white uv hiz ize then, more'n ever — when I kommenct puttin' t' gears on, eezy like. He twitct a little an stompt one foot, lookin' roun a me — thar wuz the whites o' them ize agin! I wuz a litle nervus — seemed like my rite britches-lag wuz shakin' a little. Mrs. Abe wuz standin' at the porch — lookin' on; also sum body elce stopt t' look.

I poot the plow pint into the groun' — an slapt the line, eezy like on the hoss's back — he stompt hiz foot hard, switchin' hiz tale — then he give a lunge! I stove the plow deep in the groun' — then hollered: "Hold 'im, Will — hold 'im!"

Grale hel on — but that pony wuz hard as the devil to hold — he had allreddy kickt out o' the harness!

"I wuz afrade so", sed Mrs. Abe — "I told you that hoss wouldn't work; why don't —"

"Oh, fur goodness hush! bringin' up, 'I tole ye so's' — if ye can help us enny cum out an try — don't ye see we're in a perdickamint".

"I'm afeared to',, she sed.

"Well, we're sorter afrade rite now ourselves'" 'turned Grale.

We let that skeered pony cool off a bit, rubbed 'im an eezed the harness off. Then I led him up ιo the barn.

Az I went on up t' the little barn I thawt I hyeard Mrs. Abe singin': "Onct We Getherd Dazies —" an so foarth; an I got t' thinkin', *she's a-singin' that fer me;* caze onct we getherd 'em an she "tide 'em roun."

To make a long story short: The hoss didn't cum out o' the stall mutch fer 'bout 10 days or 2 wks. — when I swapt 'im off. Dick Smith at Hazelwood rode down t' see me one day, said he hyeard I had a hoss what he mout like, a good saddel hoss. He also sed he just felt shore he had the good ole steddy work hoss — which I needed fer plowin' an workin' in my one hoss wagon. "Here he iz," sed Dick —

try 'im if ye want to; he'll work enny whirs. An I notis ye have sum childern," koncluded Dick, "jist the very hoss fer childern."

Well, we soon traded — "'eab'm t' boot;" an I wuz well pleezed — so wuz Dick. I had good servis out o' my gray hoss — an finely made back sum o' what I'd lost on Slew-foot Jackson.

But this ended my hoss tradin'.

THE LATER UNCLE ABE

NOTE: The following Selections Are from the later Uncle Abe, beginning about 1950 — when he had begun "visitin' an' fishin' in Floridy rite mutch"

"Hit's Fun To Cook" — YE-AH?

Yeah, I red that, 'fore I come over to Asheville an' went to batchin' for myself — oh, I woodn't be batchin' for ennybody else!

I got along with my cookin' purty well ontil I had that dreem t'other nite — I drempt about grits, an' it seemed as tho they woodn't let me have enny, cravin' 'em like I wuz, when I woke from the nite-mare 'bout 5 A.M.

"The 'terpreta-shun o' that dreem is, that I need grits," sez I — "I need 'em for my systern, no doubt." So, before I got up to kinnel the far I de-sided that I'de jist major on grits. Well, I pored out what I thawt wood be ample suffishent for a man 5:11½ x 144 an' haungry at 5:30 A.M. I had forgot whether I orter put the grits on in cold water or in scaldin', so compermized by usin' warm water. Then I sot the pan on a hot stove (I have diskivvered that vittels air better cooked on a hot stove) an' sot down myself to read. I hadn't more'n got started in good when my grits biled dry. "I'll fix ye this time," sez I — an' pored in 'bout a qt. of lickwid.

Well, purty soon them grits wuz cookin' up a storm — an' then all at onct a-bilin' over! I hurrid with another pan, pored ½ of 'em in it — an' I'm a lire, fokes, if they didn't soon fill both pans. I'll git the dish-pan reddy," sez I — "jist in case." Them wuz the multiplyinest grits that ever hit the pan! "I've shore nuff majored in grits," sez I — "jist call this Grits Week." By dinner-time they had turned a lite blu an' had a top or crust on tuff as sole-lether; then I de-sided to call it Blu Grits Wk., or Grits Blu Week.

Then, as I stood back a-surveyin' my wondrus work, I rea-lized thar wuz no way out — nothin' I could turn them grits into. My instruckshuns hadn't sed ennything 'bout a grits pie, grits dressin' or grits konsole — so no more majorin' in grits for me!

A Few Hints:

Still I larnt a rite smart 'bout cookin' and so f'oarth over here, Mr. Editur, f'rinstance:

Don't starve for chicken caze they're hi — go to the markit, an' call for chicken noodles in the can, an' I'll g-yarantee there'll be as mutch as ½ a gizzard to the can. Course hit mout make ye a little sick; but still you'll be able to holler over the backyard an' tell the naybors you had chicken fer dinner.

If yore stove only bakes one side of the bred, don't throw out the stove — jist make one-sided biskits.

To keep up with yore naybors, dry out old coffy groun's for loanin'. This is mutch better than keepin' 2 kinds of coffy.

S'long till nex' wk.

—Uncle Abe

UNCLE ABE SEZ: A long windy speech is like the month of March — an' we're allus glad when both air ended.

APPYTITE GITS OUT OF KONTROL

Mr. Editur, Looks like I'm a-goin' to haff to fess up as to what's a-makin me look better over here — also when I go back home. When I go back to Waynesville lots o' fokes say: "Well, you're a-lookin' better, Uncle Abe." Then I say, "Thar's room fer improovment in moast of us."

I think hits caze my appytite is so mutch better — has bin fer 2 wks. It snapt back almost at onct, like a dislo-kated bone a-snappin' back into place. But hits now a-gitten out of kontrol, fokes, an' I don't no what to do. Why, I'm a-havin' to cook ½ the time to satisfy it.

Fer the past week I woodn't mutch more'n git the dishes kleened up from one meal fore a haungry pain wood hit me aig-n an' I'de haff to start right back to cookin' — maby fer the 6th time that day!

"What's the yoose," sez I at last, "I'll jist wash the dishes up onct a day, at nite, fer the nex' day's bizness."

I don't think hits a tape-worm a-helpin' me eat, Mr. Editur, caze I don't feel enny nawin' or rigglin' sensa-shun in my lower rejuns; I jist caint figger out what it is. But one thing I do no — hit's about to put me in the red. I tride eatin' more an' still more at one settin' down, but that was 'bout to back-far, seein' as how the bowil-mizzeries started up.

Nites I dream of flap-jacks an' 'lassies; shortin'-bred an' milk; pies, cake, froots, jams, jellies an' other ack-sessorys — ontil the tempta-shun throws me out of bed in a wild franzy an' sometimes a-shoutin' —

"Give me them flap-jacks, consarn ye!" An' onct they sed I hollered —

"Stop! Stop thar, you! Stop eatin' all that shortnin'-bred up!"

Ye see, I'm a-wakin' the naybors up; an' they say I'm not a-settin' the rite sample, me bein' a J. P. an' disturbin' the Peace myself. Course my appytite needed peppin' up — but not like all that, with a vengance to it!

I'm here cloast to 2 Sooper Mkts. — an' I thawt I was forchunate in that. But now I don't no — the added tempta-shun mite be wusser. I have lookt in Catalogs an' in the papers to see if thar was enny sitch a thing as appytite checker-ups advertized, or appytite re-doocers, but thar don't seem to be enny.

125

So, I don't no what to do. Enny suggeschuns from you Mt'neer readurs, or from the Staff will be welcome. Write me at 11 State St., W. Asheville, N. C.

Yores, Anxshusly,
Uncle Abe

UNCLE ABE SEES FLORIDY IN RAINY SEEZUN

"Thank the Lord!" sez I-as we landed back at my dawter's house in Hollywood that nite.

There wuz three of us, and had jist gat back a'ter the wurst downpore I'd ever seed in all my born days. Have ye ever bin in Floridy in of them fall pore-downers?

We thawt the rain had sorter let up-least wise, I did. But the Floridyites no purty well when to run an when to stay I didn't dout. Thar mite be brite skys one hour — then a flood the next.

Darkness had alreddy come on almost so—jist from the hoverin', black skys — for the third time a'ter brite skys that day, the water alredy standin' in the streets.

And lo! here it was on us onct more—in sheets of rain! But we **drove on**—for a short while only; now we pauzed —

"Looks like a flooded creek er sump'm — what must I do?" I axt my dawter.

"No, I think its just a flooded street," she replide — "gits that way here purty offen; go on thru — we've got to git out."

"Pray fer me", I replide.

So, I drove on thu—in water up to the runnin boards!

The lites wuz drownd out, we saw as we neard the other side-but on we went, follerin' the cars ahead. Finally we reacht a little fillin' stashun — an' stood in the rain (now sorter slackt up) ontil the man fixt our lites.

We made it in — we'd seen all the sites we wanted to see that nite.

JETS ROARED TOO LOW — FOR UNCLE ABE

No, I didn't 'tend the 'Merican Legion's big Parade at Miamy, caze I thawt hit wood be too big an long to soot me. But I hearn some of it; also saw the big jets swoopin' all about — 16 at a time. Women an childern wood sometimes scream out like the mischeef. Uncle Abe never did sereem; but I sorter felt like runnin' — when they'd swoop down so low over the house-tops ground seemd to shake. But maybe hit was me a-shakin'.

The Swank Hotel

A passel of us saw the swankest hotel I ever layed my eyes on. They called it Flountain Blow, er sump'in.

"Mister", I sed I to a feller settin' at the desk, "fokes must be as rich as all git-out who stay here."

He sorter laffed an sed: "No, I don't railly no how rich all-git-out is; but they don't haff t' be too rich — how much money you got?

126

"Oh, No", I sed — "don't gess I have 'nough t' git a shoe shine here". He laffed ag'in; then sed: "Here's you a picter: Thars nothin' like it under the sun, Uncle Abe"

"No", sez I, lookin' around, "maybe not eab'm under the moon an stars".

"Why, thars, so much o' that fine hotel I woodn't ondertake to perscribe it. All them pictures — on the inside an pools outside; then all yore bars, orkistrys, dance halls, hed men an foot men — runnin' here an thar. But I wood like to sleep, say 2 ours in this fine hotel".

"Well, maybe we can 'range for you to sleep 2 ours, Uncle Abe, seein' as how you comes all way down here to Myami to see our hotel. Les see", he sed, studyin' a minit, you've got 6 dollars: You'll have to have a shoo-shine — that's one buck; then you'll have to have a tie — we'll loan ye a tie;then fer the 5 bucks ye can sleep 2 ours — how's that?"

"Ye kaint let me sleep but 2 ours?"

"That rite; we'll wake ye up promply on the our"

"Then whir wood I sleep rest o' the nite?"

"You can set here in the lobby, pervided ye don't go to sleep", sez he.

"Well I gess I'll jist haff t' go out in the park t' sleep."

"Oh, No", he sed, quick as scat'! "umbody'd shore nock ye in the hed and rob ye."

"Bout the same thing", sez I, only you maybe, woodn't knock me in the hed — good bye!"

'SKELYTON' IS FOUND IN UNCLE ABE'S KLOSIT

The Bible sez that Adam & Eve wore fig leaves — to hide ther neckidness — mighty little things to hide behind; seems to me. Howsumever, sum fokes now-a-days don't ware enny more. Why, I saw 'em on the Floridy beeches with nothin on top but two 'fig leeves' an skercely nothin' on the middle — gals & men. I'd al'ays jist turn my hed, in passin' — the *men* I meen. But them harry-brested men lookt too mutch like baboons to me; gess maybe I sorter envyed them tho — as you will soon see.

My wife, Mrs. Abe, kotch me a-holdin' up a pare of gals' pantees in my room one day — an a-lookin' at em, longinly—

"What-chu doin' in here lookin' at them things — whir did ye git 'em!", she stormd out.

"Dog-on if I no", sez I, lookin up innercent like. "I found 'em in my klosit — didn't no thar wuz enny sitch a thing in here — I'd declar on a stack o' Bibles", sez I. "I wuz jist a-lookin' fer an ole pare o' pants t' put on fer pickin' blackberry in — an found theze purty things hangin' in thar."

127

"Yes, 'purty things hangin' in there' — "I see", she sed — "looks like you had some purty gal in here too, since I bin gone", I cood see she wuz mad as a hornit.

"Hold yore 'tater", sez I — gess I can explane."

"Well Ye'll certainly *haff* to explane" she replide.

"Thars not ben a purson, feemale that is, on this place while ye wuz gone — 'cept by cuzin over the street — course you woodn't 'spishun her don't 'spose —"

"Oh, no", she broke in.

"Wate a minet", sez I — "jist thawt o' sump'm" —

"No, you needn't try to think up anything to try to git out of this— I have a no-shun to go out an' see if enny o' our naybors saw a woman, maybe slippin' in here some nite—"

"No, don't let this out to the naybor women, *pleeze*. Why, it's now 'bout one O'clock—they'd have the biggest skandel out of it you ever h-yeard by two o'clock ennyway. But you cut me off minet ago; you didn't let me explane what I started to say."

"Well, what wuz it?"

"I started to tell you I wuz gone two nites also while you wuz gone. An also our gals had two other gals visitin' them. Now coodn't it be that one o' them left that — this", I sed, holdin the purty little pantees up?

Rite then I saw a little smile form on Mrs. Abe's full lips. "Come on", I sed, "Aint-ha a-goin' to the naybors, nor to the law—ar ye not goin' t' pack up an leave yore old man — of long standin?"

She had her hed down a little — I thawt I cood see the smile growin bigger—

All at onct Mrs. Abe jumpt up, run over—flopt down on my lap an give me a hug an kiss—

"I coodn't keep it from you enny longer", she sed. "But you wuz ketchin' on ennyway—you wuz rite. One o' gals left it here, she foned about it."

"Well, I never thawt you cood do a little plot and play well as that", I sed—that's wuth a kiss *for you.*"

"Well, I must run an wash the dishes—scat thar!", she hollered— "cat's on the table alreddy."

She jumpt up an run into the kitchin.

"THINGS GITTIN' ALL RONG"

Dear Editer an' all, If things dont git better round here soon I'll haf to go back to Floridy. Hain't had no peece o' mind fer nigh onto 3 weeks. Raily I think some o' the men fokes here have entered into a spiracy ginst me.

Here's the way hit is, best I can deskribe; Over at the Coart hous t'other day Albert Walker wuz a-settin' thar, with 5 or 6 'round 'im (men I mean), all a—talkin' —

"Why, hello, Unkle Abe! What under hy heb'm an' Tom Walker's matter with ye?"

"Nothin' don't reckon—feel alrite", sez I.

"Well, you look like you'de done fell off 100 lbs—wha-wha-wha!"

"No, if I'de lost that mutch Unkle Albert, thar would jist be 32 lbs. of me left standin' here—I'de way a little more'n that don't y' think?"

"Well, not mutch more"— (wha-wha-wha—te-he-he!—That wuz the crowd a-laffin')

Now, Mr. Editer, that's why I think they've entered into a spiracy; caze I know hit wuzn't that funny—not to me.

The men mosl'y say I look bad—want to put me in a class with themselves, I reckon. But most of the women say I look good—that's puttin' me in same class with them. Oh, Boy! Well. I al'ays did think more of the women ennyway, their judgmint, troothfulness an' all.

NOISES IN THE STOVE

Then thars another thing bothers me lately: Ever time I drap off to sleep behine the stove these here coal days, purty soon sump'n goze—"boo-oom!" bout like the hous had caved in.

"Sakes alive! what wuz that?" I axt Mrs. Abe jumpin' up (I mean I jumpt up)

"Stove jist made a little noiz", she replide.

" 'Little Noiz ' ? Sounded like a 6000 millymeter canon! Maybe hit wuz a air plane fell clost by; b'leeve I'll go out an' see."

"Maybe you'de better have yore pills changed."

"Pills—pills! why woman, what pills?"

"Yore Floridy Pills," she replide. "You're back up here now—attytude mout be a-causin it."

"Well of all things under hy heb'm—attytude! That Doc down thar didn't say hit wuz my attytude; said it wuz probl'y my livver. I gess my attytude's bout as good—"

"Wait-wait a minet!" Mrs. Abe intersected.

"No, dont 'wait-wait' me. . . Well what is it?"

"I didn't say attytude", she replide, "I said *altitude,* means elevashun, up or down."

"Oh, I see", sez I, camin' down. Now you mout have sump'm thar. The elevashun here's prob'ly too hy fer my Floridy pills. I'll jist tell 'im I want Westurn N. C. Altitude Livver Pills, my age & so foarth."

"Yes, an' be shore to tell 'im bout the noizes you've bin a-hearin' in the stove, also bout the bad nite mares. I gess he cood stir ' up sump'm speshal for that; an' also—"

"Wate now, good 'oman," sez I intersectin', "le's jist take one thing at a time. Besides, I think if I leeve of corn bred an' butter milk, souse-meat, sour craut, ingurns, apple sass an' ginger bred, the nite mares will stop. As fer the man made noizes, woman-made—al kinds, I s'pect I'll have them rest o' my life."

But a'ter all, good fokes, hit jist seems like ever'body's a-goin' crazy. Now, this haint pursonel—I s'poze you're sanitary alrite, But I found it like I sed all up thru Floridy an' Gorgy. "Shorely", sez I "I'll find 'em more sanitary when I git to Haywood". But, no— hit's 'bout the same.

Ski-high prices, that's what's a-runnin' folks crazy. That's why Unkle Abe wuz cryin' out in hiz sleep, "Stop 'im! Stop that man—*we haf to eat*-to live, an' (some of us) live to eat". That wuz the man I saw in my dreem a-raisin' prices—the Al' flashunary devil. The farmer sez hits' not him, an' the re-tailer sez he's not guilty—well I hope kongres finds the gilty skunk.,

Yores trooly, Unkle Abe.

UNCLE ABE CHARGES LISTENING IN OVER 'PHONE

Well, fokes — howdy!

I hate to tell you that when my troubles seemedt'be about over, rite then I up an' have tellfone diffyculties; also froze in, slippin' an' slidin', et cettery. Jist seems like ever'thing's gone haywire on my hill top. Sumbody called me threw the fone—

"Whooze this?", he axt. "This you, Uncle Abe?"

"Yes, this is the 'riginal. Jist who air you?"

"This is the tellyfone company," he replide.

"You meen to tell me you're the hole company yourself? You air some gy, ain't ye?"

Then he busted out mad-like: "Now none of yore wizecracks, Uncle Abe. I called you up to tell you you'll have to be keerfull with yore langwidg over the fone."

Rite then I sorter got het up, too, Mr. Editer, an' I shot rite back: "Have you bin a-tappin' my line—I see, you're a sabatoor, meddler, er sump'm like that. I kno Mr. Mock woodn't auth'rize you to do sitch a thing as that—tap my line an'lissen in—caze he's too much of a gentleman—"

"I'll give you to understan' I'm a gentleman, too, sir," he sed.

"Jist what persishun do you hold over thar?" I axt him.

"Well, I manage my end," he mumbled back.

"Well then, I guess you're 'bout the 25th 'sistent manager," I sed. "Didn't kno they ever got that low-down. But ennyway, seein' as how you're at the fone, I'll 'dee-send to talk with you. Now what about my langwidg?"

"Well, you shore did bless that heater man out over the fone 'tother day," he said.

"He made me mad—jist like you did," I replide. "An' I'm a-goin' to see what can be done about lissen' in on the fone. Now, in the furst place, I speak nothin' but the purist English, Victorian English— an' on back to Queen Lizzybeth the furst—that's the purist.'

"You meen fokes cood cuss over the fone back then?" he axt.

"They didn't have fones back then; but course you woodn't kno," I replide. "Besides, I hain't cussed over the fone—not since 1917-18. But when I git mad, I come awful close to it, you see. Why you don't kno what a seeryus charge I can put aginst you. Hit's a bad thing to tap, meddle or lissen in on a persun's privy line—you done jist that, tapt or somehow lissend in on my combinashun-privy line."

"What's that?" he axt.

"Well, you wood call it a reg'lar line; but in Queen Victoary's day an' Sir Walter's they wood call a line like mine a Privy line—with a capital P, see? That's more important—are you a-lissening?" I axt him.

"Yes, I wuz jist a-thinkin'", he replide.

"Thinkin' what?" sez I.

"A line like yore's does sound awful important; an' if I've done ennything rong, I'm sorry—"

"Jist forgit," sez I. "We all make mistakes."

Now, good fokes, I hope this end my televitis-heater-langwidg an' dreemin' trubbles.

This is 'bout as bad a winter, so fur, as we've had, ain't it? Jist set me to wonderin' if some of my ol'frends air standin' it alrite. Fellers older than myself—like: Albert an' Lawrence Walker, Joe A. Chambers, D. A. Howell, G. A. Rathbone, Jim Singleton, C. W. Medford, Dave Boyd, Boone Medford, Tom Rogers, Tom Fincher and others. O. K., I hope!

UNCLE ABE PRESHYATES GOOD FRENDS

Kind Reeders,

I don't kno jist what I'm goin' to do with all my good frens. I got so menny I thawt I'd classyfy 'em: In the fust place I put my *very* bes' frends—them what meet me a-smilin', pat me on the back (some few women hug my neck). They never say: "Loan me 50¢".

2nd class: This class, while maybe not feckshonate, I kno to be my good frens—all wether frens.

3rd class: My fair-wether frens. I still hole on to 'em—caze a fair-wether fren is better'n none a-tall.

4th class: In this class (small), I put my "Loan-me-50¢" fellers. I'm a-trying t' git rid uv all 'em. Thars jist 1 still holdin' on—I'm a-goin t' shoot him. (He's a-bummin' on the candydates now; but a'ter 'leckshun I'll haff t' shoot 'im).

131

Now, Mr. Editer, this is goin t' be a sort of Luv Letter, speshly to the wimen—an' ever body what's stuck to Uncle Abe in sitch a fine way. (Ye all kno what a hard row he's had); but now I can sorter let up—an' say, Glory be! (But no braggin'— no sir-ee) caze ever kine wurd an kompliment goze strate to Uncle Abe's hart—not to hiz hed.

In all my 'Uncle Abe' peeces, I spoze I menshuned 500 peepul, menny in a jokin' way. An' in all that number only 2 or 3 got sorter mifft. Y' kno Haywood fokes injoy good holsum yoomer. This cuntry wuz settled, fust of all, by a good, thrifty class o' peeple — English, Skotch-Irish, Dutch, German (an a few French) peeple.

Now jist look what a good ballence that is: English for stick-to-it ness an' also kulcher; Irish for free-hartedness, good spirits an' pluck; Scotch for thrift an' closeness (jist a little too mutch so); German for ingenuity an' downrite progressive, smartness an' goodness of hart. Now (last) the French. For gayetty an stubborness (I hope the French won't git mad at Uncle Abe for puttin' them under the Germans an' others) —caze you see gayetty an stubborness goze t' make up a good ballence.

Course, there's more or less stubborness in all peeple, maybe,— most peeple enny way.

My dad use t' tell uv 2 men on Crabtree what fell out— O, they got terribul crost up, as you'll see: On meetin in the road, if thar wuz room, one uv' them (maybe both) wood leeve the road (jump the fence an' go thru the feel); but if the road wuz too all fired nar t' git out, eech one wood slap up the hosses, turn hiz hed an' grit hiz teeth.

Now, fokes, ain't that a hell-uv-a-life to live?

The bes fee-losofy I kno uv to live by is to luv peeple. Fact is, luv (eether spelled by Uncle Abe's dickshunary or Webster's) is the greatest thing in life.

I've got so, folks, I try t' think like Will Rogers sed: "I luv ever boddy." Why sumtimes I think I eb'm luv the "50-centers."

So, in closin, Uncle Abe's 84-year-ol' hart reeches out t' y'all, an I can trooly say with Tiney Tim: "God bless ever boddy!"

Uncle Abe

UNCLE ABE

Loozes Hiz Specs — But Gits Fish

Melbourne, Florida. — I see by the papers, Mr. Editer, hit's bin cold as all git-out up thar. An I want to tell you we've bin gittin' some of it down here, too.

Seein' me with my overcoat on 'tother day, a man sed to me, sez he: "That's not a good 'vetisment for Floridy, mister." Then I sed rite back to him, "Well, hit's the best I can do — onless you heat up yore state a little better: looks like you fokes cud bild up some smudge fires, or sump'm."

Seems like I'll jist haff to stretch out my time down here another week. I've allreddy stretcht it out so long I'm about stretcht out an' dry-cleaned myself. (But so noboddy will be oneazy, I'll say I'm not in jail . . I'm not a-writin' this from the jailhouse).

Unle Abe went fishin' a few days ago — an' had the best luck yit. That is, I had good luck a-fishin', but awful bad in other ways — caze I lost my specs. Reckon I jist got so all-fired ecksighted over my fishin' I didn't hardly no which eand of me was up; so went chargin' throo the bushes — an' didn't no when I lost 'em!

Then a'ter that I tore a britches lag haff off. Then I sed to myself, *What in tarnashun is the matter with me today — kain't haff see!*

When I got back somebody sez to me: "Uncle Abe, didn't you ware yore specs a-fishin'?"

"Why, yes," sez I.

"Well, they're not on yore noze — that I can see."

So I recht up frantic like, an Heck — no specs!

The Lost Is Found

Two days later, an a'ter I had kickt myself all over the place — in walks another fisherman to my roomin'-place. 'Is Uncle Abe here?," he axt. "I saw him a-lookin' for his specs t'other day; well, I found 'em," sez he.

My lan'lady called an' I run down — an' bless yore soles, fokes, thar wuz my specs!

I felt like huggin' the man rite thar. But I remembered seein' two fishermen a-huggin' each other onct (they wuz drunk), an' I sed rite then I didn't ever want to see anything like that again. So I thawt we'd best put that ackt off until nex day — when we went fishin', an nobody wood be a-lookin' on.

Fishin' On 41 Cents A Day

I jist want to give the Haywood fishermen a hint of my new fishin' formulay. Caze, when I git it reddy to copyrite, hit's shore to be the cheapest fishin' plan ever put before the publick — 41 cents a day.

Hit calls for only 23 cents for lunch an 18 cents for bate. I'll also gyarantee that no fisherman will haff to pick enny berries to splice out on hiz lunch — or be a-runnin' up and down the creek bank a-beggin' bate.

O'course, I kaint di-vulge too mutch of this plan rite now. Howsumever, I'll say that it takes little ground-space on which to spred this 23-cent lunch. An furthermore, thar won't be enny hungry fishermen (or wimmen) standin' aroun', thinkin' they're goin' to git a hand-out.

Fourtee-Foot Fish

No, this is no fisherman's yarn — no 100% stretch. This fish what I saw here, few days ago, had washt ashore on Melbourne beach. An it was shore a whopper — 14 feet long an 600 lbs., a fair estymate. Some sed it was of the whale fam'ly. (Four or five whales were found dead on the shore here a few years ago, you remember).

Well, this is a-nuff Floridy fishin' yarns, I'm shore. Caze hit will soon be spring up thar in ol' Haywood — an I'll be back I hope, to jine Mayor Davis, Vaudny Massey, Seay, Nick Medford, Bill Bradley, an a thousan' other fishermen.

Yores Trooly,
Uncle Abe

UNCLE ABE REFUSES TO PULL OFF 'HIZ PANTS'

Mr. Editor,

I come down here to 'scape the cold — an' was railly injoyin' the fine weather here — then here comes a cold spell an' knockt it up for a week. I wore my overcoat a time or two, also my hat; but I _ could see folks sorter makin' fun of it, so I pulled it off. Then when I could still see a few sly smiles, I thawt, *hit must be my hat,* an' quit wearin' it also, my coat. But — dogone me! if some o' these bare-leg fellers didn't look at my pants as if to say, why don't you pull 'em off?

Now, I'm tellin' you, Mr. Editor, I'm not a-goin' to take my pants off — no, siree! These here ganglin', knot-kneed men can go half neckid if they want to — not me. 'Course, we men folks can skuze the purty gals, seein' as how they want to show off a little; but I think some of the men look worser than a ol' ape would, traipsen along the street. They're not near as purty as the long-legged flamingos, caze tall as they are, they can stand on one leg an' plume thireselves with 'tother foot. I've never seed the neckid-leg men try that.

Well, I jist missed seein' a missel go up for a few minets. When Uncle Abe got thar, the long spiral of smoke still trailed in the sky over the Atlantic. That thar big missel ('bout 70 ft. long) travels faster than all git-out!

Pourin' In — An' Pourin' Out

Folks are pourin' in here — also quite a few are pourin' out. Jist a gineral down-roar, up-roar — grind, clash an' clank, whiz an' whir — rush an' roar, boom an' bust! The fust night or two I didn't git much sleep — thought I'de haf to change my sleepin' place. But a'ter studyin' over it, I wonderd where I'd go to — onless I took to the swamps, an' I was afraid of the snakes an' 'gators there.

My old armydilo kep me awake two or three nites — he come rite under the floor and went to rootin' about, snortin' an' blowin' hiz noze. I jumpt up an' down on the floor rite over him — but he'd jist start in again soon as I quit stompin' an' hollerin'.

Hain't Sunshine All The Time

So, folks, hit ain't fair skies, flowers, fruits, good fishin' and sunshine all the time — no, siree! Floridy has some downs — well as ups. The vegetable crop was hurt bad in the low-south part of the state durin' January cold spell. But there is a good crop of citrus in the state — an' it's not hurt.

I got in a few days fishin'; but got sorter discouraged durin' the cold spell an' give it up. Now I'm jist 'bidin' my time, for a few days longer — when I hope to be back with Y'all.

—Uncle Abe

"OL' HAYWOOD BEST A'TER ALL"

Hello! Haywood fokes:

I'm a-comin' in — near the fust of April. I've bin here in Floridy a leetle over three months — long anuff for enny nacheral, dide-in-the-wool Tarheel to be away from his Caroliner hills, yes Siree!

Course, I'm glad I 'scaped all that cold wether; but with all our cold, hit's purty hard to beat Ol' Haywood.

The Broke Wing

T'other day a crowd of us was fishin' on Big Indian River. "Looky yander," sed a lady, — "at that pore ol' pellycan." We lookt, an' thar it was driftin' along in the water — with a broke wing draggin' behind. But that big ol' bird lookt bold an' sassy like, as if to say "you kain't lick me! !"

"A strange bird is the pellycan —
His beak holds more than his bellycan."

But ennyway, it was a pittyful site. An' then I thawt about how fokes are flockin' into Floridy — the old an' young, rich an' pore, even the sick an' crippled. They come here, some o' them, with stars in their eyes — a lokin' for pleazure, for health, an' wealth.

But some of them are in a pittyful plight — like the ol' pellycan. They are driftin' with a broke wing, so to speak — driftin' with the tide, on out to sea.

But that's too sad — I hear a mockin' bird a-singin' this mornin'. The mockin' bird is Floridy's state bird. The rattlers are also out. With the spring grass that's growin', the flowers are in bloom an' the froot's beginnin' to grow.

Hit's also rite now a good time for fishin' — but I'm a-leavin' it all. Caze I've had some purty good fishin'; I've also visited about, played aroun', rested, et an' slept.

"— I Eats All But Cat"

Yisterday I went fishin'; the big ol' porpisses went fishin', too. They fisht out in the deeper water, 'bout 75 feet from whir Uncle Abe sot, wallerin' an' snortin' to beet the band. They sorter skeer a feller sometimes, when thy flop to th surface sudden-like.

I don't do enny sport fishin' or deep-sea fishin' — jist the ol' fashon kind, with a pole — from the cauzeways, peers an' bank. I ketch different kinds — blues, blowfish, cat, crab, mullet, brim, sheephead, sailor's choice, trout, yaller tails, an' whiting. Most o' theze are rale good, others are purty punk.

The Negroes here eat about all kinds — "cept salt water cat," as one told me last week. I had some yaller tails. 'Do you want theze here yallers?", I axt him. "Yes, sir boss. I likes 'em," he anserd.

Then a little later on I kotcht a crab. 'Do you want this thing?" I sed.

"Yes," he replide. "I eats all kinds, 'cept this salt water cat — they jist hain't no 'count."

135

I don't rightly know how to de-scribe a blowfish — onless I say hit looks like a cross between a fish an' a frog. But thars no frog what can blow hizself up like the blowfish can, no, siree! Yisterday I got a stingeree. They are very dangerus to git off the hook, onless you fust kill 'em.

Well, I gess, Mr. Editer, you can see by this letter that my hart's now turned back to 'Ol' Haywood' an' the fokes up thar — yes, siree. An' I must go!

Yores trooly,
Uncle Abe

THE BALSAM PROFFET

Now here kums my ol' friend W. H. Jones of Balsam.

An' by the way, Henderson is now a wether proffet. Ye kno what that is. He sez he hit this winter pine blank, an' haz hit uthers endurin' past few yeers.

Bro. Jones can also rest on hiz larls as a former Alderman uv Waynesville, The purty . . . when it wuzent as purty as it is today. It wuz him I think what helpt to git the furst fountins installed, one at the coart hous an' one in Frog Level . . . an' Waynesville haz bin wet ever sense.

Howsumever, Bro. Jones takes gratest pride in bein' the wether proffet uv Balsam . . . lives up thar above ever boddy elce, ye see, whar he can reed the elements, watch the groun' hawgs, the wether burds, the bark uv trees an' all the uther shore sines . . . then jist make up hiz Allmanick months a-hed.

Shucks, we cood do without waterin' places an' sitch like but we coodn't do without our wether proffets . . . so few uv 'em enny way ye kno.

Jist one favor we'll ax Bro. Jones . . . aiter this when he sees one o' them awful Scott's Cr. fluds a-comin' this way we want him to broad kast in time fer our Frog Level an' Cripple Creek sitizens t' git on higher groun'.

"Wish ye'de tell our legislaturs an' state offishals how to ballence the budgit, Unkle Abe", sed Verlin Camel, "that's sump'm they orter kno."

"Now, sense you've named Cripple Creek, Unkle Abe", sed Frank Davis, "we want ye to see about gitten em a better road bilt down that bank back of yore offis, so's they kin git down".

No, Frank, its not the gitten down part that's so hard, it's on comin' back out . . . that's when they need han' rails — fer 2 reezuns.

"Be Shore Yore Sins" — *An' So Foarth*

"Be shore yore sins will find ye out", the Scriptures say . . . an' so quoted Monte Stamey one day last wk. when he took a no-shun to preech to a krowd of us.

"Amen — an' gloary be!" sez I, "which meens that jist as shore as ye drap yore sick kittens off at sumboddy elce's doar, jist so shore will sicker ones be lef' at yore doar."

Then I took the flore an' tole 'em how I de-sided to git rid of a sick kitten one day las' summer in the yoozyal way. Well, I thawt I'de got by with my trick, an' so had fergot all about hit ontil one day a little while back . . . when, on gitten up one mornin' I found 2 sick kittens at my frunt doar, also 1 sick pup.

"Why did ye say that a feller will git back sicker kittens than he takes off?" axt sum one.

"Cauze that's what the Apossel ment when he sed, 'Sow to the wind an' reep the whurlwind'."

Well, fokes, sum uv you, Noah Harrison, f' instance, have thawt Unkle Abe wuz a little too hard on the Townsend Plan; but I think you'll find when the thing blows over that I'm about rite.

Gess sum uv you have alreddy h-yeard about Kongress goin' to investygate the hole Townsend skeem . . . goin' to try to find out whar all them thar nickels an' dimes have gone to that hav' been pade in by over 2 millyun peeple.

Well, it's all verry strange — Look at the papers:

Judge fines a Joory 10 bucks apeece fer tossin' a coin in order to de-side on the verdickt . . . woman shoots herself 'cauze she thawt the komicks wuz a-makin fun uv her . . . moovy stars, prize fighters an' baseball players a-makin moar munny than the president of the U. S. . . . Lag o' Nashuns (that's what I call it) still in sesshun —— an' a-gitten nowhir . . . an' last but not leest, Nelson Galloway's grasshopper — which giv up the goast last Tewsday at 9:45 E.S. Time.

Yes-sir-ee — heep big snow! Who sed we don't hav the "Ol' Fashun" winters enny moar? We've had about 2 uv 'em this winter.

But aiter all the snow wuzn't hardly as deep as reported — Unkle Rube Coman sez that who ever reported it to be 30 inches in Canton must a-mezured the driffs.

The Cawze Uv-It All

Don't gess we'de a had the last bad spell if Unkle Abe hadn't a-sent out hiz last "Sines O' Spring" Predickshun . . . a lot o' peeple have bin a-axin me lately why I up an' dun it. Well, all I kin say is that I've never node them sines to fale before.

But that ain't it, Mr. Editur . . . the rale cawze of all this last disturbence in the elements wuz the fackt that me an' Ikey, Wayne Rogers, Chan Burress an' Sam Bradley fent fishun the day befoar an kotch so many suckers — spechly Ikey, — that we left too mutch vackyum in the waters uv the Lake — all uv a suddent, ye see, an' got the disturbence startid.

Unkle Abe Gits Loaded Up

It happened like this:

I wuz up on Kamp Branch an' Allen's Cr. a-lookin' aiter the intrusts uv the Mount'neer — an' I'm a Sun of a Gun if neerly ever man I went to didn't want t' pay hiz subscription in korn meel an' 'taters! Well, ye kno, a man can only yooze jist so mutch korn meel an' 'taters,

137

speshly when he's alreddy got pell-agry. So aiter a while I got mad an' swore I woodn't take enny moar spuds nor korn meel neether.

So, at the nex place I tole the man that I thawt the Editur's shoes wuz a-gitten' a little bad, an' that my britches wuz alreddy wore into a hole at the seet . . . an' we 'lowed as how he mout help us out 'bout 1 buck —

"Not got eny munny", sed he, "but I can let ye hav' sum 'taters —"

"Taters, hell no!" sez I. "an pleeze doant menshun korn meel — I've alreddy got my ol' Ford full o' both.

Why, man, I've got so mutch korn meel. I'm liabul now to be 'rested on suspishun."

Then he changed hiz t'backer to the other side —

"Lem-me see," sed he, "may-be the ol' woman's got a doller."

Well, I node rite then that a doller wood purty soon chang hans . . . an' it did. I tell ye, Mr. Editur, "the ol' woman is offen our best bet.

"Unkle Abe's a little hard fer me t' reed," sed Dock Bigham, "but I allus stick to it till I git it all red".

"Ortn't to be hard for Dock", replide sumone — "that's the way he tawks."

"Goin' to re-sindy kate it?" axt E. K. Herman. "Yes, E. K., an' how about gitten you fer my Bookkeeper an' Privet Sickatary?"

HERE'S TO THE GAL OF TODAY

Ol' preechurs shout thar aint no hope,
    That our modurn gals air gone —
Gone to the dawgs, er sumwhir elce,
    Since modurn ways air on.
With pettin' partys, paints an' sitch.
    The dance, strong drink an' shows,
They swair she's "on the road t' ruin —
    Whir it ends noboddy noaz".
Sum parints seem to think the same,
    But "pleed an' hope an' pray" —
That sumhow Sis will weaken not
    When kums that evil day.

But —
    Here's to the gal of post-war days,
    An' the gal of the gran' New Deel;
    I giv this toast to her sterlin' worth —
    An' to tell her jist how I feel:
    You're az good a-stuff az yore parints wuz —
    Maybe stronger an' moar wize;
    An' you'll sail rite throo with colurs up —
    You're o.k. in yore Unkles ize!

Re-leef Selebrates

Well, the lokal Re-leef got pade off last Thurs. an' we heer the boys hugged eech others necks an' selebrated the blessed Event that aiter noon an' nite.

The Mayor's Coart had a kongested dockit on Fri. folerin', the majority of the dee-fendants bein' on the federal pay-role, it wuz reported.

One dee-fendant lackt 4 bucks havin' all the costs, but sed he'd make it up out uv hiz nex check.

If this wuzn't a free kuntry we mout set up anuther Alfybet fund, say W. A. T. R. A. (Watch All The Rest Administrashun) to find out how they spen' their munny.

Times is a-gitten good don'che see, under this hyear Rozyvelt minnustrashun. Sum o' theze ol' fellers have alreddy started to soin' their wile oats agin. It won't do, fokes, it won't do!

The Plezzur Of Makin' Up

I no a cupple that quarl an' fite all the time — more than Unkle Abe duz. They throw stove wood, cheers an' flat arms at eech other . . . even run eech other roun' the hous with boocher nives.. On rainy daze they put in full time.

One day when Unkle Abe wuz passin' by Miz Batcher wuz a-runnin' John round the hous with a boocher nife. John cood outrun 'Eafy', so in about one round he'de be rite behine hiz wife —

"Eafy, Eafy," he'd shout, "I'm a-tellin ye t' lay that boocher nife down — caze the law sez it's a dedly weep'n."

But Eafy woodn't lissen — she wood jist turn on John — an' start him 'tother way round the hous. Finely Eafy got so tard she codn't run — "Now, looky here, Eafy", sed he eezin' up, "le's tawk a spell. We can settle our bizness 'thout bringin' a boocher nife into it."

So, 'tother day I met 'em aiter they'd razed the flag o' trooce an' made up agin . . . walkin' arm in arm. But what made the hole thing so hot, the woman wuz a-singin', "Best times I've ever had have been with you."

I didn't no fer shore whitch "times" she had refference to, the boocher nife days or the make-up minits.

AN' THE POSSUM'S GITTEN FAT

"When the frost is on the punkin,"
    An' the possum's gitten fat
An' the grapes out in the medder —
    Then we no 'bout whir we're at.
It's gitten 'long up in October
    Chillin' shades an' all o' that,
"When the frost is on the punkin'"
    An' the possum's gitten fat.
No uther time is like October —
    Oh, how I like its' bracin' air!

Makes me feel jist like a millyun —
　　'Tis then I never take a dare.
An' oh, sitch goodies in Ma's kitchen!
　　'Round 'bout whir the cupboard's at,
"When the frost is on the punkin'"
　　An' the possum's gitten fat.
Then's the time the squirls git sassy,
　　Bark so brave upon the lim';
Gess he, too, likes this fine wether,
　　An' what the harves' meens to him.
With skool an' play — an' a little study,
　　Chesnit hunts an' things like that —
Well, that's why I like October,
　　When the possum's gitten fat.

Well, fokes, requests hav bin a-pilin' up on Unkle Abe endurin' the past 2 wks. France Millner wantz me to "rime off" hiz one-legged hen — will try to reech you nex' week, France.

Also, Charley McCracken an' Chas. McCrary hav bin axin Unkle Abe to say sump'm about that man on Fines Creek — thay call him Dal, who woar so menny clothes one winter.

Well, boys, I kaint git to all theee requests in 1 week. Besides, ye must remember that Unkle Abe is not a poleece, town council, traffik cop, street sprinklur, and publick promoter — mutch as I'de like t' be all 5 of theezze. But Ile try to kommodate them Fines Cr. fellers — so hyear goze, boys:

Thar wuz a man on Fines Creek
　　One summer shed his cloze —
He coodn't stan' the heet, ye see,
　　So, he pulled off to hiz toes.
An' then, as winter-time drawd nigh,
　　He coodn't stan' the frost;
So he startid wearin' overalls,
　　Moar soots than he had lost.
Still this-hyear man on Fines Creek
　　Cood not keep out the kold;
So, he goze rite down to Norman Jeems
　　Whir pants an shurts wuz sold.
An' sez, "Giv me 4 moar of overalls,
　　An' shurts about the same —
I'm a-goin' t' keep the kold wind out,
　　As shore as Dall's my name.
An' never changd, the winter long,
　　An' slep' in all them cloze;
How hot he got, how bad he stunk —
　　Well, the pole cat only noze.
An' did he shed hiz cloze nex' spring?
　　Yes, the spot may still be found;

140

All that wuz found uv what he wore
        He left upon the ground.
Thay found 12 straps uv overalls
        An' 6 neck bands, thay sed,
With buckles an' buttons still intackt —
        That's all he had to shed.

Mr. Editur, I must giv one uther observashun uv the Fair that I omitted las' week:

Thar wuz one ol' man frum Rush Fork a-watchin' the Dizy Dangle. Well, when the swing startid up that ol' man commenct to open hiz mouth sorter slow, an' as the swing got faster an' faster, the ol' feller opend hiz mouth wider an' wider ontil it lookt like he had reecht the limit. Then as the swing startid slowin' down hiz mouth commenct to cloze agin.

"Well, mister, you'll not ketch me on that thar thing", . . . an' he walkt away.

CORNFIELD PHILOSOPHY

Tolerance, Where Art Thou?

"Going to church are you?" A lady public school teacher asked a little girl.

The girl said she was.

"What church do you attend?"

"The ——————— church", replied the girl, "where do you go?"

"Me? Oh, I attend the ——————— church, that's all the church there is," the lady teacher said in reply.

Now if this had taken place seventy-five or a hundred years ago it, at least, would not have seemed so much out of place, improper and narrow. Because back then the Baptist and Methodist preachers often "dug in',, as it were, on their respective battlefields and snipped, cross fired and bayoneted each other front and rear . . . never giving quarter nor asking any. And, of course, the members, following the example of their leaders, did likewise.

But in this 20th century day of more advanced ideas, liberalism and tolerance of both thought and action — well, it was hardly to be expected, especially from a teacher.

Rank intolerance like that is dangerous running rampant in the community. Do you not think so?

The late Phillips Brooks said that we should be more afraid of the littleness than the largeness in life. Now it is not necessary to go into the littleness of all this contention and argument about certain church practices and beliefs. If you want to be a "whole-soled, four square, dyed-in-the-wool" Baptist, Methodist, Presbyterian, Mudhaead, Holy Roller or What-Not — why, you can be it without having to snub, insult or hurt the feelings of your neighbor's child. To be loyal is all that's required, or should be required, of anyone; loyalty does not imply hatred, jealously or bigotry.

And let us remember, also, that from childhood on through life there are many qualities, duties and responsibilities that we are called upon to exercise before that of loyalty to the doctrines of a certain church: Christianity, love, truth, obedience, honesty, neighborliness, good citienship, etc.

I so loathe, abhor and detest this thing of church intolerance. I have always let my children attend Sunday School and church where ever they wanted to attend; and furthermore have told them to join what ever church they desired to join — if different frome mine, okey.

MILLNER'S BANTY HEN

Now F. C. Millner's got a little hen
    With jist one lag, fer shore;
A banty hen with one lag gone —
    An' she stays rite in the dore,
With a cluck! here, an' a cluck! luck! thair,
In the yard, in the hous an' ever whair.
An' this little hen had little chicks,
    Four chicks, or hit may be five;
An' bein' banty chicks, ye see,
    Thay air every mutch alive.
So it's cluck! cluck! here, an' peep! peep! thair,
    In the hous, in the yard an' ever whair.
"Shoo out o'hyear!" sez Francis' fokes
    "Less ring this ol' hen's neck."
"No, sir," sez France, "she's my pet hen,
    An' mine to keep, by heck!"
With a peep! peep! here, an' a cluck! cluck! thair,
    In the corner, in the dore, an' on the stair.

Up on Bald Cr. I found a man a-doctorin' a ol' white mule. "Too mutch frost-bit corn," the man replide in ansur to my queschun.

"It will be too bad ef he dyes," sez I, "oanly 30 yeers old, you not dun yore fall plowin' an' so foarth."

"Yes, I'de be sorry fer the mule, — an' me, too," the man sed. Aifter passin' on, I wundered at the man's remark, 'bout goin' to be sorry fer hiz self too. I calkylated that ef the mule dide, the man wuz a-goin' to foller soot.

It's wunderful, Mr. Editur, what attachment theze mountain men offen hav fer a houn' dawg, hoss flash — an' the wimmen, Yes, sir-ee!

On the gris' mill at upper Crabtree is the follerin' sine:

"GRITS AN' GRAVY—COME IN"

Now, thars nuthin' I cood add to this, fokes, nur take away . . . it's about komplete.

JIST LIKE A MAN

When I went to Bob Jeems hous the childurn wuz a-shuckin' corn —

"Whir's Bob?" I axt.

142

"Hed o' Bald Creek," one uv the boys replide," sed he'd be back in a few minits."

"Well, when he sez that, how long is he yoozly gone?" I axt.

"Sumtimes all day an' nite,' sed the boy.

Then I went on down to lower Crabtree an' found John Nolan' plowin' in rye. Ever boddy else over thir wuz a-komplanin' about the groun' bein' so dry an' hard that thay coodn't git eny grain sowed. Well, John had the advantage of em all . . . he had sandy river land an' a steer to plow with.

RE-LEEF MILK

It's sed that thars nuthin' new under the sun, but thar is — it's a speshul kind o' milk to ween the Re-leef fokes on. Doc Turpin wuz a-showin' it to me tuther day.

"Jist got it in," sed Dock, "it's speshul prepaird to taper theze hyear Re-leef fokes off on. Sorter like weenin' a kaff, ye no, mussent ween it all at wunst."

"How mutch do they allow 'em, Dock?" sez I. "Oh, I don't no," replide Dock, "depen's on the age an' so foarth, I reckin' Direckshuns is on the can."

Well, the papers say that pe-anners air comin' into stile; thaive bin out of stile in the sitty endurin' the past few yeers, ye no.

An' that reminds me, I acks'ly hyeard a parler organ down at Wes' Canton tother day. Ever time I hyear one o' them things my mem'ry goze back to S. S. picknicks, crowdid R. R. stashuns, pink ice cream, hall trees, 10¢ shaves, tite korsets — an' "In the Shade of the Old Apple Tree."

"How menny seegyars duz the Mount'neer start ye out with ever day?" axt sumboddy.

"Not a one," I replide, "thay don't even allow me to yooze the tackle rope enny more."

SEES IT THROO

Boice, come on! play ball, play ball fuh babies . . . Have a drink, have a lunch! . . . Yes, sir, they're hot — all hot . . . Rite this way, fokes, have yuh pickchus made . . . Here's whir yuh see the alligatur gurl — bahn rite hyear in you own state . . . Hey! hey! this way, see the monster alive! Ah-boo-boo! — Princess Mite, Princess Mite, fokes, an' her . . . only a dime — ten cents, a dime!

It's a-ringin' in my yeers yit, Mr. Editur . . . I woke up las' nite groanin' like the "monster alive", Buh-la Buh-la haz bin aiter me, an' oh, well I kaint tell it all; I think I'll haff to go back to the Big Bend in ordur to git a rest.

143

Well, fokes, if you've got all the dust out of yore eyes, we'll
sorter re-vew a few of the hi spots — an' sum that wuzn't so hi.
Wenzday noon the boss handed me a pass t' the grate Event (he'de
yoozed the best uvit) an' sed, he — "Unkle Abe, now hyears yore
pass, an' I want ye to see the hole wurks 'er bust . . . an' write it up
jist as it is — I'll stan' by ye throo thick an' thin!"

"Gloary be!" sez I.

Well, I went throo it all 'cept in 2 places, I lost mu nurv at the
Loop-O-Plane, an' by the time I got aroun' to the negro minstril, the
wether had turnd warm an' I node I coodn't stan' the odur. I had
finely bolstered up nurv 'nuff to try the Loop Wenzday nite, an' wuz
a-waitin' my turn when some ol'-made skool teechurs got in. Well,
thay got so skeerd that the noiz of their hollerin' drowned out all the
rest . . . An the opperator, he seem t git sorter oneezy like; gess he
thawt thay wuz goin to faint. They sed one uvem shore nuff did faint
— or the nex thing to it. So, Unkle Abe lost his nurv fer good then.
Thats too excitin' an' stimilatin fer ol'-made skool teechurs an' Unkle
Abe.

On good authority, 'bout 3000 wittnuses, we no that the sky wuz
plum clur an' kool that nite . . . an' they say that it shore rained out
of a clur sky — yes sir-ee!

"Orter hav sumbody to take keer uv a feller's munny while he
goze up", sed a sertin Haywood man.

"Never mine the munny", sez I, "jist look aiter the bat-wing."

You wuz all wittnuses to the fackt that the shows an' sitch like
at the Fair this yeer wuz prepaird to take keer uv the munny.

A good number of you will also bear me out in sayin' that when
a man is stood on 'iz hed in the Loop, its' hard to hole on an' keep
hiz bat wing in the inside pockit frum fallin' out. —

Bang-flap-bang! Tap-tap-bang! . . . . boys that bat wing shore
did make a racket — ontil it broke. That show wuz put on by a acktor
frum Jones Cove.

An' did the crowd laff! I thawt Hew Lutherwood wood take a fit.

"Rite this way, fokes! See Princess Mite, smallest muther in the
wurl' an' her 7 oz. . . Five cents, a nickul, boys, — it's only 5 cents.

An' look a-comin' yander! If it aint W. D. Smith an' Ed Russ
a-ridin' 2 big bulls. That wuz one uv the best free acks at the Fair,
follered kloce by Unkle Abe's ride on the Dizzy Dangle.

"Did ye not git skeerd, Unkle Abe?" axt Mrs. Crawford. "No",
sez I, "but when that thing got to its fastest I had a awful strang
sensashun abou the middle . . . Graceful rider, ain't I?"

"Ye shore air."

That nite Unkle Abe rode the Ferris wheel . . . hadn't bin up in
one in a long time.

An' bleeve me, I thawt that man never wuz goin'a let me off! Aiter I'd dun got the wurth of my munny, an' then sum, he kontinude to ride me. I think they acksly fergot 'bout me bein' on thair, an' thair wuz so mutch noiz I coodn't make 'em heer. That wuz Wenzday nite, an' as I hadn't yit changd under cloze, I neerly froaz to deth. I wisht a duzzen times I had sum o' them cloze the clown pulled off — then the thing startid to slow down. Never agin!

"Now sum of you fokes think I'm to be pitted', sed the allegatur woman to a crowd of us getherd around her, "but sum of you are reely worse off than I am."

"Ye kin look over this crowd an' see that," sez I.

"Now effen I jist had me a bat wing, I'd take this heh Fair in," sed an ol' Waynesville cullord woman as she made her way throo the gate. She went on up to the merry-go-round, follerd kloce to a good-sized crowd that wanted to see what she wood do. Ocnt on the merry-go-round, she soon shet her ize an' begun to laff.

"Jist as neer heb'm as she wants to be," sed sum one.

"Swing low, sweet charry-ot, comin' fuh t' carry me home" . . .

I'll now intedooce ye to the judges of Singin kontest: Wade Noland, Albert Walker and Uncle Gene Corzine. Nuff sed.

Well, Cline Bramlett shore stuck to hiz post like the soljer he is them cold nites. I axt Cline Wenzday nite if he didn't want me to go an' git him sum o' the cloze that the clown pulled off, but he 'lowed as how he thawt he cood make out.

But the funnyest thing wuz the way Depty Shurfs blossomed out at the fair . . . an' ever one had him a stick. Re-minded me uv the cattle sails, only the Depty's stick has a crook.

"Don't be arrestin' fokes by the holesale like this, boys", sez I, don't beet up the pore devils like that . . . this is the furst rale Fair we've had in a long time — let 'em injoy it."

"Alrite, jist as ye say, Unkle Abe," replide Bob Welch — then we all went back to look at the "crap game."

Nex yeer I want to be a Depty Shurf, Mr. Editur. But the order wuz good considerun' sitch a large crowd — an' that's no joak.

Now, look! Here's a crowd getherd aroun' the "Iron-jaw" gamlin' dee-vice. Vice, that is rite an' I'm not jokin' when I say that sitch a thing as that ort not to be 'lowed at our nex Fair. "Iron-jaw" is rite . . . cold, crooel, hartless . . . it never failed to rob the childrin and inexperienced if they stayed with it only a short while.

The dog an munkey show wuz good — most educashunal uv them all. The free trapeeze ackts wuz also good.

An' now fer the Follies, whitch Ed. Russ sed he wantid Unkle Abe to see — an' report on. Ye see, fokes, our Editur wuz jist a leetle

145

bit backerds 'bout goin' in in broad day lite an' he allus had hiz wife with him at nite. They woodn't let me in on the nite show — sed it wuz too hot fer ol' men an' childern, so I had to wate till the nex day.

Well, I felt like I had bin sold — fer 15 cents, on comin' out. I wanted to come out at the back uv the tent instid of the doar, but thawt I mout git shot by a Depty Shurf, so I braved the frunt.

To tell the trooth, that show wuz almos' flat . . . Wuzn't mutch dancin' to it, mos'ly suggestiv movements an' kontorshuns of the boddy — all 'cept the fan dancer; this an' a few cheep, flat jokes.

But, summin' it all up, this show orter also be kondemned along with that Iron-jaws thing. Shows like that have a tennency to tempt an' leed astray ole innersent men like Unkle Abe.

IN DE-FENCE OF THE PLUMMERS

This letter is in part of a de-fence of the plummers of Waynesville an' ever whir elce; caze they've bin joked about an' im-pozed upon too mutch. To begin with, Unkle Abe will say that he's done repented uv hiz cuss words 'bout the plummers las' winter an' haz got on the good side o' the ones he don't yit owe an' haint tride out — I dun that when I red the sines an' saw the kold spell a-startin' in.

So fer this winter I haint needed a plummer, 'cept fur a short time — the time wuz short becaze he fergot sum o' hiz tools an' haint cum back yit. In the meentime Mrs. Abe fixt the rezvoir with a stick uv stove wood. The plummer foned from sum whir in town an' sed that if the stick, what my wife fixt the thing with, wuz still workin' alrite to jist let it stay — sed he gessed it wuz as good a job he cood do ennyway. Now don't tell me they's no onnest plummers!

Furthermore, plummers air a sympathetick, konsiderate lot of gize. When ever boddy's pipes freez up at the same time, we kaint blam the wethur man fer treatin' us all alike. Then we kaint blame the plummers fer treatin' us all alike, by leavin' the jobs unfinisht till they git aroun' one time; nur fer leavin' a tool at eech place to go back aiter when thay start on their 2nd round. Ef we'de bin without work a long time we mout strech the Golden Rool to the breakin' pint too.

Besides, plummers haff to work in the meenest kine o' wethur (I woodn't a-worked a tall this las spell). Thay also haff to take a lot o' gab. If sum ol' dame or man in pajammers, robe an' a seegarette — in hiz mouth I meen not in hiz pajammers — I say, if sitch a ol' dame or guy as this wuz to begin lordin' it over you, with the thee-momater standin' at 2 above, an' us with our hans an' feet in the mud, water an' ice . . . well, we mout kommit murder. Yes, sir-ee, I tell ye they air a pa-shent lot!

Hyears about the way sum fokes tawk to the plummers:
"No, the cut-off aint there — man kaint ye remember nuthin'? Didn't ye put that cut-off in las winter?" sez ol' man Doe.

146

"Weren't me," replize the plummer, "mout a bin my unkle er brother, brother-in-law er neffew — thars 12 uv us at the shop."

"Well, he sertin'ly looks like you," sez Mrs. Doe, her hed a-stickin' out at the kitchun door. "He wuz a short, thick man in ovurall soot an' about 2 weeks of whiskers on hiz face."

"Well, we all ware ovurall soots — haff to," replize the plummer, "an' ef you had to work in the kold slush like we do, gess you'de ware yore whiskers 2 wks. —"

"Now, non o' yore sassy tawk, young man . . . daddy air ye a-goin' to let a plummer tawk to me like that? Besides, he's jist a-killin' time."

"Ah, hush up, Marthy, maybe the man's a-doin' the best he kin."

"What do ye meen — who d'ye think wood move it? Line's rite whir it's allus bin . . . think the cut-off wood be sum whirs elce, a-settin off to hits self? I no more 'bout plummin' than that", sez Mr. Doe.

"Well, ye mout a got up in yore sleep at nite an' mooved it . . . or maybe the hous haz bin mooved —"

"Now, looky hyear young man, I didn't call ye over hyear to make brite remarks . . . I called ye to fix my pipes; now, ef ye kaint fix 'em jist say so an' I'll git sumboddy what kin."

Now this shows what grate provokashun plummers haff to ondure, Mr. Editur. I gess most of us wood pick up our Stillson rench — I meen send fer it — an' throw it throo the ol' dame an' ol' guy, pajammers, seegarette an' all. And I think John Queen wood ackcept a plee o' manslawter an' reckommen' mercy.

KOLD WETHUR, THIS

Layin' all jokes aside, fokes, this haz bin the wust kold spell Unkle Abe haz wittnessed since 1917-1918. It's bin so cold part of my hens. (I meen Mrs. Abe's hens) have jist sot up on the roost all the time nite an' day — all 'cept the ones what froaz to deth an' fell out.

"Lissen, what's that a-goin' — thump! ever onst in awhile?" sed Mrs. Abe to me 'bout 5:00 o'clock on the mornin' uv Dec. 31st.

"Aw, taint nuthin' but the froaz hens a-droppin' off the roost," sez I, "go on back to sleep."

Now the hens what cum off the roost faird somewhat better, still they had to set down an' skeet about on the ice to git the feed that wuz throwed out.

Unkle Abe had to skeet sum to in ordur to git to the cow barn — but not egzackly like the hens did. But, in gitten' back frum the cow barn it wuz up hill, so I had to git down an' krawl on all 4's most ginerally.

KORNFIELD FILOSOPHY

"Peeple air a hole lot like sheep," sed Lee Noland tuther day. "Thars allus a few leedurs in ever kommunity, an' when the leedurs start the rest follers."

147

"Good thing the floo don't strike all the famly at the same time," sez the Town Wag. "As it is, thars yoozly a-nuff well ones to wate on the sick ones till all famly gits throo with it."

Now that times air gitten' better, menny fokes hav startid loosin' their heds agin. No doubt a lot o' them wood like to re-kall sum of that mis-spent Christmas munny alreddy.

FOOL DRIVERS

Waynesville (not so purty rite now aiter the freez) Jinuary 13th.

Well, fokes, yore Unkle Aberham is still alive an' gallopin' about . . . gloary be!

But I mussent fergit that I ment to rite about fool drivers — whitch the Mount'neers is printin' a peece about nex wk. I hope you will reed it.

Now, did ye ever think about it, we hav checkt or kontrolled ever bad dizeese, ever crime, ever rackit . . . in short ever grate danger, even war itself better than we hav the rekluss, criminal drivin' uv automobils. We air allowd to shute a mad dawg — now ain't it too bad w're not allowd to shute the fool driver? We air also keerful to keep a smallpox pashunt konfined an' the publick away frum him, yit the law won't let us konfine the fool driver an' tag 'im as bein' dangerous to society.

Ever man an' woman that is konvickted of drivin' on the rong side, keerless or drunk or at too fast rate of speed, cuttin' in an' out, whippin' aroun' when the ways not clur, falin' to give a signal, etc, an' who thereby cawzed an acksident orter not only be denide the rite to drive a car but orter be sent to jale. Then whin he's out o' jale he orter haff to ware 2 sines strapt to hiz neck like this:

I SURVED 6 MONTHS IN JALE FER DRIVIN ON THE RONG SIDE.

Or whatever the sentence an of-fence mout a bin.

Unkle Abe is so afeerd hyear lately of bein' killd that he tops hills at only 10 miles per, an' allus cums to a full stop, befoar he rouns a sharp curv . . . if the fool drivers seem to be out that day I git out an' git me sum rocks (ye see I doant carry a gun) then go aroun' the turn to see ef the way is clur uv fool drivers an' drunk drivers. (Now the only differents I can see 'tween the plane fool driver an' the drunk drivers is that the drunk one is 2 fool drivers in 1.)

I also toot my horn ever ten steps as I roun' jist ordinary curvs — an' pray as I toot.

So, now ye see if ever boddy wuz as keerful as Unkle Abe thar woodn't be enny collizuns, runnin' off banks, an' so foarth — no, sir-ee.

NOAH'S FROG

Well I reckon Noah Harrison's the latest to go into the freek bizness. No, it's not a 3 lag chickun nor a horn tode, nor a dubble barrell calf — not even a pettrifide snake, but a yaller frog with all its feet growde together — yes, sir-ee! An' that's not all . . . that frog wuz berried 9 ft. back an' down (boath ways ye see) in a solid clay bank. Still not all — reed on, bruther: That frog seemin'ly had no air, no water, no food, no lite, "no nuthin," as the Arshman sed. Now that frog wuz sum hermit weren't he?

"Well, wood it moove about mutch," I axt.

"Moove? Now I'm tellin' you," sed Noah. "Why, that wuz the moovin'est frog I ever seed.

Kornfield Filosophy

Well, fokes, I see by the papers that Wm. H. Lord, the sleepin' man of Springfield, Mass., haz intered on hiz 10th yeer of kontinued snoozin'.

I bet he'll hav plenty of dreems to tell ef he ever wakes up.

"How's yore car-eckter, Bob," sed sum one to Bob Burnett tother day.

"Good accordia' to my way uv lookin' at it," sed Bob; "but I don't no whuther it wod stan' the coart test er not, seein' that the coart test is what a man's naybors say."

I notis that the Ethiopeens hav grate hopes of the raney seezun (whitch begins thar in eerly summer) of helpin' them out vs. the Italyuns. Seems as tho it wood be better to look at the good Lord now ruther than to the Leeg of Nashuns.

Feb'y turm of coart will soon be hyear — the time when the Haywood politikal pot allus begins to bile, an' whin sumeone yoozly thows hiz hat in the ring.

It's A Strange Ol' Wurld

Unkle Abe haz bin a-reedin' rite smart here lately, tryin' to make out the hed an' tale o' sump'm: but Ile be dog-gone ef I kin do it . . . the more I red an' studdid the more I got konfuzed. Sumtimes I think we wood be better off if we didn't no enny thing an' didn't hav enny thing — jist sot back like we wuz in the ruff stone age, ye no. Then it wood be grate fun to slowly evoloot up, up throo the long senturies agin to the New Deel, Il Duce, an' hiz Ethiopeen War, the wunderful Leege, Bruno, Dr. Townsend an' hiz 200 bucks an' Mae West — grate Scotts! (But thatz only when I hav the blooz — St. Louis, Bloo Ridge Mt. — er sump'm.)

HALLOWE'EN IN WAYNESVILLE

How air ye all an' how did ve injov Witch Nite? It went off all rite hyear in Waynesville . . . Unkle Abe an' the rest uv the yung

fokes had a fine time. I mozied over to town aiter supper jist to smoke my seegyar an' sorter see the sites ye no, whin all onct I felt the ol' time sperit cum over me . . . an' I had to jine in — yes, sir-ee.
An' gloary be!

The childern shouted, "Hello, Unkle Abe!" on ever hand an' I hollered back at em. (But ye no, fokes, Unkle Abe is not ½ as old as he looks ter be . . . ef he wuz he'de a bin ded 100 yeers ago.) One good lookin' gurl wuz a-goin' to hug my neck, but she changd her mind on 2nd look —
"Hello, Unkle Abe, I no ye; but I bet ye caint gess me", sed she.

An' uv all the spooky costoomes —
  well they wuz a site!
Hyear cums one all dresst in rags,
An' thar's anuther out in bags —
With a Hooray — howdy do!
Sum in bloomers, jammers, sheets;
Shurts, haf-pantz — all on the streets —
Makin' whoopee — hoo-ray, hoo!
Gurls dresst in pantz, an boys in gowns
My, hoo haz ever seen sitch clowns!
Sitch a Hooray — howdy do!
Ol' cotes an' caps an' masks galore —
I've nevur seen sitch like before,
Sitch a Hallowe'en big-to-do!

I notis by the papers an' the ol' made speekin' at a Yooth Kongress on "The Konversashun of Yooth." Well, uv all the irony this is the limit. Good thing, Mr. Editur, that the yung womanhood of Americky looks at yooth konvenshuns diffurnt frum what theze ol mades do, elce we woodn't hav enny yooth to konserve purty soon.

Coartin' Then An' Now

Well, fokes, I've bin a-thinkin' about theze yungsters in a gineral way o' late an' in particklar about the advantages thay hav over what we ol' fokes yoost t' hav. Fer eg. (that stans fer egzample) jist look how mutch moar konvenyent it is to coart now then it yooce to be.

Thar wuz ginerly a buggy in the bettur-to-do familys; but John who wuz a-coartin' Sal akross the mountin' an who Sal Eckspected to see about ever Sunday, did not allus show up. John wood haf sumtimes let it be nown that he wood be bac the nex Sunday pervided he cood git the yooce of "Ol' Kit" an' the buggy or Henry, the saddle hoss.

Then a gurl didn't hav mutch chanc o' gitten out on Sundays at all onless her "beau called t' take her to meetin' er out fer a buggy ride. Offen times gurls, lef to their selves on Sundays wood pre-tend to be visitin' eech uther when, in fackt, thay wood be on the look-out fer the boys. On meetin' up the boys an' gurls wood ginerly match off, then set off on the rode side an' coart.

150

No cars to drive out an' coart in? No, sir-ee! No moovies? Yes, sumtimes, but we coodn't reech em from the kuntry. A boy on goin' to see hiz gurl on Sundy most ginerly coarted her in the "parlur," but sumtimes in a bed room or in the kitchen. Sumtimes we had a ol' fashun wall-back sofy, ginerly set on strate — bach cheers, an' at a saf distance frum eech other, espechly if Dad an' Mam wuz in the jinin' room. When we thawt the ol' fokes wuz saf in bed we venchurd closer togither, held han's an whiperd "sof' nuthin's" purty mutch as they do today.

Now jist look at the differuns today! We've got cars — an even reg'ler coartin' masheens, like that catapiller kontrapshun at the Fair f'rinstance. Did ye notis how well it wuz arraigned fer coartin' in? Ever time when the masheen got up purty good speed an' the kuppels had to git closer together an' reddy to hug an' kiss . . . rite then the hood uv the thing wuz throwd over them an — well o' coars the noiz uv the thing drowndid out the smacks.

Well, did ye hyear about Grover Davis a-gitten foundered on apples? I hyeard it wuz a fackt. Seems that he went down to sum uv hiz kinsfolks tuther day an' they give him nuff apples to a-lasted moast lawyers a wk.; but Grover startid in an' had et about ½ of 'em when hiz fokes begun to git oneezy. But to their meny remonstray-shuns hiz only reply wuz —

"But jist think of the cheepness on 'em, Samanthy."

Grover, it's grate fer us town fellers to visit home fokes in the cuntry a-kasion'ly, but we orter allus be keerful t' not git foundered . . . thay doan't meen fer us to eat all thay set befoar us.

Little Ol' New York, Yes Siree!

Well, I don't think Waynesville can be beat fer big crowds on Sat. aiternoons an' nites . . . if ye don't bleeve me jist go over an' stand on that block whar the Thee-ater, Stovall's an' Sam Jones' place of bizness air.

Less take a little look at last Sat. nite: Here comes sum 3 C's boys a-makin' fer the beer stands, alreddy crowded. Did ye ever notis the difference in the way men drink their beer? One Waynesville man 'bout 65 gulps hizzen down at a-bout 2 swallers an' rushes out; but most all young fellers "tarry over their wine" to talk an' laff awhile . . . Now here comes three gurls — its' the 12th times they've gone by in 20 minets. They pass on to whir the brite lites give out, then turn an' parade by agin . . . now a lank country man passes by, pawzes an' looks around as if to say:

"Well, what's all this noize an' komoshun about enyway?"

An' now the ol' Barn Dance program from Nashville bursts out afresh — the musick never stops on Sat. nite . . . Too-toot! "Curb service out here," sumboddy shouts.

Oh, look there! A boy with an Indian made a-swingin' to eech arm. Jist opposit me they meet 2 boys, the boys turn an' shout back, "Heep fine white man, me tink-ee," an' the crowd roars . . . Now, here

151

comes a prim little woman — she scarcely looks to her rite or left, 'cept in a scornful sort o' way, as if to say —

"Look what a crowd; an' look at all this filth an' dirt — shoo! I woodn't stop here."

Lissen, what's that? Oh, the show's let out — here they come! What a clatter of feet! Sum make their way to cars, then one aiter anuther pulls out leavin' the air filled with burnt carbon . . . here's a country truck fillin' up, whole family an' their naybors a-gittin' into an open truck bed — ugh! how cold the children look! (Oh its' the Human Side out to-nite. Late shoppers worm their way throo the thee-ater crowds . . . the crowd thins out, 'cept at the beer an' fruit stanns whir they still carry on — whoopee!

Unkle Abe An Miss Rain-In-The-Face

Well, I've got an idee, fokes It's gitten' fashunable to hav Indian mades hyear in Waynesville; so seein' as how Unkle Abe is a stickler fer fashun, I reckon I'le haf to git me one.

Then, yoo see, when I git my Indian made, an she gits sorter tamed down an yoost to the place, mabey I kin indooce her to go over an parade with me on Mane Street Sat. nites. I'le let ye all no, so all who want to see the purformance can be on han'. Of korce, ef I kin git 2, one on eech arm it will be better.

Saw Big Bill an a white man arm in arm over neer the "squar" las wk. They wuz a-comin down toarg the waterin' place when the white feller stopt, took out hiz tin o' snuff, th'owd hiz hed back an let hiz lower lip have it . . . then fer awhile neether one cood tawk so's to be understood.

"When is it rong fer a man to take a glass of wine?" axt Father Lane in one uv hiz coart hous talks last week.

"Why — when a man gits so full he kaint walk. I reckon," replide a hezitatin' voice frum the reer.

Just To Point A Moral

When I wuz a boy 'long in my teens,
 Growin' up down on the farm,
I wore wool britches made o' jeans,
 An they usually kept me warm.
But sometimes on a real cold nite
 When Bill an' I'de "turn in",
We'd have to "scrunch' up close an tite —
 'Cause the cover was so "thin'.
But we knew to "spoon" each other when
 'Twas cold nights on the farm —
I'd lie close up to brother's back then ,
 And so, would keep him warm.
And then before we'd gone to sleep,
 If my back was sort of chilly,

152

"Let's turn," I'd say, "your word to keep" —
   Then we turned, me an' Billy.
Old simple lessons learned back then,
   At home with sisters, brothers,
Will help us in this life as men —
   If we'd apply them unto others
Would we be warm, warmth we must bring,
   Be cheered, then cheer our neighbor;
Be loved, then love — no other thing:
   Be helped, then give our labor.

The Christmas Of My Boyhood

Come 'round kloce, childurn an' yung fokes . . . Unkle Abe's a-goin' to tell ye 'bout Christmas back when he wuz a boy.

Skool clozed then in December, usually a week or 2 before Christmas . . . ye see it onley lasted 4 months, not countin' the 2 wks. off "for fodder."

Unkle Abe, as a boy, allus kommenct gitten Christmas well into hiz bones 'bout a week befoar good ol' Saint Nick wuz suppozed to kum 'round. It took a day or two to get in the "Christmas wood," as we called it; now the only diffrunce I cood see in "Christmas wood" an ever day wood wuz that it didn't go neer so hard with me to prepare the Christmas wood.

We didn't hav menny Christmas trees back then — no, sir-ee! Little fellers, boys an gurls too, hung their stockin's by the fireplace to be filld instid. Boys an gurls boath wore home-nit wool stockin's whitch they tide jist below the nee with a cotton string. So, ye can imagine what a site 3 'er 4 prs. wood be a-hangin' on the mantel by the wide wood fireplace.

Santy Claws back in them daze yooz'ly brawt boys an gurls strip-ed stick candy, apples, oranges, fire crackers an sweetbred. Little gurls kon--sidered themselves verry forchunate indeed if they got a cheep doll . . . an so did the boy if he got a french harp.

Now back whin Unkle Abe wuz a boy thar wuz plenty uv stores out in the cuntry, so fokes didn't haff to go to town t' buy their Christmas fixin's. The kommunity store wood be filld with shoppers fer a day or 2 befoar Christmas . . . people who had road hoss back, cum in waggins or buggys an' foot over ruff, narr' an' often muddy roads to reech the stores.

Fokes diden't hav mutch munny back then . . . they bartered or exchangd corn, chickens, eggs an' sumtimes wool, roots, erbs an dride apples for the things they needed from the store, sitch as dress cloth, shirtin', lether, coffey, sugar an' rice.

So, ye see the cuntry peepl didn't kongregate in the towns at Christmas time, or enny time, like they do today. No, sir-ee, it wuz a

153

days journey, an' frum sum parts, like Cattalooch, Big Creek an' Hurricane, it took about 2 daze.

So mutch fer the yung fokes an' things in gineral.

Now the older fokes sellebrated Christmas verry mutch as they do today, cookin' an' feastin', visitin', givin' gifts, sendin' cards an' so foarth, wuz not so mutch in stile as it is today . . . no, they diden't give ½ so mutch back then. I don't say that peeeple are enny better now or hav more uv the tru Christmas sperit, it jist wuzn't the stile an' tharfor, wuz not so mutch eckspected.

---

70 Yeers Ago

An' back in Unkle Abe's boyhood daze ever kommunity wood hav 1 or moar Christmas "parties." They wood sumtimes begin 2 or 3 days befoar Christmas but the usual time for theze parties or cuntry dances wuz on Christmas eeve, an on theze ockashuns boath the yung an' old wood atten', the yung fokes of korce, doin' moast of the merry-makin'.

These dances wood be held sumtimes in the dinin' room, sumtimes in the parler; but whirever hel', the room wood haff to be clurd of furnichur, etc., to ackommodate the crowds. The fiddlin' an' dancin' wood yooz'ly kontinue till 2 or 3 o'clock, sumtimes till chickin crow.

But aiter all, it wuz the same Christmas sperit that mooved fokes back then, an yooz'ly made them happier, less selfish an' better 'bout Christmas-time, as it does today, only it wuz in anuther generashun an' under sumwhat diffrunt kustoms.

Whir's Goldsmith

Well, when I went down to Clyde on the Pidgin las' wk. I met a hoast of fren's, amung them Tom Green.

Now, Tom got to ree-flectin' on bygone daze, as is hiz habit, ye no.

"I can remember the time of the June Flud, back when I wuz a mere boy," sed Tom, "when all theze bottums whir Clyde is wuz under water. That wuz befoar the R. R. wuz bilt throo hyear an' thar wuz oanly 3 houses hyear.

Then the konversashun led up to Clyde of the brite t'backer daze. "'Clyde wuz the bizziest place in the state fer its size," sed Tom. "Rite as 2 rabbits," sed John Shook.

"It's the trooth ef ye ever did tell it," sez I.

"Why neerly all of the 'tbacker an' all uv the cattel razed in Haywood Co. wuz shipt from Clyde then," kontinued Tom.

"Yes — looky yander!" sed sum one a-pintin' toarg the deepo, "Look at that ol' deepo platform, how that thick floarin' is wore an' skyard . . . that tells the tail."

Well, it wuz neerly trane time, so Unkle Abe mozied on out toarg the deepo. On the way I passt Unkle Dock Smathers's 2 fine gray

154

hosses hitcht to the waggun in frunt of the barber shop neerly asleep (the hosses I meen) while Homes Plott wuz a-baskin' in th' sun.

Jerry Liner Haz Kompetishun

But thir's one new bildin' goin' up in Clyde . . . kum to think uv it, thar's only 1 in Waynesville. But the differuns is, Jerry Liner haz neerly a score of workmen on hiz bildin' in Waynesville, while thar's one lone boy at work in Clyde. He's a-diggin' out fer the foundashun with a mattock an a-rollin' out the durt with a wheelbar. But the boy is fathful an' if he can only git a new leece on life he'll maybe git that hole finisht.

Tromp — Tromp — Tromp!

Well, fokes, have ye hyeard about Unkle Zack Davis, havin' a new way to git hiz trench silos trompt? Hiz neffew, Frank wuz a-tellin' about it here last week.

Frank sed hiz Unkle Zack wuz a-worryin' 'bout how to git hiz feed trompt down as it wuz blowed in from the cutter —

"Why, Unkle," sed Frank, "haint ye done hyeard about how they git their silos trompt in the west?"

Hiz unkle sed he hadn't.

"Jist let yore milk cows, dry cows — eny kind of cattle tromp it down, bigger the better. Ye jist put 4 or 5 hed in, 'cordin' to the size of yer silo, shet em up an' yore trompin' problem is over with . . . all ye haff to do is, see that the cattle git water reg'ler," Frank ecksplaned.

Well, Unkle Zack follered instruckshuns to the letter, Frank sed . . . the cattle furst filled up on the green corn, got hot, drunk water — modisty forbid me goin' into deetale eny further, but ye no the rest uv the story. "But, Unkle Zack wuz not to be outdone," sed Frank. When he saw what he'd dun he jist kep the cattle in thar, sed he wuzn't a-goin' t' let eny little upstart of a neffew git the joke eny further on him."

> Ol' France trod out her grapes by foot —
> An' the wine wuz good they say.
> But silage feed trompt down by cows —
> Well, Oscar, you take it away.

Homes wuz a-sittin in frunt of hiz shoe shop. I rouzed him up with the yoozal queschun —

"How's bizzness?"

"Bizzness — hell," sed he, "I've not made hiz ackquaintence yit.'

Jist then a purty gurl past by fer the 3rd time in 20 minets.

"Whooze that purty skirt, Homes?"

"Durned if I no," sez he, "she passes here 10 or 12 times a day."

"Well, if I didn't hav anything elce to do, I'd shore try flirtin' with 'er," sez I.

I went into the watin' room, rapt at the tickit winder, an' shouted, "How long till trane time, pleeze?"

No anser . . . jist the tick-tick-tick-tick-tick-tick of the telegraph insterment on the inside. So, gitten no anser, I went aroun' to the side

155

winder, peept in — an' what do you think? No agent anywhirs, an' the door wuzn't lockt.

Well, it's a good thing to hav them bizzy daze to pint back to, thawt I. Jist then the trane pulld in an' I swing aboard.

Goodbye, Clyde of the bizzy days
Goodbye the Clyde of yore;
Fond mem'rys, fine foke an bottum lands —
But them bizzy days are o'er.

A BIG CHRISTMAS

Gee whiz — what a big C'rismus we've jist gone throo! Unkle Abe don't remember ever seein' one to come up with it. It wuz the fattest, fullest, fastest, friendliest, costliest, coldest, ravinest,, rip-snortinest, bizziest, biggest — an BEST I think we've ever had. Yes — sir-ee — an' gloary be! fer it showz better than eny thing elce that "happy daze air hyear agin."

No. I never seed sitch a spendin' Crismus in all my born daze — ef noboddy haz eny munny fer about 30 daze, it will be becaze we spent all our December salary an' giv an ordur on Jinuary as well.

An' ever boddy in town seemed to be on the streets the week, befoar Crismus, yes, an' all the cuntry fokes seemd to be in town. Then munny wuz a-flowin' like "Noboddy's Bizzness" (skuze it). On Sat. an' Monday befoar Crismus I don't bleeve thar wuz nuff of the cuntry peeple staid at home to slop the hawgs, an' in town not a-nuff to turn in the far alarm.

Well, Unkle Abe took a trip endurin' the hollydays — an' what do ye think? The trane wuz so krowded that he wood a-had to stood up ef he hadn't a bin an ole' man. While on this trip an whil smokin' one o' my 8 inch see-gyars (8 inches moar or less), I fell to meditatin' an reflecktin' a little bit on the past 12 months. "Cood a-done better, maybe a darn site better," thawt I.

"Still," sez I to myself, "aiter allowin' fer the weeknesses an' mistakes kommon to mankind I reckon I ort not to komplane; speshly sence I didn't let eny of my 12 dizeezes git me down, also manidged somehow to keep out of the bred-line.

I like to think that with 2 expectshuns everboddy has took the jokes an' jibes in this kolyum in the verry best of yoomer — jist like John Boyd does.

BIG SNOW, TOO!

Whoopee! bigges' snow on the ground rite now we've had in sevril yeers. Ever big snow that cumz Unkle Abe is re-minded of the shore

156

nuff "Big Snow" of 1886 when it snode fer 4 daze. It wuz more than waste deep fer a man — mutch too deep ye see fer little boys an' gurls to git out in.

It took the men fokes a long time to kut roads throo that snow so's they cood reech the places they had to, wood pile, cow barn, etc.

FOUND THE RITE KLIMATE

Accordin' to the story, Gene Sutton, who had bin workin with the CCC boys on Mt. Guyot, kum to town an' walkt into one of our barber shops.

"What's the matter, Gene?" axt sum buddy.

"Oh, I'm sick, tard, week, hungry sleepy an' moast froze to deth — I reckon the alteetude up thar don't agree with me, er sump'm," replide Gene. "Hav ye got a good fire?" he axt as he made hiz way toarg the reer of the shop.

Well, Gene went to sleep, an' the boy "run the heet" on him thinkin' they wood make it so hot he coodn't sleep. But not so — Gene slep 12 hrs. by the clock, an' they had to moove him by foarce on closin' up that nite! He found hiz alteetude.

HOW IS IT OUT YORE WAY?
By UNCLE ABE

Wisht ye cood see at my house —
Sitch a fam'ly, grashus me!
There'll be konflict in Opinyuns,
No matter what the subjick be.
If Nell sez white, Jane sez it's black,
An' vice a verce, ye know;
If Willie sez a thing's one way
Fay quick replies, "Not so."
If askt to stay, they want to go;
To go, then home's the place;
An' if they're told to take more time
They quicken up their pace.
Each has a temper of its own —
An' a tallint quite distink;
But the hardist thing fer them to do
Is to hold their tungs—an' think.
Sumtimes, 'tiz rare, they try to ackt
Quite nice, an' then to love;
'Tiz then I say, "Why bless their soles—
Quick, Ma, bring out the dove"!
But when I say to Ma, "Alas,
It seems we've made a mess."
"They're by it honist, Pa," sez she,
Like us, no more no less."